DATE DUE

PROBLEMS OF AMERICAN SOCIETY
Bernard Rosenberg, General Editor

| *Civil Liberties* |

Civil Liberties

WILLIAM SPINRAD

Quadrangle Books | *Chicago*

33460

Library of Congress Catalog Card Number: 73-101075
SBN 8129-0140-1

Preface

When I accepted the suggestion that I write a book analyzing recent civil liberties problems in America, I saw my task as a systematization of a vast amount of material already written on the subject. Instead, I discovered little that was directly useable. Most of the voluminous literature, whatever the historic scope, seemed to contain either summaries of laws and their judicial application, value statements of prominent intellectuals, descriptions of individual events, or, occasionally, reports or estimates of popular attitudes. Very few writers had seriously addressed themselves to a crucial question: Which features of societies, or of a particular time in a specific society's history, were responsible for the relative presence or absence of civil liberties? With appropriate modesty and apprehension, I thus found myself something of a pioneer.

Fortunately, some published material existed which could provide a beginning, as the reader will find in the text. Furthermore, much of it was devoted to the serious threats to civil liberties in the United States in the 1950's, frequently referred to as the "McCarthy Era." The bulk of all empirical research ever done in the area of civil liberties is classifiable under the "Mc-Carthy Era"; several writers had presented explanations of the phenomenon which could readily fit into a sociological orientation to civil liberties problems. An appraisal of those data and those ideas provides the basis for a major part of this book. Once the design of the rest of the work had been formulated, appropriate material was uncovered, much of it in unforeseen and relatively obscure sources. I hope my own efforts will somehow spur interested scholars into adding a little more, or will encourage those citizens concerned about the subject to press for more serious analytical efforts. The issue is certainly of sufficient significance.

When I first started the book several years ago, an appraisal of current political trends and their possible impact on civil liberties was to be included as a kind of speculative addendum. Since that time, these tendencies have produced a serious "crisis of legitimacy," which has necessitated a fairly extensive chapter. Of course, the continuation of these severe political conflicts means that supplementary material continues to appear. To add new and up-to-the-minute details, even to append special footnotes, would be an arduous task and would not alter my basic analysis.

This book would not have been possible without the assistance of many people. Among those who helped, by such contributions as suggesting sources or critically examining some parts of the manuscript in draft, were Gordon Haskell, Al Nash, Alfred Young, Martin Spencer, William Preston, Alan Westin, Donald Koster, and Laura Clarke. Of special value were the many ideas of Murray Hausknecht, who offered useful suggestions for almost every part of the work. Bernard Rosenberg thought up the entire idea in the first place, and Ivan Dee of Quadrangle Books painstakingly examined the entire draft and suggested many necessary revisions. Several graduate assistants at Adelphi University, Brian McBride, Barry Perlman, Charles Napoli, Yitzchak Dekel, and Linda Rouse, helped locate bibliographic sources and assisted in the complex tasks of editorial revision and proofreading. In addition, Thelma Miller not only performed all of these chores but gathered most of the data and wrote up the basic draft for the discussion of "movie censorship." The arduous assignment of typing and other clerical duties were expertly handled by Linda LoDuca Torre, Wendy Shinn, Helen Slavin, Marjorie Leotti, and Patricia McGrath. A special acknowledgment is due my wife, Leah Babitz Spinrad, who not only exhibited the typical patience of a spouse throughout the long process of the book's composition but actually read much of it and offered many needed suggestions for its improvement.

W.S.

February 1970

Contents

12 The Problems of the Mid-1960's:
    The Crisis of Legitimacy *178*

PART 3. CONTINUING PROBLEMS

13 Censorship *209*
14 Academic Freedom *235*
15 Some Other Issues: A Miscellany *259*
16 Civil Liberties in Private Organizations:
    The Case of the Labor Unions *278*
17 Some General Propositions *292*

    Notes *307*
    Index *351*

Civil Liberties

Part One

The sociological analysis of civil liberties

1

Aims and ideas

The founding documents of the United States state that the "bless-
ings of liberty" are an essential purpose of government. The Bill
of Rights is a legal and symbolic embodiment of that declaration,
and, nevertheless, the maintenance of civil liberties remains a
perpetual problem. As Roger Baldwin, co-founder of the American Civil Liberties Union, said "No fight for civil liberty ever
stays won." [1] Efforts to curtail civil liberties, which are often
successful, have obviously always been present. In the two decades since World War II, we have seen a series of serious threats
to the continuation of civil liberties; according to some observers
they are as severe as any in the nation's history. This book is an
attempt to analyze some of these recent and current civil liberties
problems from a sociological perspective. Our intent is not to
narrate the events but to try to explain them and to ascertain the
relevant social factors, including those factors that can be defined
as "legal" or "political" in nature, that may be responsible for
the relative existence or absence of particular civil freedoms in
the context of the various challenges. Hopefully, the result should
mean not only a better understanding of the specific subjects

considered but also a contribution to a "sociology of civil liberties," a type of orientation to such problems for which there are surprisingly few explicit precedents. Most of the work published on civil liberties concentrates on the legal-juridical features—laws and their administration. This orientation has produced an overwhelming emphasis on Supreme Court decisions. Another commonly emphasized approach insists that the state of civil liberties depends on public attitudes. This approach is often an addendum to the approach that stresses Supreme Court decisions. Both approaches are very limited. To understand what happens in the domain of civil liberties demands the same kind of intellectual pursuit appropriate to any other inquiry into social events, that is, a search for all consequential variables.

WHAT IS INCLUDED AND EXCLUDED

Our attention is directed toward specific types of questions while excluding many others. We do not emphasize problems of "democracy" in general, although civil liberties are essential to a stable and continuing democracy. Civil liberties actually comprise the "negative" side of democracy, freedom from restrictions, rather than the "positive" side, popular participation in the selection of government and in governmental decisions. The focus is further narrowed. There is little attention to *civil rights* per se, which, in the meaning which has become conventional, is roughly synonymous with the idea of "equality." Within the domain of civil liberties, we are directly interested only in those rights defined as *substantive,* the personal rights which no one, especially the government, is permitted to violate. We are essentially concerned with those rights covered by the First Amendment to the United States Constitution and similar provisions in state constitutions, which can be summarized as the *freedom of expression* and *freedom of association* to implement that expression.[2] These rights, are, in legal language, distinguishable from *procedural* rights, or the idea of a fair and just process for ascertaining criminal guilt or its functional equivalent, usually called "due process of law." In the

Constitution, these rights are covered by several other amendments as well as in the body of the Constitution at several points. In practice, due process is a necessary condition for substantive freedoms, for they will be protected only in the absence of arbitrary, authoritarian, or capricious penalties.

Other kinds of issues that many would describe as involving "liberty" or "freedom" are also excluded. Economic freedoms, whether defined as right to a job, property rights, right of economic welfare, and so on, are significant political and philosophical questions but are outside our direct concern. Similarly, many other political disputes, which contenders may pose in terms of concepts of liberty, are *policy* questions not directly relevant to freedom of expression and association. For instance, in extending our analysis to freedom within a private organization such as a trade union, arguments over the stipulation that all workers must join a union is considered a collective bargaining issue, and thus outside the province of civil liberties. The right to oppose the union shop, within and outside the union, however, poses a civil liberties question.

The emphasis is on freedom of expression and association from external restraints, even though the motivation for, or likelihood of, saying anything or joining with others in the first place does at times become an essential element of the analysis. The purpose is to examine external deprivations, or threats of deprivation, that can limit such freedoms. Formal legal penalties are most publicized and most important, but they are not the only sanctions that can curtail these freedoms. The government does not have to arrest a publisher, because it can simply remove his publication's mailing privileges. In fact, the refusal of a newsdealer, under particular pressures, to sell the publication can effectively limit expression. Fear of losing a job may silence a dissident voice as readily as a possible jail sentence. Freedom of expression and association may be further contained by intimidation, harassment, slander, or extralegal violence. In other words, "private" as well as government suppressions are part of our analysis.

Even if the question of motivation, that is, the social factors that stimulate people to want to say anything or join with colleagues to propagate their views, is not central to our analysis, it cannot be ignored, especially since it is affected by external deprivations. For instance, it is obvious that an atmosphere of authoritarian controls, in which free expression is penalized, will be likely to diminish the desire for such expression beyond the fear of being punished. In fact, the lack of communication about opposing views can limit interest in even thinking dissident thoughts, as some have claimed is typical of totalitarian societies. Similarly, the lack of meaningful channels of communication, even without conscious efforts to limit their use, becomes a subject for analysis, if only peripherally.

The specific problems investigated represent, in each instance, an *area* of civil liberties dispute and/or threat. The impact has been fairly extensive and those involved as "disputants" *relatively* numerous. These problems are not only the most significant for society but there is also likely to be more usable data about them. Some of the problems that warrant thorough analysis were time-bound, specific features of a particular historic period, despite the general applicability of the events. Other problems were more continuing, with obvious historic variations. For many reasons, a large part of the book is devoted to a discussion of what can be loosely defined as "McCarthyism," the range of civil liberties problems induced by the Cold War in the decade or so after World War II. The events of the "McCarthy era" were, at least as seen by many observers, the most serious threat to civil liberties in recent America. Furthermore, analysis of what transpired permitted the utilization of the most extensive empirical investigations and theoretical contentions by social scientists of anything that can be classified as civil liberties. It thus furnishes the setting for our most meaningful dialogue with other published ideas.

An obvious follow-up was an appraisal of the immediately *current political scene,* which also poses a threat to freedom of expression and association, including some comparison with the earlier phenomena of McCarthyism. The two most important continuing kinds of problems that seemed to prompt sufficient explanation were *censorship,* actual attempts to ban or control communication content, and *academic freedom,* essentially the ability of those in academic institutions to express themselves freely without harassment. With one exception, a variety of other problems should best be left to a *miscellaneous* section. The application of our analytical ideas to the internal workings of one type of private organization, *labor unions,* seemed very appropriate and, in terms of our own interests, extremely important.

In essence, we are presenting a modified "case history" approach, that is, an examination of particular types of civil liberties problems in specific situations within a single social-political system, including its own unique history. Of course, the objective is to develop some conclusions, resembling general propositions, applicable at least to this society and, in some ways, to the macrocosm of all human society. Despite this last, ultimate purpose, references to other societies and to earlier American history appear, primarily, as a basis for an analytical scheme and, to some extent, as material for comparisons. To analyze the "cases" meaningfully required more than an array of information. Enough writers have achieved this aim. A method for systematizing the material, a *model* which would facilitate the search for the social variables that affect the maintenance, extension, or limitations of civil liberties was necessary. An historic backdrop is an obvious source for such a model. In order for the examination of history to yield the most relevant clues, however, some previous set of ideas is still essential. Available literature, which dealt with the reasons for the relative presence or absence of civil liberties, was probed. What was teased out of the comments of others was thus combined with some of our own initial impressionistic observation to develop a preliminary framework.

WHAT IS IN THE LITERATURE

It is not necessary to document the fact that a vast amount of published writing on the subject of "liberty" exists. When the term is narrowed down to comprise only what can be defined as "civil liberties," the available discussions still remain immense. Even when further limited to "freedom of expression and association," a review of the existing material is a herculean task. Despite the quantity of material available, very little of it is relevant to our purposes because most of it consists of value affirmations, that is, philosophic statements about what is "good" or "bad" about particular liberties, historical narratives, reviews of the ideas of political leaders and prominent intellectuals, or legal-juridical discourses. For those interested in a sociology of civil liberties, of the social factors that enhance or diminish such liberties, the available ideas appear to be incredibly, and to the author, very surprisingly, meager. Several empirical investigations offer valuable data, particularly those conducted in the 1950's. Beyond the above, the relevant literature consists, for the most part, of either ad hoc comments or elaborate essays. Systematic presentations are very rare. What has been described as man's "noblest cry," a fundamental civic value that has, presumably, stirred the passions of the best minds and the most dedicated citizens in so many eras, has hardly been analyzed with either vigor or rigor.

Nevertheless, it is possible to cull, from what has been written, several clues for the development of our preliminary formulations. Take, for instance, the vast amount of legal-juridical discussion. This preponderant emphasis seems to imply that civil liberties are almost entirely a matter of constitutions, statutes, judicial rulings, and so on.[3] In the United States, this has meant an inordinate attention to Supreme Court rulings, even to the details of language used. The result is, typically, a set of formalistic presentations with minimal relation to social reality. A sociological interpretation must seek to disclose the basis for laws, court actions, and so forth, and, more importantly, their impact— how do they actually affect the prevalence or absence of civil liberties. Legal features, however, possess a self-evident importance. If nothing else, they set the fundamental standards, at least in relatively democratic systems, by which the state, the only agency in society that can use force legitimately, operates in relation to its citizens. The pertinent proposition that emerges is: one of the *necessary* conditions for the existence of civil liberties, including freedom of expression and association, is the formal stipulation of individual rights, accompanied by a regularized and "fair" system of dispensing justice with appropriate procedural safeguards. Perhaps the converse presentation is more useful: civil liberties are unlikely in the absence of meaningful legal safeguards. The other dominant motif in writings on civil liberties, frequently stated rather casually, is that appropriate popular attitudes and values are also necessary. Sometimes also assumed to be a near truism, an extreme version rests on some variant of the idea that societal decisions, especially in democratic systems, are a result of the expression of an inclusive "consensus." For example, Robin Williams, in his short discussion of civil liberties as part of a general analysis of *American Society,* asserts that the existence of such liberties requires that "a large proportion have real emotional reactions against the violation of those rights." [4] The research concomitant of this approach is the attempt to disclose public opinions on civil liberties questions. The result, as later described, can be quite disappointing to libertarians, that is, widespread "intolerant" attitudes show up in the American public and those of other democratic nations. Similarly, historical accounts pinpoint the widespread sentiment for suppression of free expression throughout American history.[5]

Nevertheless, some concordant popular values are necessary, for example, some acceptance of the belief in much of the population that people have a right to express themselves freely. Without this belief, there would be little impetus for free expression, and legal protections would be inoperative. In actuality, the relation between popular opinions and the relative prevalence of civil liberties is quite complex. A more precise delineation awaits our more extensive examination of the relevant data.

Many analysts, on the other hand, are not only less interested in popular opinions but also tend to regard them as important barriers to freedom of expression and association. This type of "aristocratic" or "elite" analysis has come from a variety of spokesmen with differing political and intellectual bents. In essence, the maintenance of civil liberties is assumed to be the task historically assigned to independently powerful and humanistically cultivated people, asserting their rights in opposition to the "masses," the leviathan state, or both.[6] To give a recent example, many analysts of McCarthyism perceive it as a result of the intervention of the mobilized mass populace into the autonomous provinces of specific "elites" and/or the latter's failure to act as responsible "elites." [7] Some of these analyses go further. They assert that tendencies toward "equality" are particularly dangerous to civil liberties because they diminish the independent power of elites.[8] A possible variant of the position holds that civil liberties is dependent on the "virtue" of the rulers, the dedicated elite, and, to some extent, other protagonists in political society.[9]

Opposed to the emphasis on elites as the bulwark of civil liberties is what might be termed the "radical democratic" doctrine—freedom is possible only with a wide dispersal of power, including the resources which provide for meaningful exercise of power.[10] Most of the people will not be capable of expressing themselves, individually and collectively, unless they have some means for protection against the mighty, whatever the basis for that might. Interestingly enough, Robin Williams also expresses this idea very succinctly with his additional requirement for civil liberties: "those whose rights are violated must have the power to strike back." [11] What is implicit in this orientation can be described as the proposition of "indivisibility of freedom," that is, liberty or restriction will tend to spread from one sector of society to others.

The "elite" and "radical democratic" explanations actually have one theme in common. They are joined by a common belief in the need for many independent centers of power in society as bulwarks for civil liberties. The dispute is between the emphasis on the importance of a few individuals in such positions of power against the dispersal of power potential throughout society. Both points of view become different versions of a proclamation for "pluralistic" rather than "unitary" social structures as libertarian requirements. But there is a significant underlying argument. The "elite" doctrine accentuates a pluralism of "autonomous spheres." Liberty is dependent on the rights of the elites to operate in those spheres without external intervention. The "radical democratic" doctrine perceives liberty as grounded in the pluralism of open political conflict of many groups, each with an appreciable power base.

Determining which approach is more pertinent is not an immediate necessity. Both sensitize the analyst to the importance of *specific people* in determining the fate of civil liberties, above and beyond the legal formulas and the generic popular values. For their actions to result in a "libertarian" output requires, not only the resources to defend their freedoms, and those of others, but also the *motivation* to want to. This need not mean that their beliefs are more libertarian than others'. Our first elaboration on the subject of relevant attitudes and values is in order. Other orientations, not so readily classifiable, may prompt a demand for free expression and association, for oneself and/or others.

The pragmatic "ulterior" approach, which accents what freedom is "good for" rather than its intrinsic virtue, has been a matter for philosophic dispute. As an analytic departure for determining why people seek freedom, it can also appear to be extremely important.[12] This is particularly true of the quest for "knowledge," of whatever type. From this standpoint, not only is free discourse the objective condition for acquiring wisdom, but also enough people accept this dictum to provide a foundation for the existence of freedom of expression. Of course, this has become more pronounced with the development of scientific inquiry. This type of analysis can be further extended. The demand for civil liberties may have quite a peripheral origin, not associated with their inherent values in any form. People simply want such liberties in order to propagandize their own beliefs, maintain or extend the position of their groups within society, and so on.[13] Simply stated, the demand for civil liberties is a concomitant of other, somewhat "peripheral" quests.

From a similar perspective, those who strive to restrict freedoms can be spurred by other considerations besides obvious anti-libertarian attitudes. Restrictions are sought because of perceived threats to power positions, "entrenched interests," or strongly held values. This is particularly manifest as a reaction to the upsurge of the previously downtrodden or alienated. Opponents are suppressed because they are then denied legitimacy, and the entire structure becomes more inimical to civil liberties because the opposition will also deny legitimacy to those in power, sometimes in anticipation of the suppression deemed likely. This is what makes civil liberties so difficult to maintain in any type of "revolutionary" situation. Similarly, analysts of the "garrison society" point out that the mobilization for external conflict is inimical to internal liberties.[14]

A summary of what has been thus far presented is aided by an examination of the many contributions to the general area of the "sociology of democracy." One of the most succinct and empirically grounded discussions is that in Seymour M. Lipset's *Political Man*.[15] Lipset, by comparing contemporary nations and using particular indices of democracy, correlates "stable democracy" with such things as the extent and pace of economic development, accepted legitimacy of both democratic governments and political opposition, amount of education, and size of mass media audience. A consolidation of the list would add up to the ability to satisfy both the economic demands and the quest for political participation of much of the population and generic agreement about the rules of the political game.

How is this related to our perspective? Remember, we are interested in the "negative" side, the lack of restrictions of freedom of expression and association. Furthermore, our emphasis is on problems within a generally functioning democratic system. Finally, if comparisons between societies can provide useful clues for our purposes, they could well include comparisons among democracies, and even among different types of authoritarian political structures. Lipset's analytical scheme, and those of others who have attempted something similar, cannot be directly transported for our analysis, but they do allow for the adoption of some well-developed and verified principles of political sociology in somewhat translated form. The following is a possible formulation: freedom of expression and association is enhanced when a social-political system is generally accepted by the populace, and when the right of opposition is both permissible and viable. Of course, much of this will be further expanded.

All the foregoing suggests the following initial analytical scheme for a sociology of civil liberties: freedom of expression and association is dependent upon some formally stated legal protections with structures for enforcing them; some prevalence of beliefs in support of and in accord with such liberties; enough people who are motivated to extend and defend them and, because of some features of their social position, capable of so doing; and a social-political context permitting the right of organized dissent. Antithetical conditions result in the absence of, or at least the diminution of, such liberties. The major dispute thus far revealed is whether elites or larger publics, properly motivated and with appropriate resources, are relatively more important as bulwarks for civil liberties.

Actually, one man has come closest to a comprehensive statement of this entire formula, including a way of reconciling this argument. Alexis de Tocqueville, writing about the United States in the early nineteenth century, foresaw a danger to liberty from the absence of an independently powerful aristocracy. He saw, however, the possibility of an alternative in various value and structural features as well as in the popular pluralism of such things as local governments, voluntary associations, and the many independent newspapers. And he also saw the dangers from militarization and the type of political controversy that can challenge legitimacy, such as the slavery question.[16]

Additional variables also suggest themselves but did not, at the outset, seem to fit obviously into the scheme. One involves the question of channels of expression, the idea that freedom would be hollow without some mechanisms for communicating to a significant audience. The second type of variable includes the psychological elements associated with motivation, particularly the general psychological aspects of a society or a situation that encourage assertion of the right of expression, acceptance of its curtailment, or the desire to suppress others' rights.

One final set of ideas, not directly connected with the subject of civil liberties, turned out to be very important for our analyses. Since the focus on the behavior of specific people, the relevant *social actors,* and their impact on actual events seemed an advisable perspective, a "decision-making" orientation seemed appropriate. Each civil liberties "problem" was viewed as a series of political-type decisions which tended to curtail, maintain, or extend freedom of expression and association. Therefore, a model for analyzing decision-making in society was also in order. The basis was the author's own discussion of "Power in Local Communities," a review of the literature on power and decision-making in American communities.[17] What emerged was, for the purposes of this book, a set of variables that can determine who has what effect on community affairs. Included are such things as the roles, values, interests, motivations, and resources of particular people and groups. Of particular importance is the concept of the "saliency" of an issue to any contestant, with the accompanying proposition that, whatever else was involved, the degree to which one "cared" about questions at issue would have great impact upon what was decided.

Before this initial scheme can provide a usable model for analysis of concrete recent problems, it must be further developed in the light of other historical experiences. An historical survey, furthermore, not only reveals some of the "lessons of history" but also supplies some necessary background material for examination of later events.

2

The lessons of world history

A comprehensive history of freedom of expression and association on a world scale is hardly possible in this book, nor is it appropriate. A very capsulized survey, however, suggests some further interpretations about the bases for such freedoms. Accordingly, the emphasis is on a few selected historical "facts" in what can be called the "prehistory" of our subject, that which antedates the founding of the American nation, with particular concentration on Great Britain, the national society from which the United States emerged in effect.

The initial requirement for the existence of this type of civil liberty is some form of motivation for dissent. If the society is so constrained and the culture so contained that there is little stimulation for dissent, as in the usual depiction of ancient despotisms, the entire question has little meaning. Whatever has been true in other societies, the potential for dissenting voices seems typical of those that can be included in the "Western"-tradition nations of Western Europe, the civilizations from which they directly descend, and the nations they have influenced. In all of them, some element of open disagreement has been a conspicuous part of the historical record.

LEGAL FOUNDATIONS

Codified legal protections of the rights of free speech, press, assembly, and so forth, are fairly recent phenomena, even though people have sometimes exercised those rights without such formal stipulations. For instance, the free discourse in classic Athens did not rest on a formulated bill of rights. Yet legal protections have played an important role in the development of civil liberties, especially the insistence on procedural rights in criminal prosecutions. Whatever internal freedoms existed in ancient Rome, both in the republic and the empire, largely depended on the systematic legal system, including some emphasis on due process, which can be considered a precursor of what has become an essential ingredient of modern relatively libertarian systems. Similarly, medieval Europe, with all its authoritarian features, is part of the libertarian heritage. The emerging doctrines and procedures of regularized and stable law, with varying forms in different places, were the beginnings of modern due processes. Furthermore, even if men were rarely legally free as individuals, they became increasingly free constituents of legally autonomous cities, universities, or special church bodies, providing some haven for the open declarations of individual and collective minds. The universities were the most important and symbolic expression of such freedoms. As protected enclaves for religious scholars and students, their autonomy from local governmental controls permitted a wide range of freedoms, including intellectual freedom.[1]

British history is even more illustrative. Procedural liberties were both prior to and a foundation for substantive freedoms. The tradition of "common law," whatever its hoary origins, gradually established a fairly "just" method for criminal prosecution. In the extreme formulation of an early English jurist, even the king could not violate the laws as handed down by customary practice and strictures. Although this dictum hardly set the prevailing mode for some time, it illustrates the kind of legal norms that have played such an important part in the judicial system of the country which, in turn, has been so significant in the maintenance of free expression and association. Some of the legal defenses against suppression were enacted into statutes: other defenses, which were part of the unique Anglo-Saxon political culture, were merely customs that became legally binding.[2] Thus, the end of "prior censorship" of printed works was simply a consequence of the termination of government licensing. Nevertheless, it resulted in a formally accepted rule, which also became the de facto law in this country.[3]

One could add countless other examples from this and other societies. The historic evidence buttresses our initial contention that definitive legal restrictions against suppression and procedural safeguards are, in most situations, essential to freedom of expression and association and may, in some instances, stimulate their actuation. In the absence of such legal "subsystems" freedoms are unstable and very uncertain at best, whatever the other conditions. Their diminution in ancient Greece was facilitated in some measure by the lack of appropriate legal norms.

On the other hand, suppressive laws in a society with some degree of freedom do not necessarily curtail expression and association in every instance, but they do provide a legitimate basis for such suppressions. The crime of "seditious libel" in England, also prevalent in early America, goes back to common law precedents but did not become significant until the early eighteenth century.[4] Under the specific contemporary conditions, the charge could include anything interpreted as likely to create disloyalty to the government or disorder. Under the hazy formulas used, the mildest critic was subject to severe punishment. The judicial stipulations made the dangers more pressing. The truth of printed charges was no defense; in fact, the more truthful, the greater the libel. The severe suppressions and oppressions of the era of the French Revolution and the Napoleonic wars utilized these, and a few later formulas, as their legal justification.[5]

LIBERTIES AND QUEST FOR KNOWLEDGE

One of the most quoted and argued about libertarian pronouncements is John Milton's "Areopagitica," written as an attack on
the restoration of censorship. Some critics have recently pointed
out the limitations in the famous poet's defense of the rights of
free expression.[6] More important for our purpose is the rationale
behind his opposition to at least some types of suppression—his
belief that "truth" and "virtue" will win out over "error" in an
open contest. The validity of this hazy contention is immediately
irrelevant. It symbolizes the many historic illustrations of the nexus
between the existence of some freedom of discourse and the desire
to acquire knowledge. The quest for rational wisdom was a basic
motivation for the extensive political debates, intellectual conflicts, and political disputes in ancient Athens, much of which
were quite "open" despite the lack of concrete legal protections.
The concept of participating citizenship demanded free dialogue.[7]

Whatever the legal framework for the medieval universities,
they existed because of the growing quest for learning, most of it
religiously inspired but later stimulated by the reawakened interest in natural science. The Renaissance intensified this type of
motivation, with a resulting extension of the notion of free intellectual discourse to other circles. Under the impact of the Enlightenment's faith in the search for "reason," the values of free inquiry
and free discussion became a generically applicable philosophical
doctrine. The belief that this type of civil liberty was essential for
a knowledgeable population, in whole or in part, and this in turn
was important to the society, was a principal impetus for its
creation, extension, and maintenance.

TANGENTIAL MOTIVATIONS FOR FREEDOM

Other types of historic motivations for freedom of expression and
association are less directly associated with libertarian values.
The exercise of religious dissent developed in the Reformation
not out of an acceptance of religious toleration but as an assertion

of rival orthodoxy. Fear of despotic rule over *themselves* compelled social and political notables to affirm their prerogatives to discuss and collaborate freely. The development of the British Parliament is a conspicuous example. Demands for complete citizenship from a previously deprived group can be combined with an encompassing plea for general civil liberties. The concomitants of the rise of one relatively "deprived" group, the bourgeoisie, has been sufficiently detailed in many historical accounts. The world of the "free" capitalist entrepreneur fitted in with a "free" political system. Even the libertarian rhetoric was affected; to this day, it is conventional to speak of the need for a "free market of ideas." To remain viable, political parties and factions have had to proclaim the virtue of their type of "free" association.

Of course, those who demand their "rights" are frequently making a claim for their own group exclusively, sometimes explicitly denying these rights to others. But the "indivisability of freedom" principle is usually operative, if not always immediately. Magna Charta was merely a codification of some of the power of the feudal nobility vis-a-vis the king. The doctrine of parliamentary autonomy was a later extension. Under the Tudors and the early Stuarts, the aristocratic Privy Council was expected to engage in free debate, a privilege not given to anyone else. The elected House of Commons, however, began to assert its independent power, including the right to untrammeled discussion.[8] The establishment of parliamentary immunity supplied an ideological justification for more comprehensive freedom of expression.

Scholars outside the medieval university gradually assumed the freedom granted its members. Divergent religious doctrines, each claiming an exclusive orthodoxy, ultimately led to religious tolerance. To emphasize again the British example, the fear of any kind of despotism, particularly after the civil wars of the seventeenth century, compelled acceptance of the legitimacy of many divergent viewpoints.[9] One result was a plethora of independent newspapers.[10]

POWER

Viable freedom of expression and association requires a power base, however obtained. The independence of the medieval universities was legally formulated, but it was real because of their interstitial power position. They furnished, to both the international church authorities and the still weak kingly powers, an additional check on feudal nobles and city governments.[11] The general decentralization of effective power at the time, despite the official authoritarian system, could readily provide a haven for the dissident, as long as it did not involve any proscribed heresies. If intellectual discourse in the Renaissance and Enlightenment was relatively free, it was, at least partly, a result of the protected status of court intellectuals. Early capitalism brought an extension of freedoms because, among other things, property ownership meant some de facto liberties. In England, the widespread dispersal of newspaper ownership was a very relevant illustration. The internal freedoms of the English Parliament and political parties was bolstered by their power potential, a ready defense against usurpation by state edict or rival groups. Similarly, most religious bodies had some access to the powerful in society and possessed their own popular resource in the size of their followings.

RESTRICTIONS OF FREEDOMS

Suppression of existent freedom of expression and association was typically a result of the kinds of situations listed in the introductory chapter. Generally, liberties have been curtailed under pressure of perceived threats to the legitimate power-wielders, either from internal dissidents, foreign "enemies," or, frequently, a combination of both. In fact, the time-honored formula has been to brand the domestic dissenter as either a conscious or unwilling enemy agent. Even when not explicitly stated, such beliefs are commonly the actual motivation for suppressions. For instance, charges of heresy are closely associated with defense of power positions. Historic examples for all of this are manifold.

To begin with the most famous case in classical Athens, Socrates was found guilty of "corrupting the youth" at a time when the disintegrating Athenian community was surrounded by the Spartan armies. In the fashion which has been so common in human history, his dissenting ideas were deemed a danger to the need for stabilizing the existing order, maintaining the legitimacy of the government, and mobilizing the populace against the enemy.

The period of the burgeoning modern world, most characteristically identified with the Renaissance, the Reformation, and the rise of the national state, was marked by two very contrasting tendencies—the development of some of the bases for modern libertarianism and intensified suppression. The Renaissance brought an intense interest in learning and expression as well as an avid search for scientific information—some of it under the protection and sponsorship of the newly powerful political rulers —which could be widely diffused as a result of the invention of printing. The Reformation resulted in an obvious break with the previous religious monopoly.

The contrary tendencies were also very apparent. The political power-wielders were creating, or desiring to create, centralized and effective states. Dissidence was perceived as a serious danger to that process. The major contending religious groups had to defend their respective orthodoxies against all opponents by ideas and by force. In this continuing contest for allegiance and power position, temporal and spiritual conflicts were fused. Open dissension, however capriciously defined, was anathema to this drive toward an encompassing garrison atmosphere. The British experience was very illustrative. In a land which had been slowly evolving toward one of the world's libertarian symbols, treason trials and heresy hunts, with the specific targets dependent on the current power incumbent, prevailed for well over a century. In Italy, cradle of the Renaissance, Bruno was executed and Galileo humiliated by church authorities because they expounded the depiction of the solar system originally devised by the Polish monk, Copernicus. Their proclaimed cosmology could be, and was, readily absorbed into any type of theology. They were victims of the Catholic Counter Reformation, caught in the cross fire of Protestant-Catholic power politics.

Official British reaction to the French Revolution and the Napoleonic wars was a typical manifestation of overreaction to a perceived danger to a legitimate social order and the powers it proclaimed. Anxiety about possible Jacobin and anti-monarchical tendencies resulted in a wide range of suppressive policies, legal and extralegal.[12] Because they were prompted by fears induced by the situation rather than extensive turmoil within British society, they were no longer conspicuous after the Napoleonic era. The point is that concern about conceivable external-internal threats, in a somewhat ambiguous situation, may engender "panic" suppressions not appropriate to the actual dangers.

CIVIL PEACE

Internal dissension, especially in the presence of external conflict, can upset the stability of a political-social order, may challenge the legitimacy of power-wielders and the dominant ideologies, and may, therefore, be suppressed. In addition, that very suppression may further exacerbate the internal conflict, intensifying, to use traditional terminology, "civil strife." The desire to maintain "civil peace" may thus, under specified circumstances, demand the official toleration of at least some divergent organized beliefs. In essence, this was the major reason for growing religious "toleration," especially in England. Mass revolutionary parties may be similarly unhampered, particularly in "nonrevolutionary" times.

SUMMARY IDEAS

A few seminal ideas emerge from this historical survey, suggesting elaboration of our earlier preliminary scheme and providing an appropriate backdrop for a discussion of American history. Free-

dom of expression and association is clearly dependent on specific social conditions, including proper motivations. People want
these civil liberties because they see them as necessary foundations for the quest for knowledge, because such freedoms allow
them to maintain or extend their social positions, and because
they permit the appropriate atmosphere for the kind of social
order they prefer. Those who pursue or proclaim the need for
free expression maintain that right only in the presence of some
power, their own or others, capable of defending or asserting that
right. The pluralistic basis of libertarianism is thus further amplified. Suppression is stimulated by a perceived threat to a power
position and to the values that are presumed to make that power
legitimate, especially within a garrison society in the midst of
assumed serious external danger. Nevertheless, organized dissent,
even in these contexts, may engender the right of more dissent,
both as an accepted value and as a legally approved option. Suppression would bring more disorder than that which results from
continued permissiveness. Thus, many are led to accept this value
as a promise of freedom—that the welfare of the society, or its
strength, will be best enhanced by a free play of ideas.

The history of Britain up to the nineteenth century discloses
even more specific conditions for freedom and unfreedom. The basis
for freedom of expression was established by such things as: a
traditional system of due process, detailed in common law; a
powerful Parliament zealous to establish its collective independence and the individual freedom of its members; an acceptance of
religious diversity as a solution to internecine conflict among
contending sects; a popular press with widely dispersed ownership
and editorship; a vigorous intellectual life, with many people committed to the value of intellectual freedom; a fear of despotism
born of many struggles against powerful monarchs; and a small,
but vigorous, group of genuine democrats. One should also add
that Britain was the country that first developed capitalism with
the accompanying features already discussed. Freedom was limited
from time to time by such things as the fear of internal revolution, realized twice in British history and later threatened by

events on the Continent; the general fear of popular demands by the varying government elites; the frequent concern about religious heresies, even if the domain of the heretic became increasingly delimited; and the anxiety about maintaining the monarchy, common to so much of the leadership, with memories of the Puritan Revolution and the specter of what happened in France always before them. With the comparative stability of so much of the nineteenth century, these anti-libertarian factors were less operative and one can speak of the nation as generally exhibiting a relatively high degree of civil liberties since that time, especially freedom of expression and association. The history of the United States has been somewhat similar in many ways.

A continuing historical survey would certainly be valuable, especially since it could readily lead to a more precise depiction of relevant variables. The existence, absence, or wavering status of civil liberties from time to time in different places could be correlated with other significant features. For instance, twentieth-century history, in amplification of previous tendencies, indicates that the "revolution of rising expectations," the demands of the previously subservient for a more equitable share of whatever society has to offer, can pose a threat to civil liberties if the power-wielders are, for varying reasons, unwilling to yield to the demands of the new assertions, or are, in fact, incapable of yielding under the existing order. In addition, unstable regimes, as in the case of the "new nations," may, in classic form, readily squelch dissent, whatever the original ideology of the government. A more extensive historical sociology of civil liberties would also have to consider such things as the phenomena of totalitarianism, including the reasons for and effects of the ebb and flow of suppressions; the many cases of instability in more or less democratic regimes and the effect on freedoms; civil liberties and revolutionary changes; and the impact of large-scale warfare. Many more could be readily listed. This would require another book, although some of it will be implicit in later discussions. The foregoing account will suffice for the immediate purposes.

3

Civil liberties
in American history

American society has possessed a legal basis for civil liberties, especially since national independence. The provisions of the United States Constitution as well as similar items in state constitutions are more than formal statements in official documents. They have furnished the legitimate operating guidelines for all branches and levels of government, whatever the many violations in practice. The other most emphasized foundation for freedom, the appropriate values, also seems to be an ever present feature of American history, at least as measured by the public assertions of political leaders and intellectual spokesmen. That opposing views have also appeared does not gainsay the vast amount of libertarian sentiment. In the absence of systematic historical data, it is reasonable to surmise that much of the population did support such beliefs in some manner, as indicated by the vast amount of free expression in the historical record. Our historical survey is, then, of a political-social system with both a legally normative and a value commitment to freedom of expression and association, as well as, in general, the appropriate social foundations.[1] What is the actual reality and what are the explanations for the relative presence or absence of freedom at different times?

In assessing the amount of freedom existent—as an historical overview or as a judgment about specific historical junctures or particular groups—it is very easy to make exaggerated assertions. A professional civil libertarian will quite naturally accent the abuses; an adherent of the "American Celebration" will concentrate on the comparative lack of widespread suppression. Both are equally right and wrong. In fact, both tend to agree on most historical details. The dispute is usually one of verbal tone. More importantly, both are irrelevant to a social scientific analysis, which should be directed toward the reasons for whatever freedom or restriction is observed at specific historic junctures. Unfortunately, many otherwise valuable discussions are marred by this type of composite appraisal. It is sufficient, as a kind of truistic aside, to declare that the exercise of civil liberties and their curtailment have both been part of the American pattern. The revelations of "revisionist" historians, exposing the vast amount of nonlibertarian ideas and practices at the very beginning, even among the Founding Fathers, supply some useful data. But they are not the source from which to devise a sociological interpretation. The writings of Leonard Levy are one of the most quoted examples.[2] His prevailing theme is that both colonial America and the early Republic exhibited little adherence to either libertarian values or practices—a duplicate of the situation that prevailed in Britain at the same time. For instance, he points out that there were few published pronouncements either by the prominent or the obscure that consistently affirmed any belief in the inclusive right of free expression. The need to maintain order or the right of individual people or governments to be protected against slander and libel were considered sufficient reasons for prosecution and conviction of those who said the "wrong things." In practice, this frequently did occur. Ironically, even those previously convicted of such offenses were in favor of penalizing others for similar offenses.

"Legislative trials" for seditious libel, with little protection for the accused, were as conspicuous as court trials under common law. "The actively suppressive power was exercised by an unlimited discretion in the legislature to move against supposed breaches of parliamentary privilege!" [3] Attacks on royal appointees were permissible and, in fact, were almost encouraged by legislative leaders. "Freedom of the press was, in other words, a useful instrument for the expression of legislative prerogative." [4] The very privilege the legislatures thus achieved, however, was what made attacks on their operations and personnel considered as "treason." Carrying his description to the American Revolution itself, Levy reiterates what many other historians have detailed— the vigorous suppression of Tory sympathizers, with legal, illegal, and quasi-legal methods, much of it approved by leading patriots.

In his account of the adoption of the Bill of Rights, he insists that the First Amendment was not originally interpreted to mean what it has subsequently meant. Proponents variously explained it as a restatement of the "no prior restraint" principle or as an assertion of states' rights; that is, seditious libel was something for the states to handle exclusively. Expansion into a more thoroughly libertarian doctrine came from the struggle between the Federalists and the Jeffersonians. Initially, the Jeffersonians applied it as an argument against the acts of the Federalists, such as the Alien and Sedition Laws. Later, the Federalists used the First Amendment as a protection against the threats against them by the Jeffersonians in office.

The last suggests another feature of the analysis of many "revisionists"—the debunking of the libertarianism of the presumed most libertarian Founding Fathers. Jefferson is the favorite target. In another work, Levy disclosed examples of the almost Machiavellian notions about ways of suppressing opponents suggested by the author of the Declaration of Independence and the man whose words are so frequently quoted in support of pleas for unlimited freedom of expression and association.[5] His "backsliding," most of it stated rather than practiced, is thus another indication of the effect of political realities on the politician in a specific situational context, whatever his general philosophy.

Other scholars have refuted some of his contentions.[6] Our objective is not to judge the validity of either position. A more pertinent observation is the fact that Levy ignores the sociological backdrop implicit in his account. As part of this limitation, he fails to appreciate the concept of "indivisibility of freedom." For instance, the privileged position of comments made in the legislatures was historically a vital base for more extended freedoms. The legislator's ability to talk without restraints could and did readily become anybody's right to do so. Ability to criticize royal officials provided the atmosphere for demanding similar rights for criticizing all public officials. Procedural protections under common law cases permitted much expression with few restraints. Even the permissibility of religious dissent, which Levy agrees existed, encouraged other types of dissent. A little freedom tends to produce a lot of freedom, especially if there are appropriate conditions—parliamentary opposition to royal governors, the existence of many independent publications, vigorous organized political disputes, many independent power bases, an interested and involved citizenry, and so on. That the implementation of the Bill of Rights was a result of political contest should have been a central point in his presentation.

Any purely "ideological" interpretation of civil liberties is, at least, very limited. Other historians have sought a more comprehensive explanation in terms of the relevant social factors. One of the most ambitious attempts is that of John Roche.[7] His analysis discounts the possible legal and value foundations of freedoms in early America even more than that of Levy. Civil liberties were primarily a product of the existence of many fairly autonomous pluralistic enclaves. None had power outside its own domain, and the dissident member, tyrannized by majority opinion, could readily shift to another group or even to a distant place. In the urbanized America of more recent times, civil liberties are even more pervasive because of such things as the impersonality of social life and the resulting indifference to the ways of one's neighbors; the accompanying impersonal norms of bureaucratic administration; and the increased intervention of the federal government, with its system of nationalized, impersonal due process of law and substantive justice.

A critical historian, William Preston, alleges that Roche's formulations may be "too pat . . . too optimistic." [8] Again, such disputes are outside our immediate concern. One feature of Preston's critique is, however, very germane. Although Roche's accounts dwell on the many examples of political self-assertion and political conflict in defense of civil liberties, he does not sufficiently accent them in his general analyses. Something else is also lacking. Despite his precise delineation of the problems of each specific period, his theoretical formulations exhibit an inadequate sensitivity to the ebb and flow of freedom and suppression, which would mean a greater concentration on the *situational* features that affect such changes. Interestingly, Preston exhibits the same sort of failing by his listings of the many restrictions at all times. Such "muckraking" accounts fail to distinguish between episodic "nuisance" curtailments of liberty and the "pervasive" types that have a significant impact on society, a distinction that will underly most of our later discussions.[9] It is necessary to correlate the relative presence or absence of civil freedoms with the particular political-social context at a given time. To elaborate our analytical scheme further and to provide the appropriate historical background, the rest of this chapter is devoted to that explicit task.

"FREER" TIMES

The early nineteenth century, the period covered in De Tocqueville's observations, was, in general, a time of comparative absence of external restraints on freedom of expression and association. The most conspicuous exceptions were the difficulties encountered by a few unconventional religious dissenters, like the Mormons, and, surprisingly, for some contemporary observers, the pressures toward conformity in academic institutions. One of the most striking examples of intense, "free" declarations of hostility to official government policy was the discussion about the Mexican War. Among the most critical, during the actual conduct of the war, were two of the country's leading political notables, Daniel Webster and Henry Clay. It was obviously a serious political controversy, involving the vital issue of extension of slavery, party conflicts, and so on, and, yet, these dissenters were apparently unhampered.[10] Generally, in this period, values, laws, and social conditions were all coordinately responsible for maintaining the right of free expression, no matter how sharp and potentially divisive. The nativist, Know-Nothing movements tended to foster a spirit of intolerance, but, whatever the general political impact, they did not seem to have any significant pervasive effect on freedom of expression and association. Those in honored and strategic positions, such as legislators and prominent literary figures, were especially immune to suppression. But the general situation was also favorable. The Republic seemed stable and could presumably stand such divergencies, especially since they usually did not challenge the accepted verities. Of course, all this changed as the slavery question became more pressing.

The immediate post–Civil War period, despite the heritage of violent conflict, including the attendant suppressions and the current political turmoil, witnessed little limitation of freedoms, except for the barring of Confederate leaders from public office. In a famous decision the Supreme Court ruled that participation in the Confederate cause, for instance, could not by itself be justification for barring a lawyer from his practice.[11] The strains of Reconstruction in the South, and the reactions to it that ultimately resulted in the second-class citizenship of Negroes are, in line with our specified orientation, outside the scope of this volume because they cover the area of "civil rights" rather than civil liberties. In most respects, there were few restrictions on freedom of expression and association in the nation at that time. A relatively stable nation, immersed in the pursuit of economic expansion, produced little significant dissent and little reason for checking dissent.[12] That, too, was to change with the challenge of the incipient labor and radical movements.

Similarly, the 1920's, following the vast national mobilization for a European war and probably the most extensive suppressions in the nation's history, were a time of comparative freedom, despite contemporary caustic accounts and the fervent activity of the recently formed American Civil Liberties Union. Some features of the earlier atmosphere remained, especially hostility to "foreigners" and radicals. The former, which included a revived nativism, was accompanied by a desire to forget the "foreign" war into which "we had been dragged." The new conservative "normalcy" was predicated on domestic tranquility.[13]

American radicalism was at low ebb in the 1920's. Still, it did exist as a vociferous voice, and there were situations of widespread dissent against the official order—as in the Sacco-Vanzetti case, sharp industrial disputes, and so forth. There was the existing revolutionary government of Soviet Russia and revolutionary movements throughout the world, particularly those in the Communist International. Legal, and some illegal, suppressive acts of these few voices did occur, producing several famous court decisions relevant to First Amendment freedoms. Only a few people, however, were concerned with radicalism or anti-radicalism in the days of Coolidge prosperity and the experiment of the Kellogg-Briand world pact to outlaw wars.

Problems of intolerance were evident in these times. The continuing nativist sentiment, best personified in the strong Ku Klux Klan of the early 1920's, was bent on stamping out "alien" ideas. Labor unions were commonly included in the category, and the few attempts at new organizations were met by legal and extralegal suppressions. Nevertheless, the nativist and accompanying religious fundamentalist fears were not primarily about political dissent, of which there was so little. The tenor of the times prompted a return to anxieties about religious heresy and an intensified concern about "immorality." Efforts to suppress freedom of expression were directed primarily at "improper" literature and presumed anti-religious doctrines. The most publicized action of the ACLU in the entire decade was its involvement in the famous Scopes "monkey" trial, its handling of the defense of the Tennessee schoolteacher who taught about biological evolution in opposition to the state law. Accounts of the struggle for "liberty" in this period dwelt upon the perpetual contest with the otherwise unidentified "mob" rather than with "entrenched interests" or governmental power.[14] Most of the restrictions of the 1920's were of the "nuisance" variety. Only the pressures against unions and the censorship of "immoral" communication can be defined as somewhat "pervasive."

During periods of comparative stability, especially after an era of intense turmoil, including war, threats to freedom of expression and association, though present, are not encompassing and do not affect much of the population. Peace and prosperity in an expanding economy limit the incidence of challenges to the political-social order and the legitimacy of its power-wielders. One must look at "crisis" situations to locate the more serious suppressions.

CRISES AND CIVIL LIBERTIES

The first serious threat to freedom of expression and association in the history of the Republic came early. The impact of the French Revolution and the Napoleonic wars was felt in this country as it was in Britain, exacerbated by the domestic conflict between the Federalists and the Jeffersonian Republicans— Democrats. The Federalists saw many of the Jeffersonians as infected with "dangerous" Jacobin doctrines. Concern about "foreigners" or anything foreign was widespread. The culmination was the Alien and Sedition Act of 1798, which permitted the deportation of aliens by executive degree and continued the tradition of "seditious libel," punishment for "malicious attacks on Congress or President with attempt to defame." [15] Critics were sent to jail by the Federalists, even for attacking the act itself. The act expired in two years and was not renewed by the victorious Jeffersonians. (President Jefferson pardoned all prisoners and fines were repaid.) The major effect was actually the wrecking of the Federalist party, facilitated by the somewhat milder suppressive techniques of the Jeffersonians in office against political opponents. The respective denials of civil liberties were assertions that the opposition was illegitimate, a comprehensible manifestation of the internal and external insecurity of the new nation. After the War of 1812, the "stabilized" society contained few stimulants toward extensive suppression, as previously described.

Later, the exacerbation of the slavery question inevitably posed a very serious threat to the maintenance of freedom of expression and association. The implicit issues covered such features as property rights and resultant power positions, varying interpretations of legitimacy (such as state versus federal government), sanctified values on different sides, and, ultimately, the very continuity of the nation. To the power-wielders in the South as well as those whose beliefs were akin, abolitionist doctrines were quite appropriately regarded as revolutionary proclamations. Most southern states passed laws abridging public discussion on the slavery question. The major result was to prevent any discussion whatever of any aspects of the slavery problem, which extended to the universities. Beyond the legal strictures, informal action, frequently by vigilante groups, was conspicuous in both the North and the South, and it was further intensified by the tide of nativist sentiment. Special citizens' committees were set up, which became a type of secret police. They sought to prevent any anti-slavery expressions, checked on mailed material, and investigated visitors to their areas. In the North, action against abolitionists was mostly extralegal—riots in many cities, destruction of abolitionist presses, and assaults against abolitionists.[16]

What happened to civil liberties during the Civil War comprises a very important episode in the history of American freedoms. It was the most serious "crisis" of them all. The impact of mobilization for armed conflict, however, is left for later consideration. The comparative "tranquility" that followed, at least as far as civil liberties issues are concerned, did not last too long. A new legitimacy crisis emerged with its attendant suppressions, involving labor and "radical" organizations, which represented a form of self-assertion by the "downtrodden."

The curtailment of the civil liberties of labor organizations, the suppression of their rights of association, remained a significant civil liberties problem until well into the 1930's. Symbolically, a Senate investigating committee which studied the question in the 1930's was officially called the "Senate Committee on Civil Liberties." The difficulties of radical organizations were different at different times. Some labor leaders might object to the identification of labor and "radical" groups so closely together, but their respective struggles for the right to exist without legal and extralegal harassment tended to be joined until the post-World War II period.

All branches of government participated in the process, and many extralegal and nonlegal tactics were applied.[17] The courts assisted by regularly issuing "injunctions," which could make various types of union action in contempt of court. The executive branch was most involved. Action ranged from that of President Cleveland in calling out federal troops, which, in effect, broke the Pullman strike in 1894, to local police running labor organizers out of town. Legislative acts were, at least officially, more concerned with radicalism and will be later discussed.

But the suppressions by the "private government" of employers were even more persuasive. In some "company towns," the company made the laws and its private police force enforced them. Freedom of expression and association essentially was by their sufferance. There were also economic weapons available—the "blacklisting" of those who joined unions or even spoke to unionists and the "Yellow Dog" contract by which a prospective worker promised never to join a union. Extralegal violence, including murder, could come from public or private police or any unofficial group of citizens. The record has been sufficiently detailed in many places. It may be difficult to accept this history from a contemporary vantage point, to appreciate to what extent the assertion of labor's right to organize was of central concern to libertarians for a long time. The American Civil Liberties Union devoted much of its effort in its earliest days to that goal. As a lingering manifestation of this tendency, the Congress of Industrial Organizations (CIO) was not permitted to hold a public meeting in Jersey City until the Supreme Court ruled such denials unconstitutional in 1939.

Although civil libertarians have been firm in their defense of the right of labor to organize, the various techniques to thwart those rights has not only been a result of the recalcitrant power of vested interests. They, too, have been able to make appeals in value terms. By nature, unions are opposed to the notion of individual contracts, a time-honored American value frequently sanctified by the Supreme Court. Unions are frequently organized by "outsiders," seem to disturb the apparent social peace, have been identified with "foreign" ideas and were, at least in the early stages, frequently disproportionately supported by immigrant groups. Violence on both sides was a frequent concomitant of labor struggles.

All of this was even more true of "radicals." The first to be involved were the anarchists.[18] The historic event that set off the campaign against them was the famous Haymarket Square bomb explosion in Chicago in 1886, which actually occurred during a labor rally. President McKinley was assassinated by a man publicly identified as a presumed "anarchist." As a result, New York State passed the first state anti-sedition law under the heading of a "criminal anarchy" law. The law stated that it was a criminal offense to advocate either by speech or writing the doctrine that organized government should be overthrown by force or violence, or by assassination or any unlawful means. It was also unlawful to join any organization or attend the meeting of any organization that advocated overthrow of the government. In 1903, Congress passed a law excluding even "peaceable" anarchists from entry into the country. Several other states followed the example of New York shortly thereafter, although there was little prosecution under such legislation for some time. For instance, the New York law was not applied for almost twenty years until it became very appropriate to the atmosphere of World War I.

The difficulties of the anarchists were compounded in the case of the "revolutionary syndicalist" labor organization, the Industrial Workers of the World.[19] Its members were physically assaulted by both police and private groups, arrested for fictitious offenses, and denied procedures of due process. Above all, various local governments even denied them the right to meet; an extreme manifestation was complete prohibition of street meetings in San Diego in 1912.

Fears about radicalism sometimes extended to the social and political critics identified with the progressive era. This rarely led to legal sanctions but it did produce other types of suppressive behavior, such as harassment and even dismissal of critical professors.[20] The World War I period produced even more severe actions against the "radicals" and, ultimately, against unions. As a result the "radicals" were effectively reduced to recalcitrant remnants, and the unions to a collection of "redoubts" in a few industries in the 1920's.

As the Great Depression succeeded the era of normalcy, the nation probably faced its greatest crisis in peacetime. Among other things, the legitimacy of radicalism and unions was again a pertinent issue. The intense economic slump engendered an understandable fear for the established order, with its large-scale unemployment, riots, the spectacle of the Bonus March on Washington, and so forth. The radical movement began to revive although it still remained a very small part of the populace. Industrial strife was part of the process of the growth of a legitimately accepted trade-union movement in the middle and late 1930's. The contestants in the intense political turmoil in much of Europe had their supporters in this country. Partly spurred by the New Deal, there was a searching for new political ideas. The depression was never completely overcome until World War II. Through the respectable approach of the Popular Front, the Communist party had developed some significant influence in the late 1930's. From what is conventionally defined as the other end of the political spectrum, growing "rightist" movements presented the fearful prospect of quasi-fascist totalitarianism. Intense ideological conflicts were an integral element of the intellectual landscape.

Although nothing resembling a revolutionary crisis ever developed, the possibility of severe internal conflict seemed an ever present danger to many. Yet there was comparatively little of the widespread official suppression that might have been expected from the situation.[21]

An ACLU report might complain, in effect, that this was the worst of times, a posture quite appropriate to its function. Arrests and prosecutions, which were apparently in violation of the First Amendment, did occur. But the Supreme Court first assumed its role of defender of the rights of expression and association against government encroachment in those days. "Radicals" were harassed in other ways, including vigilante action. Although, considering the decade-long turmoil, the extent of suppression does seem rather minimal. And, by the late 1930's, labor unions were made legitimate by and large. Rather than being curtailed by legal restraints, they were now in many ways protected by statutes, administrative procedures, and favorable court rulings.

A thorough probing of the reasons for the comparative absence of external restrictions is beyond our scope although several major ideas suggest themselves. Despite the domestic and foreign strains, value commitment to all democratic principles acquired a unique saliency in the light of the specter of totalitarianism throughout the world. Legislatures and courts codified some of this into law. The dangers of a widespread significant challenge to the political-social order abated by the latter part of the decade. On the other hand, the need for civil peace, intensified by the drive for national coordination behind recovery programs and, later, mobilization against external enemies, made suppressive actions, if desired, a far greater risk. Furthermore, much of the dominant Democratic party leadership sought to avoid any behavior that might antagonize any section of its political supporters. The acceptance of union "rights" was, in some measure, a reflection of their growing strength and their resultant weight in the "New Deal Coalition."

To the historian of American civil liberties problems, what is perhaps most significant about the 1930's is the distinctive suppressive techniques that emerged and became pervasive phenomena in the post-World War II period. The legislative committee investigation into "subversion" and the extensive use of the "loyalty" concept, particularly as applicable to government employment, were not unknown previously. They became significant forms of attempted suppression of radical dissent in the 1930's and later developed further into the characteristic style of the cold war epoch.[22] Finally, Congress in 1940 passed a law which was also to loom so important later on, the Smith Act. The major section, modeled on the old criminal anarchy laws, states, in essence, that it is a crime to advocate, or knowingly distribute material that advocates, or help set up an organization that advocates violent overthrow of the government.

World War II had an atypical effect on domestic disputes and civil liberties. The nation was effectively unified and suppressions were few. The end of the war brought its unique problems and responses to them, which provide the substance of later analysis. One final point, however, is in order. The immediate, current period creates its own special type of legitimacy crisis, which is the subject of a separate chapter of this book.

In the cursory review of world history, the most serious threats to civil freedom occurred in the setting of armed conflict or preparation for such conflict. In the United States there have been enough of such situations to warrant special attenion.

CIVIL LIBERTIES AND WAR

At the very beginning, the internal tensions of the Revolution produced their attendant suppressions of suspected Tories. The era of the Alien and Sedition Acts, in the midst of European wars and revolutions, saw a continuation of the same tensions. Armed conflict, here and abroad, was associated with an actual or feared legitimacy crisis in a new, unstable political-social order. Since then, the impact of war and warlike situations on civil liberties has varied. "Small-scale" wars—the Mexican, the Spanish-American, and perhaps the War of 1812—have stimulated little restriction. When the conflict required large-scale mobilization—military, economic, demographic, and even ideological —the dangers to internal freedoms have been endemic. Yet each experience has been somewhat different.

Civil War

The suppressions that took place during the Civil War are generally considered one of the most serious limitations of civil liberties in American history. It may seem odd at this time that the degree of curtailment was much greater in the North than in the South. Shortly after the firing on Fort Sumter, by executive order, President Lincoln directed that the mail be closed to "treasonable correspondence" and suspended the writ of habeas corpus (which was later ratified by Congress in 1863). As a result, people could be arrested, both by civil and military authorities, on suspicion of "disloyalty" and kept in military prisons without trial. The most widespread efforts occurred not in the border states, but rather in the Midwest, where anyone who indicated any sympathy with the Confederate cause or favored a negotiated peace might be jailed.[23]

Some historians, however, imply that the justifications for restraints were patently evident and the degree of suppression was rather mild, from this vantage point. The military crisis was almost constant until the last period, and opposition to the war was open and widespread. Understandably, there were many southern sympathizers by kinship and friendship, particularly in the border states and the southern portion of the midwestern states. Nationality groups, particularly the Irish and even many of the pro-Republican Germans, were openly hostile. Newspapers not only criticized the administration and asked for immediate peace, but in effect some also took the southern side, declaring that the federal government could not keep states in the Union by force. Some of the leadership of the Democratic party, particularly in the Midwest, assumed some or all of these positions. Conscription efforts were often met with armed violence, including murder. Secret organizations assisted the southern cause and even planned a rebellion in the North. In other words, the need for an unprecedented national mobilization, the maintenance of the political system under which it operated, and the legitimacy of the political authorities were subject to extensive, continuing challenges in the midst of a very uncertain military situation.[24]

Except for the arbitrary acts of military detention, the legal suppression, however, appears to have been comparatively limited. There were "private" acts against dissenters, particularly violence against the opposition press, frequently by Union soldiers on furlough. But there were few prosecutions of opposition publications and politicians whose utterances might, under other situations, be readily interpreted as inciting sedition. Apparently, only those directly involved in conspiracies—from helping deserters to forceful opposition to conscription to quixotic plans for armed rebellion—were prosecuted, and sentences were generally mild.[25] As already indicated, the end of one of the most violent internal armed conflicts in human history terminated the suppressive atmosphere.

World War I

World War I, and the period immediately afterward, brought the most serious threat ever offered to American civil liberties, including freedom of expression and association.[26] The majority of the population was apparently committed to staying out of the war, as were most of the prominent political leaders. After the United States entered the war, open or covert opposition remained strong, either to the war itself or to specific manifestations of it—conscription, bond sales, and so on. The opposition came from a variety of motives, for example, pacifism, isolationism, several variants of radicalism, and Irish and German hostility to Britain; it included every tactic from simple rhetorical statements to encouragements to evade the draft. In addition, the very act of mobilizing for a global war was obviously a new national experience. The statutory method for dealing with real or feared dangers was primarily the Espionage Acts of 1917 and 1918. The texts were officially concerned with military matters—interference with the war effort or recruitment, and so on. But they were extended to civilian activity and included indirect censorship by the government. According to some court decisions, it was a crime to advocate heavier taxation instead of bond issues, to insist that a referendum should have preceded the declaration of war, to present a film about the American Revolution because it might cause disaffection with our ally, or to criticize the Red Cross or the YWCA. There were also many state laws. For example, it was a crime in Minnesota to discourage a woman from knitting socks for soldiers. Even opposition to war bonds made one liable to prosecution. It was in the classic tradition of suppression based upon fears of upsetting the national unity, mobilization, morale, and so forth, in a time of external conflict on a scale previously unknown in American history. With appropriate historical irony, all of this occurred under the administration of the man who was probably quite sincerely dedicated to "making the world safe for democracy."

Anarchists and members of the IWW were, as a continuation of previous trends, particularly subject to suppression, and leaders of the Socialist party, officially in opposition to the war, were almost as severely harassed. The Russian (Bolshevik) Revolution intensified the process. Dissent now implied not only interference with the war effort, but also danger to the social order. Any oppositionist could be and was accused of sympathy with the Bolshevik Revolution, and any labor dispute could be defined as a prelude to insurrection.

There was some justification for this attitude. Radicals did expound their sympathy with the Russian Revolution, and it was offered later on as an example to follow by some propagandists, particularly by the new "Communist" groups. But the proponents of this view were generally seeking an "education" for the future and not an immediate incitement, and those who sought to stop them knew they were not acting immediately to prevent any planned violent action. The restrictions were generally designed in response to fears of what might happen later.

Among the many sentenced to prison terms under these acts

were the Socialist party candidate for president, Eugene V. Debs, and the IWW leader, William Haywood. The elected Socialist congressman from Milwaukee, Victor Berger, was refused his seat while under indictment. The Post Office removed material deemed in violation of the Espionage Acts from the mail, typically without a court appeal possible. Among the material excluded were the radical magazine, the *Masses,* the Socialist *Milwaukee Leader,* and even the famed scholarly work by economist Thorstein Veblen, "Imperial Germany and the Industrial Revolution," published in 1915.

Under the impact of the Bolshevik Revolution, the suppressive acts became more pervasive and thorough during the last months of the war, and even more comprehensive after the armistice. Extralegal action was more pronounced on the side of the government and its opponents. People were killed by vigilante action and bomb throwing. Labor disputes, at a time when there were few unions in the major industries, involved the basic question of the legitimacy of such organizations, whether part of the American Federation of Labor or the IWW, and assumed the character of a civil war in those turbulent times. Seattle was gripped by a general strike. The most serious government action of the entire era followed, that is, widespread rounding up of both suspected individuals and less culpable aliens, which was carried out under the direction of the man whose name began to symbolize the period, Attorney General A. Mitchell Palmer.

The tactic was the omnibus dragnet, the unofficial formulation of the doctrine of guilt by association. Arrests were made without warrants, and property searched without search warrants. For those people, the nation appeared to be a police state with midnight raids, incarceration in crowded uncomfortable quarters without food, or denial of rights to communicate with relatives. Occasionally, visitors to jails where these people were kept were arrested themselves. A state legislative investigating committee in New York turned its attention to the Socialist party and attempted to close its Rand School. This committee inspired one of the most patently suppressive actions of all—the refusal of the

Republican-controlled legislature to seat four elected Socialist delegates in 1920, an action publicly denounced by the 1916 Republican presidential candidate, Charles Evans Hughes. The legislature further passed a law with an inclusive restriction from the ballot of parties with "policies that tend. . . (toward) subversion," which was vetoed by Democratic Governor Alfred E. Smith.[27]

From this vantage point, it is difficult to comprehend or even to believe the extent of violation of all the liberties in the World War I period. Nohing like it has ever happened in the United States, before or since. It is particularly ironic that the United States was mobilized in what had been proclaimed as a crusade to extend democracy. Perhaps the difficulty of convincing many Americans that this was what the war was really all about produced the strictures of the early period. Later, the fear of the spread of revolutionary ideology to America, which was believed to be a coming possibility by people of varying political tendencies, impelled the characteristic panic reactions.

What were the immediate and long-range results? All movements that could be defined as radical severely declined in support, and the IWW was completely crushed. The labor movement took a long time to recover, even though the American Federation of Labor ostensibly was not directly involved. The depoliticalization of the "lost-generation" intellectuals of the 1920's may have been partially created by the repressive atmosphere. (One of the few "latent" beneficial results was the formation of the American Civil Liberties Union, initially organized to oppose militarism and to defend the rights of pacifists.)[28] For civil liberties themselves, the following period, the era of "normalcy" or "wonderful nonsense," depending on personal emphasis, exhibited both the comparative absence of restraints and the special problems earlier listed.

World War II and Afterward

World War II occurred in an amazingly "free" internal atmosphere for so vast a military undertaking, especially after the political turmoil of the 1930's and the divisive national debate on foreign policy before entry. The only prosecutions under the old Espionage Laws were those of a few people judged to be Nazi sympathizers, and their convictions were overruled by the Supreme Court. Three other events were significant. Most flagrant was the forced evacuation of the Japanese-Americans from the West Coast. This act, although widely regarded as a serious threat to civil liberties, is outside the scope of our discussion. It involved violation of several procedural rights and perhaps of the Thirteenth Amendment proscription against "involuntary servitude," but it was not directly related to First Amendment freedoms. The other two events concerned dissenters at opposite ends of the political spectrum. Twenty-eight pro-Nazis were tried for violating the provisions of the Smith Act relating to the armed forces.[29] On the other side, the leaders of the Trotskyite Socialist Workers party were convicted of violating various sections of the Smith Act.

There was so little suppression during the war because there was so little opposition to it. The strongest basis for opposition, the "isolationist" sentiment, readily succumbed to the patriotic consensus, whatever the continuing political disputes about foreign policy. Unlike the situation during World War I, radical dissent hardly offered any threat. The Communist party was "superpatriotic." Other groups were minuscule in numbers and influence. According to many observers, the SWP prosecutions were not motivated by fright over revolutionary potentials but by the desire of the national Democratic Administration to placate prominent union leaders in conflict with SWP spokesmen.[30] Quasi-fascist groups had lost their possible audience base, the isolationist patriots.

The end of the war coincided with the beginning of the cold war and the new suppressions that ensued. Analysis of this set of phenomena comprises a major part of this book. One of the basic themes will be that the civil liberties problems of the post-World War II era, which lasted roughly for about a decade, were unique, although some of the tendencies that were evident in the

1930's were continued, as indicated in the proliferation of legislative investigating committees and the expansion of the "loyalty" criteria for government employees.[31] (To some, the tenor of the times became apparent with the prosecution in 1948, and later conviction, of Communist party leaders for violating the Smith Act. Actually, the more characteristic style of the period was evident one year earlier when the attorney general issued his list of "subversive" organizations; membership in such organizations was a possible criterion for judging federal employees as "disloyal.") For the first time in American history, external restraints against freedom of expression and association were much more severe long after a war was over than during the conflict itself. To anticipate the later discussion, the underlying, initial explanation is that "peace" did not come after the end of armed hostilities and that the nation bore many of the marks of a permanent garrison society.[32] The Korean War was an intensification of an existing political-social situation, which required few qualitative changes. In this instance, organized war was very clearly, in accord with Von Clausewitz' classic dictum, a continuation of politics by other means.

Some critics of the post-World War II atmosphere have, in their fearful reactions, assumed a superficial similarity to other presumably similar periods. Our analysis, which emphasizes the historically specific character of the era, is, in many ways, a refutation of the more typical appraisals. Among other things, some have exaggerated the extent of *direct* intimidation. Comparatively few were actually imprisoned.[33] New restrictive legislation passed by Congress, particularly the McCarran Act of 1950 and its later elaborations, turned out to be meaningless, except symbolically.[34] In contrast to what was typical of earlier suppressive periods, vigilante actions were rare and generally confined to the earlier part of the period. The most bizarrely restrictive statutes, which were generally local, were also enacted in the half dozen years after the end of the war and had little direct impact.

Despite the many incidents of difficulties in academic circles, as later accounted, professors were relatively "free" to express themselves, in and generally outside the classroom. Unlike previous suppressive times, existent labor organizations were generally unaffected. The campaigns for Negro civil rights met few external threats to their expression outside the South. Actual government censorship of politically dissident literature, that is, barring it from the mails or prosecuting those responsible, was almost unknown. A new harassment did develop, however—the insistence of the Post Office that specific foreign publications could be received only by written requests. Another unique annoyance of the times was the denial of passports to "suspect" individuals by the State Department. The characteristic, quintessential civil liberties problems of the period, however, were those that grew out of the legislative investigations and the elaboration and extension of "loyalty" and "security" criteria as tests for employment. These comprise the specific problems of the McCarthy era, a conventional appellation that we will apply only euphemistically. It is misleading and dangerous to portray the idea of one individual as responsible for or as a complete symbol of such a historical situation.

Obviously, the relationship between American wars, including the cold war, and the state of civil liberties has varied with each specific war. Our summary analysis of the lessons of American history will include some attempts at explaining the differences. More will appear as part of the extended discussion of the cold-war era, especially the contrast with the World War I period. The specific impact of the war in Vietnam is left for the chapter devoted to the current difficulties.

SUMMARY ANALYSIS

This sketch of American history has depicted the existence as well as the relative absence of freedom of expression and association at different times and in different situations. It furnishes an historical backdrop for the later discussions, allows for significant comparisons, and permits intelligible references to earlier details in subsequent discussions. We have dealt with the highlights, particularly in discussing problem situations. That is why we emphasized threats to freedom that were more inclusive and relatively lasting, and paid little attention to the singular and episodic events often detailed in discussions of civil liberties. As with the general historical descriptions, it also suggests further analytical insights.

In analyzing the American experience, the acceptance of some generic adherence to libertarian values is an initial postulate, fully realizing, of course, that it has often been a superficial and limited set of beliefs, readily qualified or even obliterated by other considerations. The legal background has also been essential, above all the various provisions in the Bill of Rights, and the structures and procedures for maintaining those rights, both substantive and procedural. The operation of the judiciary system, although frequently overemphasized, has been significant, particularly in recent times. A unique American constituent is the system of judicial review, the right of appellate courts to set aside acts of the legislatures and the executives.

Other variables seem to emerge as foundations for freedoms, generally in line with what was previously suggested. The motivational factor appears ever more important. For whatever reasons, many varied types of people have desired, with some zeal, to express themselves freely and join with others. Furthermore, with all the obvious limitations, resources have generally been sufficiently available. With all the types of concentration of power and communication mechanisms at different times, there has typically been enough pluralism to supply a sociological grounding for meaningful individual and collective dissent and power to defend the right of dissent. This has taken the form of both openly political bodies and those which are politically relevant, that is, their efforts involve them in something resembling political conflict for which freedom to spread their ideas is indispensable. The almost complete freedom of religiously diverse faiths and organizations has been a specifically American aspect of such pluralisms. In refutation of John Roche's thesis, defense of liberties has depended on the pluralisms emerging from open conflict rather than those that rest on either isolated enclaves or mutually indifferent publics.[35]

The basis for typical threats to civil liberties can also be summarized briefly, either in the form of specific statutes, other actions of some branch of government, or behavior of private individuals and groups. The traditional American value system includes many anti-libertarian elements appropriately noted by many observers: orthodoxy (as in fundamentalist religions), xenophobia about anything strange and foreign, or conformity in essentials. The contradictory elements in the American ethos have always been present in some form: individualism and desire for uniform external behavior, a spirit of tolerance and fear of the heretic, or a stress on the value of learning and anti-intellectualism. As summarized by Francis Biddle, there are two strains in the American tradition: "the individual urge to freedom and the opposite longing to avoid exercise of choice, to be safe." [36]

The concrete manifestations of suppression, particularly those that have been inclusive and far-reaching, may rest on these anti-libertarian values but also have more specific motivations. The most important stimuli for widespread suppressions in American history have been the following, and sometimes interrelated, perceived threats: (1) to the exercise of power, (2) to the legitimacy of the social-political order, and (3) to the functioning of a militarily mobilized or garrison society. The anti-union suppressions clearly illustrate the first threats, and to some extent, the second. The denial of rights to opponents of slavery in the antebellum South was an almost paranoid defense of both power and legitimacy. The suppression of the Civil War and World War I periods was a response to fears about the success of the mobilized nation in its wartime operation and the maintenance of the legitimate government under the strain. The restraints of the cold war were a peculiar attempt to maintain a unique kind of national mobilization, as will be further explained.

Note that none of this is a sufficient explanation by itself. They are all variables, and what actually occurred was a result of a combination of factors. For instance, the absence of significant dissent was a primary reason for the general maintenance of freedoms in the most mobilized period in United States history, World War II. The suppressions during the Civil War may have been fewer than some think was appropriate because the dissenters were so numerous and powerful. The necessity for some "civil peace" behind the lines prevented more forceful actions, despite the provocations. On the other hand, during the World War I period, the vast amount of opposition to the war did not make the radicals and pacifists either more acceptable or powerful, as indicated by the fact that there was comparatively little popular protest against their treatment.

One other significant interpretation is reinforced by this history. Values, whether directly libertarian or only conducive to libertarianism, such as dedication to knowledge or a humanistic philosophy or particular types of political orientation, may be necessary but are not sufficient bases for civil liberties. Freedom can suffer when specific situations lend themselves to other emphases, especially when suppression is encouraged by the role demands of those in power. Even the most virtuous and wise can succumb. The most extreme example was Jefferson's suggestions for thwarting his political opponents by nonlibertarian methods, few of which were realized in concrete acts. The chief executive most associated with suppression was the academic scholar and morally fervent democrat, Woodrow Wilson. One can also add the names of Lincoln, or even Franklin Roosevelt, whose administration had very little provocation for its few suppressive wartime actions. The point is that good and right-thinking men, even in positions of power, do not by themselves determine the amount of internal freedom existent in a society. A sociology of civil liberties is necessary, and these historical accounts have helped build a foundation for such a sociology.

To continue that development, it is necessary to examine more carefully the legal aspects. For the United States this means, above all else, an examination of judicial rulings and opinions, primarily those of the United States Supreme Court. What the judges say is relevant in many ways to a sociological interpretation. If nothing else, their decisions are significant data, legally binding formulations about what can or cannot be done by the government and citizens. Assessing the function and significance of court rulings becomes another essential task, especially since they constitute the major content of most writings on American civil liberties, and, to many, the major source for the defense of such liberties.

4

Courts and civil liberties

It is impossible to discuss recent civil liberties problems in America without more than minimal attention to the operations of the courts. If one accepts the proviso that appropriate legal statutes, structures, and processes are essential for internal liberties, this does not adequately explain why the subject demands extensive discussion. The unique American practice of judicial review by "higher" appellate courts not only furnishes a substantial part of so many civil liberties commentaries, but it is also, according to many, the principal and perhaps the only mechanism for protecting those liberties. In this popular view, all that one can hope for from the legislative and executive branches of government is a relative neutrality, an avoidance of too many suppressive actions. The only law deemed beneficial to liberty is the United States Constitution itself, and perhaps the provisions for the Bill of Rights in state constitutions.

If nothing else, such points of view suggest a limited historical perspective. The apparent assumption of a libertarian role by the Supreme Court is a comparatively recent phenomenon because the Court was formerly considered the protector of property rights and not the bastion of personal liberties. With rare exceptions, it did not use the power of judicial review to protect freedom of expression and association against governmental encroachments until the 1930's. The process actually began in the Court under the leadership of Chief Justice Hughes. Many of the libertarian decisions emanated from this Court and were written by some of the same justices, frequently castigated as the "nine old men" who obstructed New Deal legislation.[1] The argument can be phrased much more strongly. The Supreme Court did not declare a single act of Congress unconstitutional under the First Amendment until 1965.[2] In essence, the voiding of acts of the national legislature as well as the executive branch has been mostly on procedural grounds, with statements that the stipulated practices were "arbitrary," "vague," "artificial," "unreasonable," "overbroad," and so on.[3] Frequently, the courts have not ruled on a law itself or other general actions of some government agency, but instead have set aside the penalties of particular individuals or groups under the specific procedures utilized. Furthermore, many of the fervent judicial declarations quoted by libertarians have actually been minority, "dissenting" opinions. The courts have been conspicuous in declaring statutes in clear violation of the First Amendment only when considering state and local laws.

In contrast, the other branches have not been as despotic as sometimes believed. One legal scholar, Wallace Mendelson, went so far as to exclaim that since "Congress has killed thousands of bills reflecting every imaginable form of bigotry, intolerance, and demagoguery; the Supreme Court has not yet struck down a national measure on the basis of any provision in the First Amendment. As Madison anticipated, the Congressional batting average is about .999. The Court's is .000." [4] This assertion is obviously overstated since it was made in the context of a specific argument against another legal scholar, who demanded more intervention by the courts in such cases. The courts are involved in civil liberties cases in the first place as a result of legislative and executive acts. What is important is that they have been so reluctant to void those acts until very recently.

Yet the other branches have been more libertarian in their actions at certain times. The courts did not set aside the Alien and Sedition Acts; they were simply allowed to lapse by the victorious Jeffersonians in the White House and Congress. The courts did exercise some restraining force on suppression by disallowing some Civil War provisions, but only after they had become generally irrelevant after the war. The courts generally upheld World War I repressions while the executive branch under President Harding released many of those convicted. Governor Al Smith and his legislature were responsible for getting rid of the Lusk Laws in New York State. The courts were notorious in thwarting the freedoms of labor organizations by the use of injunctions; congressional legislation terminated this practice. The efforts of the LaFollette Committee in Congress and the resulting Wagner Act did far more to protect labor's freedom of association than any court rulings. One can add many other examples. It is sufficient to point out that any branch of government can either be suppressive or relatively libertarian.

Nevertheless, an examination of relevant higher court rulings is appropriate at the outset, not only because they occupy such a prominent place in the ideas of scholars and libertarian ideologists, but also because they do constitute significant and legally binding decisions by people who, more than any others, have the assigned task of defining legally permissible behavior. Essentially, the judges, although basing their arguments on legal dicta, "balance" the differing sides in generic value conflicts as symbolized in legal norms. Especially in recent times, what they consider allowable legal action within the Constitution (as well as other laws, common-law precedents, and so on), what they declare void under the process of judicial review, and what acts of the legislature and executive they avoid any judgments about under the doctrine of "judicial restraints" not only establishes the range for possible subsequent acts but may also set the tone of legitimacy for even thinking about such acts.[5] Even a "minority opinion," particularly in the Supreme Court, can have a significant effect on other opinions, especially, and with an obvious logic, on the opinion of other judges. In fact, the decisions of the Court have extended beyond the bounds of government acts to encompass what goes on within private organizations, such as unions and universities.

What follows is a layman's review of some important court decisions relevant to freedom of expression, most of them pertinent to the civil liberties problems to be analyzed. The purpose is both to poinpoint the legal principles enunciated and to assess their actual significance.

"SUBVERSION"

Challenges to Legitimacy

Most important and also most publicized are the many "cases" in which the judges are asked to "balance" the importance of freedom of expression and association against presumed threats to government legitimacy. In effect, the courts decide whether national and state statutes that bar specified types of utterances and organized activity, and their applicability in particular instances, are in violation of the Bill of Rights. Actually the courts have only *voided* state laws. In fact, a 1956 Supreme Court decision formulated the principle that all state regulations in this area were unconstitutional since they preempted the "supreme power" of the federal government.[6] The court rulings and other judicial opinions in cases involving federal legislation have usually dealt with the questions of whether they could be applied in specific situations without violating the First Amendment and whether the proper judicial procedures had been followed.

The much quoted statement of Justice Oliver Wendell Holmes in a World War I decision has become the classic formula. Involving the case of a man convicted of distributing a printed appeal to avoid the draft, Holmes declared that a government has a right to protect itself from "substantive evils" when a "clear and present danger exists." [7] Whatever the actual interpretation of the meaning of the terms, they have become almost a ritualistic necessity in many subsequent judicial opinions. The underlying rationale is that First Amendment freedoms are not protected from legislative and executive curtailment when the exercise of those freedoms represents a clear-cut threat to government legitimacy. Furthermore, the basic concept and sometimes even the precise language appear in many other judicial pronouncements that do not involve legitimacy considerations. By using this approach, any official curtailment of civil freedoms is judged permissible only when substantial evidence exists that proscribed "evils" could be an immediate result. Holmes's dictum has, however, hardly been a conclusive guide, particularly in cases of "legitimacy." Other justices, generally a majority of the Supreme Court, may or may not use his language. But they have stretched the "danger" criterion to include any situation so defined by a legislature, and the "clear and present" test could be satisfied by evidence of "evil intent" and/or "natural tendency and probable effect." The person or group responsible for a communication need only be shown to have desired an illegal flaunting of government legitimacy, such as a forceful overthrow of government, and to have some indefinite future plans.[8] This formulation provided the legal justification for probably the most publicized decision of the post-World War II period, the Supreme Court's affirmation of the conviction of Communist party leaders for violating the Smith Act.[9] The official decision used Holmes's language, even though he as well as Justice Brandeis believed it was applicable primarily in wartime, and that the existence of perilous dangers could only be determined by the courts themselves, not by statutes, and that they must be immediate dangers.[10]

To some extent, the majority of the Supreme Court accepted Holmes's formulation by the late 1950's. Its reversal of convictions of "lesser" Communists did not constitute a voiding of the Smith Act, but rather a questioning of certain procedural features. It insisted that instructions to juries must indicate a definite charge of conscious involvement in a "conspiracy," not mere membership in an organization whose leaders have been convicted as "conspirators." [11] Apparently, by such legislation as the Smith Act, governments can "protect" themselves from those who organize to advocate their forceful overthrow, even if the "overthrow" is planned for the indefinite future, without violating the First Amendment. But no one can be convicted under such provisions without proof of active personal participation in that advocacy. In fact, in two decisions in 1961, one reversing and the other upholding a conviction, the Court all but eliminated the idea of mere advocacy as a suitable ground for criminal action and specified the necessity of proving some personal involvement in plans or instructions for "forceful overthrow." [12]

Another doctrine also developed in the 1930's, the notion that freedom of speech and press occupy a "preferred status," which cannot be abridged because of any "inconveniences" that could result.[13] This principle, however, although important in some types of legal disputes, was rarely utilized in those cases in which questions of threats to the legitimacy of the political-social order were under consideration. It has been applicable mostly in cases involving state and local restrictions that limit expression and association because of some presumed "nuisance."

In summary, judicial review gradually eliminated all state and local regulation restricting First Amendment freedoms, which are designed to protect government legitimacy. Whatever the legal principles enunciated, the appellate judges' direct impact upon similar federal legislation has been, at least until the late 1950's, rather minimal. At best, they had presented a series of admonitions against potential abuses. The later Smith Act decisions did, in effect, terminate further prosecutions under its provisions. Criminal penalties under this 1940 law did not, however, by then, if ever, constitute the most characteristic civil liberties problem of the post-World War II period. Above all, active Communist party members were not the "victims" of suppression that prompted the most concern among civil libertarians. The courts' effects on the more typical techniques of the times, such as legislative investigations and loyalty-security programs, were more complex.

Legislative Investigations

The range of civil liberties problems associated with legislative committees, particularly those of Congress, will be discussed in detail in a later chapter. Relevant court decisions provide a necessary background. Generally, the right of committees to subpoena witnesses and compel testimony under oath has been upheld as appropriate to the acquisition of necessary information for legislative purposes. Most legal disputes have revolved around the propriety of specific questions asked by the investigators and the penalties invoked for refusing to answer. In a fairly early decision, in 1881, the Supreme Court insisted that the legislature cannot probe into purely "private affairs," which is the province only of the judiciary. In 1927, an important decision included the stipulation that the committee's authorization must state a proper legislative purpose, even if no actual legislation ensues.[14] In other words, the committees can demand answers to questions related to the legislative purpose as defined in the committee's authorization. This general formula has been, in one form or other, the essence of most subsequent decisions. It may limit certain types of inquiry but it leaves a wide option for permissible interrogations. Several decisions by federal circuit courts of appeals in the late 1940's, all involving tests of the legality of the House Committee on Un-American Activities' investigations and all of which the Supreme Court declined to review, legitimized committees' probes into personal "subversive" activities and associations, since these investigations were merely seeking information to ascertain whether there was a "clear and present danger" requiring appropriate legislation.[15] Questions, for instance, about Communist party membership were thus deemed proper for a possible legitimate legislative purpose in the current situation.

The definition of "subversive," of those whose "private" beliefs and activities can be legitimately investigated, has varied, depending on the times and the cases. Questions about possible Communist party membership are considered pertinent.[16] In a very significant decision, however, the Supreme Court reversed the conviction of a witness who refused to name those formerly in the "Communist movement" since the chairman of the congressional committee had not conveyed "the pertinency of the question to the subject under inquiry." [17] Other decisions have been more complicated. In 1957, the Court ruled that a state committee's questions about membership in the Progressive (Henry Wallace) party were improper. In 1963, it applied the same restriction to a state investigation's demand for the membership lists of the National Association for the Advancement of Colored People. On the other hand, a 1959 ruling affirmed the right of a state inquiry to ask an official of World Fellowship, Incorporated, to submit names of those who attended its summer camp, on the grounds that there was a sufficient possibility of the organization's association with "subversive activity" to justify such probing.[18]

The courts have insisted on other legal protections for witnesses, such as the stipulation that the committees follow their own rules. Persons who give answers that are "incorrect," that is, defined as "perjury," can be prosecuted only when the questions are legally precise. Thus, the indictment of Owen Lattimore, for denying he was a "follower of the Communist line," was dismissed by a federal district court because the terminology was too vague for a determination by a jury.[19] Of course, the most publicized effort to avoid interrogation has been the invocation of the privilege of avoiding self-incrimination under the Fifth Amendment, originally stipulated by the Supreme Court in several cases in 1955. The details of these and subsequent rulings are complex, but the essential feature is that the privilege can only be invoked when the witness may be prosecuted for his testimony.[20]

Appellate court rulings on legislative investigations have not stymied the activities of these committees but have offered witnesses some procedural protections. Actually, other types of legal actions, which are not based on general principles, have recently become more important. Contempt citations against recalcitrant witnesses were lost, or set aside, somewhere in the adjudication process.[21] In essence, any type of question defined as related to the clear and present danger of subversion must be answered by a witness, but refusal to answer need not always result in legal penalties.

Loyalty and Security

The loyalty and security programs constitute the subject of a later extensive analysis. Court rulings have, in some ways, limited their impact. Perhaps the most important was a 1956 Supreme Court decision that restricted the "security" criterion to "sensitive" agencies, but declared that employees in other agencies could be dismissed on loyalty grounds if proper procedures were followed.[22] The apparent result was a comparative cessation of such "employment tests" for many federal employees. The damage to freedom of expression and association was, however, already quite pervasive by that time, and a large number of people were still covered by "security" regulations.

In one of the first significant cases, in 1951, a federal circuit court of appeals declared that due process was not necessary in investigations because a government job is neither "property" nor "liberty." Furthermore, First Amendment considerations are not relevant since, under various statutes, an employee's politics offer legally permissible grounds for dismissal. Court decisions have generally affirmed this theme of the program's basic legitimacy despite the vigorous criticisms by individual judges.[23] The courts have reversed several administrative decisions that were unfavorable to employees on grounds of improper procedures or unclear standards. But the rulings have not been consistent and have frequently assumed the character of advisory admonitions rather than legally binding stipulations.[24] They have furnished some protection to suspect employees because of the possibility that a negative judgment might be reversed if they undertook the difficult process of litigation. Similarly, a 1951 decision on the attorney general's list of subversive organizations supplied an option for redress. The Supreme Court declared that a listed organization had the right of appeal, an opportunity later utilized by several groups.[25] This, too, required an elaborate and lengthy process. With the exception of the ruling confining the "security" concept, court actions on the loyalty and security programs have contributed to the defense of freedom of expression and association primarily through their presentation of legal justifications for potential suits by aggrieved individuals and groups.

Loyalty Oaths

Before World War II, state laws about the loyalty of employees were mostly in the form of requirements for teachers' oaths. Since then "loyalty oaths" and similar tests for public employees have spread widely, some regulations along those lines existing in more than thirty states and many localities, although in a few they have covered only school teachers. The provisions varied from the requirement of a simple statement that one does not personally advocate or belong to any organization which advocates the violent overthrow of the government to an assertion that one is not currently, or has not recently been, a member of an organization on the attorney general's subversive list or some similar list. If one regards these "disclaimer" oaths as a threat to civil liberties, the Supreme Court has, in a step-by-step process, developed into a bastion of those liberties. Initially, the Court upheld the legality of such oaths, with the explicit addendum that "innocent membership" would probably not be a legally acceptable criterion for dismissal.[26] In one of the most significant decisions in the early 1950's, affirming New York's Feinberg Law, the majority of the Court seemed to approve the entire principle of these oaths.[27] The decision stipulated that one's associates were a proper criterion for employment as a teacher, that no one had any "right" to such employment. It also, however, referred to the unusual safeguards provided in this legislation, especially the fairly rigorous administrative procedure to be used in "listing" any organization, including the obligation of formal hearings and the right of appeal to the courts.

In another case the same year, 1952, the Court, however,

began to whittle down all loyalty oaths. On grounds of due process, it declared an Oklahoma law unconstitutional, which required that all state employees sign a statement that they were not members at any time of any organization on the attorney general's list.[28] The basis for the decision was the previously mentioned concern that "innocent membership" might become a sufficient reason for dismissal. Over a period of time, the judges voided other similar laws on the grounds of "undue breadth" or vagueness.[29] Judges have upheld other disclaimer oaths, but lower federal courts have held that automatic dismissals of those who refused to take oaths without appropriate hearings was a violation of due process.[30]

Ultimately, the Supreme Court just about terminated the impact of teachers' oaths. A 1966 decision covered an Arizona "positive" oath, one "supporting" both the United States Constitution and the state constitution, which added the provision that those who "willfully and knowingly" are associating with the Communist party or similar organizations will both be discharged and prosecuted for perjury for signing the oath. The Court declared the oath in violation of the First Amendment because it did not include the stipulation of "specific intent" to commit illegal acts, an important defect in the light of the "perjury" potential. The culmination of this tendency was the reversal of the earlier decision about New York's Feinberg Law in 1967.[31] The majority of the Court declared that government employment did not assume any abrogation of constitutional rights, that a teacher's right to free expression was particularly inviolate, and again included the proviso of "specific intent." The Court has thus gradually reversed its acceptance of disclaimer oaths as constitutionally permissible; it has now made them nonoperative in effect. In this instance, the appellate function of the Court seems to be a crucial determinant of a policy relevant to civil liberties.[32]

Other "Subversion" Issues

Similarly, the Supreme Court has either blocked or eliminated other policies on treatment of "subversion" that libertarians considered dangerous to the maintenance of freedom of expression and association. It eliminated the Post Office's insistence that certain foreign publications could be obtained only by written request, and it also denied the State Department the right to refuse passports to suspect individuals.[33] Most importantly, its decisions have vitiated the 1950 Internal Security (McCarran) Act, and its subsequent elaborations, the most comprehensive anti-subversive legislation of post-World War II America. Although the acts are still in effect and attempts to implement them still occur, the Supreme Court rulings have curtailed the likelihood of meaningful application of most of the provisions, especially the major sections requiring various types of "registration"—of "Communist Action," "Communist Front," and "Communist Infiltrated" groups—the description based on the decisions of the Subversive Activities Board. The Communist party was compelled to register shortly after the law was passed. After a tortuous and complicated process of litigation, the Supreme Court, about fifteen years later in 1965, affirmed the right of Communist leaders to refuse to register. The argument was that registration would constitute self-incrimination and thus be in violation of the Fifth Amendment because people had already been convicted for such membership. Similarly, other attempts at compulsory registration of organizations under any of the listed categories have failed, either by court rulings or administrative decisions.[34] No organization has, at this writing, registered under the provisions of these acts. The acts have never been officially voided or repealed, but the major sections have proven legally meaningless.

Summary

In recent American history, the period under analysis in this volume, the appellate courts have obviously had some effect on decisions involving the contrary values of protection against subversion and civil liberties. Their rulings, however, have hardly been clearly in one direction, and the consequences have varied, depending on the specific type of policy they were asked to judge. (Furthermore, the "libertarian" trend was not conspicuous until the late 1950's, when many of these policies had become less pervasive.) In the "legitimacy" cases, those under the Smith Act, the Supreme Court first affirmed the legality of the conviction of Communist party leaders and then drastically limited the possibility of extending the principle. What is important to our analysis is that such action was a minor component of the era, affecting few people.[35] Similarly, the de facto scuttling of the McCarran Act by court action concerned legislation whose impact was only symbolic, that is, almost no one was directly harmed by its formulations. Other provisions which the courts voided—passport and Post Office regulations—were only "nuisance" features of the suppressive atmosphere of the times.

The most significant techniques were those associated with legislative inquiries and loyalty-security programs, and the courts' role in relation to these was, at best, mixed. After a while, they practically eradicated disclaimer loyalty oaths. On the other hand, they also, by and large, legitimated loyalty-security programs, although they did restrict some of their application and provided some procedural protections, usually in force only if someone actively sought to use these procedures as a basis for an appeal. Judicial review has had less of a direct impact on legislative investigations. It has not prevented the omnibus probes with their legally sanctioned penalties and other consequences. The principles enunciated by the courts have primarily provided safeguards for recalcitrant witnesses *who avail themselves of them.* In general, in the areas that form the bulk of our analysis of the post-World War II era, the appellate courts have assisted the defense of freedom of expression and association by supplying legally permissible options for those who wish to resist suppressive devices.

In other types of disputes involving such civil liberties questions, many of them discussed in this volume, court rulings have been more singularly decisive.

A major share of most legalistic discussions about civil liberties is devoted to the clash between First Amendment freedoms and other legally prescribed social demands, in which there is no conceivable threat to national security or the legitimacy of the social order, and so forth. The "preferred position" doctrine has been appropriately applicable in such contests. At issue is the dispute over the proper application of government "police powers," the right to maintain public order, safety, morals, tranquility, sanitation, and so on, against some element of freedom of expression and/or association. Usually, the regulations of states and municipalities rather than the national government are involved, and the Supreme Court has been much more apt to void these statutes than those passed by Congress. Many of the "cases" that result cover the episodic "nuisance" suppression rather than those that are profound or extensive.[36] In very recent times, because of some relevance to the Civil Rights movement, for example, and also, possibly, opposition to the war in Vietnam, they have had some pertinence for important national political questions.

How can municipalities regulate public meetings without violating the First Amendment? An 1897 Supreme Court decision permitted a local government to bar all meetings in public parks and highways. Since the late 1930's, this doctrine has been considerably modified. The general tenor of subsequent rulings has been along these lines: regulations must be "reasonable"; must not discriminate; must actually be used to regulate rather than prevent free expression and demonstration; and must, in most cases, assume something resembling an actual "clear and present" danger to public order.[37] What if "insulting" language is used, which means that the question of defamation as well as public order may be germane? Court rulings have varied. The presumed general principle was established in a much quoted Supreme Court ruling in 1942, written by Justice Frank Murphy.[38] He excluded from the protection of the First Amendment "the lewd and obscene, the profane, the libelous, and the insulting 'fighting' words—those which by their very utterance inflict injury or tend to incite an immediate breach of the peace." Nevertheless, this formula has not furnished a readily apparent guide. The Supreme Court has, in different situations, set aside the conviction of a presumed "rabble-rouser" and permitted police action against an "inciting" speaker. It has refused to sanction denial of a permit to anyone because of the effect of his previous speeches, considering such action as a form of prior censorship.[39] None of these decisions, however important to the specific people concerned, including libertarian spokesmen, and whatever the attention received in many writings on civil liberties, has any appreciable significance for an understanding of the important civil liberties problems of our times, with the possible exception of the application of Justice Murphy's language to other situations.

When the legal disputes were associated with civil rights activities in the South, the decisions were more significant. The conviction of demonstrators, under "breach of peace" local ordinances, was set aside by the Supreme Court because of the absence of any apparent threat of violence. Sit-in arrestees faced mixed reactions in appealing to higher courts until the Supreme Court, in 1966, upheld the rights of those engaged in a public library sit-in. In the language of the prevailing opinion, the action constituted a "peaceable" protest, "in a place where the protestant has every right to be" against an unconstitutional segregation. With other types of demonstrations, however, particularly those directed at law enforcement and courts, the Supreme Court rulings have been complex. Generally, convictions under local ordinances have been overturned because of the absence of obvious "breach of peace" threats or because the statutes were too "broad" or "vague." [40] In one case, however, the Court declared that, although, in line with earlier decisions, demonstrations to affect court decisions were permissible, there must be no threat of physical action. By 1966, this admonition was extended to demonstrations in front of jails, and the demonstrator's convictions were upheld.[41] In summary, the courts have legitimated some types of "nonviolent" demonstrations but not others, Whether the result will be a stifling of such activities is not yet clear. Whatever the thorny value and legal problems implicit, they do mean that some type of freedom of expression and association may be curtailed. The role of the courts thus becomes very consequential, as is likewise true of all other issues posed by recent "confrontation" tactics, most of which have not yet received higher court hearings.[42]

In some types of disputes related to First Amendment freedoms, the appellate court rulings have been extremely crucial. For instance, they have significantly contributed to "freedom" within private organizations, such as trade unions. Finally, in some areas, the principles laid down by the courts have been the *major* decision-making mechanisms, that is, their rulings have, in large measure, determined what actually happened in American society. One of the reasons is that they do not typically involve weighty political issues. Among these are the questions of libel and slander and, most prominently, censorship. Since courts are the predominant area in which such questions are resolved, an account of the more pertinent rulings is best left to the detailed analysis of these problems.

AN ASSESSMENT

An appraisal of the meaning and function of appellate court rulings within a sociology of civil liberties is relevant here. At the outset, it should be noted that the many discussions of the subject tend to be very formalistic. Court actions are discussed as entities in themselves, without even considering what brought the case into being in the first place and what happened as a result. For example, it is seldom mentioned that when Holmes promulgated his "clear and present danger" doctrine he was actually approving a man's sentence to a prison term and that the immediate result was the further legitimation of government prosecution of certain types of wartime dissenters. Commentators rarely refer to the fact that some rulings have occurred after either the relevant law or the case no longer had any meaning. What is missing, essentially, is sufficient attention to events in their historic contexts. At the beginning of this chapter, the role of the courts as the leading defender of First Amendment freedoms was challenged on several grounds—their "libertarian" decisions did not come until fairly late in the nation's history and even these rulings have hardly been so characteristically libertarian, protection of liberties has been mostly on procedural grounds, other branches of government have sometimes been more libertarian, and so on. A few summary statements on the actual functions of the courts as they affect recent civil liberties problems are in order. The analysis focuses on "higher" appellate courts, particularly the United States Supreme Court. Obviously, the actions of trial courts and "lower" appeals courts are also significant.

If this were an exhaustive treatment of the subject, we would have to begin by asking why the judges decide as they do. Unfortunately, little is available that could be helpful. In analyzing any area of Supreme Court rulings, a "deterministic" approach is very difficult. It is far more difficult in the types of cases under review. The judges are obviously not merely "following the election returns," or ascribing to a "national consensus." Often, their decisions may well be a product of the "times," of political pressures, of the influence of other judges, litigants, lawyers, or of the influences exercised on each other.[43] But none of this has as yet been sufficiently substantiated or systemized, suggesting a potential avenue of inquiry for the "sociology of law." At the moment, one must be satisfied with a traditional, working, operational dictum—the judges of the highest courts seem to act as independent minds, determining their positions on the basis of their legal and, perhaps, political philosophies.

It is easier to assay their possible impact. In First Amendment stipulations, it is something other than what Robert Dahl found typical of most Supreme Court decisions, a mere postponement of the actions of other branches or an impulsion to recast statutes to conform with the decisions.[44] As indicated by several scholars, several types of functions can be listed. Frequently, and especially in earlier times, the judges simply *affirmed* the suppressive actions of other branches. In a few of the types of cases discussed, they thoroughly *voided* potential or actual suppressive acts, by whatever legal mechanisms used. The end of state anti-subversive legislation and the effective termination of state loyalty oaths are examples. This frequently occurs when the operation of those acts has ceased to be very relevant. Sometimes, decisions effectively *eradicate* suppressive legislation by *procedural safeguards,* as happened to most of the McCarran Act. Similarly, judicial rulings have, to some extent, *limited and checked* the authoritarian behavior of congressional committees and the operations of loyalty and security programs. A corollary idea is that court rulings *provide a basis for legal redress,* as for those cited by congressional committees or dismissed under loyalty-security programs. All of these suggest another function. A series of decisions may *accumulate* into a *major impact,* even though each decision is a seemingly small-scale limitation on government authoritarianism, as further applicable to the voiding of local "nuisance" regulations. In a few situations, the courts, in line with the charge of many critics, do actually *establish* the *de facto policy* and tend to become the crucial decision-makers. The best examples are the murky areas, in both legal and value terms, of censorship and libel, which also tend to be minor issues politically in recent times.

Finally, higher court judges *establish* the tone of *legitimacy* or *illegitimacy* beyond the direct, official consequences of their decisions. As several commentators have pointed out, they have become our leading "philosophers of civil liberties," representing the "morality of our tradition," the symbolic exponents of the Constitution.[45] Their decisions are not always so clear as to be obviously legally binding but they become, whatever the varying attitudes toward specific decisions, the most prominent public "educators" in such matters. As explained by Alexander Bickel they are "leaders of opinion" and not mere "registers." But, as he adds, they "lead" and do not "impose." [46]

Whatever they do, however, is within a total political context. As Dahl's investigations indicate, other branches of government have typically circumvented Supreme Court rulings, at least after a while.[47] In many First Amendment decisions, this has not been so evident. Of particular significance to this volume was the failure of Congress to "overturn" the late 1950's Supreme Court decisions that, among other things, checked and limited the operations of legislative investigations and the loyalty-security programs, despite the vigorous efforts of some congressmen. The actions of other congressmen simply stymied these attempts.[48] Wallace Mendelson, in criticizing those who emphasize the role of the courts as defenders of civil liberties, cautions that "man after all is a political, not a legal, animal." [49] If one adds the proviso that what the judges do are also *political* acts, albeit special to them, and comprise one type of political action among the many that are performed, a central theme of our analytical scheme should become evident. Civil liberties decisions are essentially political, no matter who makes them or how or why he makes them.

One of the variables, and to many the most important variable, which may affect the nature of those decisions, is public opinion. The next task is actually examining popular opinions and appraising their significance for our analyses.

5

The relevance of public opinion

EVIDENCE FROM OPINION STUDIES

The major type of finding that many libertarian spokesmen dramatize is the vast amount of apparent intolerance indicated. The seeming conflict between widespread beliefs and the principles of the First Amendment has, understandably, cautioned any reliance on popular attitudes as the basis for civil liberties. It is most evident in regard to the rights of "Communists." As far back as 1937, a Gallup poll disclosed that the majority of American voters were opposed to granting certain rights to Communists —disseminating their literature, holding public office, holding public meetings, or even expressing their views. During the wartime alliance with Russia, the attitude toward Communists was less severe. Still, in a national sample two-fifths of those interviewed would not permit a Communist party member to speak on the radio. The figure increased to 57 per cent in 1948, and was up to 77 per cent in 1952.[1] In the most extensive national survey on such questions, that directed by Samuel Stouffer under the sponsorship of the Fund for the Republic in the middle of 1954, only 27 per cent of a national sample would give an "admitted Communist" the right to speak in their communities, almost two-thirds believed that a Communist radio singer should be fired, and about two-thirds would fire a Communist who was a store clerk.[2]

Apparently, the overwhelming majority of Americans supported the rationale of McCarthyite strictures. To accent the specific historical context, 81 per cent would not allow a Communist to speak on the radio, which was double the proportion who so responded during World War II.[3] The figure was still 75 per cent in 1957.[4] Other popular attitudes on "treatment" of an "admitted Communist" were also striking. Two-thirds believed that a book he had written should be removed from the public library, and more than three-fourths thought his American citizenship should be revoked. A little over half thought he should be put in jail. Almost two-thirds felt that the government should be permitted to listen to private conversations to get evidence against Communists.[5]

Of course, the question of rights of Communists involves many considerations and is not necessarily, by itself, a clear-cut index of libertarian or nonlibertarian attitudes. Popular opinion about freedoms for other dissenting political tendencies is hardly as restrictive, although the findings have also prompted concern among libertarians. One quarter of a polled national sample shortly before World War II would not allow Socialists the right to publish newspapers.[6] By 1953, the proportion had increased to 45 per cent, and it was still 39 per cent in 1957.[7] In the Stouffer study, the question was more precisely posed in terms of the right of those who advocated "government ownership of the railroads and big industries." Thirty-one per cent would deny them the right to speak publicly in their communities. Fifty-eight per cent would grant them this right, which means one can either emphasize the large amount of intolerance or the fact that the majority seemed "tolerant." [8] Such varying sets of interpretations are possible for many of the published findings.

When the questions were posed in more general terms, the results may also be shocking to libertarians. A pre-World War II

Gallup poll disclosed that 34 per cent believed newspapers should not be permitted to take sides during an election. A more extensive national study in 1953 found that 45 per cent would not allow newspapers to "criticize our form of government." [9] A more complex set of findings emerged from the *Minnesota Poll,* conducted in the Minneapolis–St. Paul area, probably one of the more "tolerant" regions in the nation. In a 1953 inquiry, one-fourth of the respondents would not accept the provision that publications should be allowed to print anything they want other than military "secrets," another finding that can be variously interpreted. More significantly, however, a majority believed that "certain groups should not be allowed to hold public meetings" and that the "government should not allow some people to make public speeches." [10] Phrased somewhat differently in a 1962 poll, 56 per cent felt the "government should not allow people to make speeches which contain dangerous ideas." [11] Among students in social science classes at Northwestern University queried in the mid-1950's only 57 per cent agreed, in essence, with the right of peaceable assembly of all groups without government restriction; considering the nature of the sample, this result may also be upsetting to libertarians.[12] One possibly surprising result in the Stouffer study was that fewer people would grant rights to atheists than to "socialists." Sixty per cent would deny atheists the right to speak, and a similar proportion would remove a book by an atheist "against churches and religion" from the public libraries.[13]

All of these findings should obviously lead to some anxiety among the defenders of civil liberties and should make any claims that their maintenance essentially depends on "public opinion" somewhat suspect.[14] But the "other side" must also be considered.

OTHER FINDINGS

Libertarians can find gratification in some of the findings, however. A clear majority of Stouffer's sample of all Americans would grant advocates of government ownership free speech, and more than 80 per cent of the Northwestern group believed in the essential free speech and press doctrine of the First Amendment. Whatever other attitudes were revealed in the *Minnesota Polls,* more than two-thirds of the respondents, in queries in both 1953 and 1962, supported the principle of a free press.[15]

A closer look at Stouffer's answers is also in order. Even though the study was conducted amidst the McCarthyite atmosphere, the majority did not favor the typical "excesses" of the time when explicitly asked. For instance, even though almost two-thirds thought a Communist radio singer should be fired, only about one-third would boycott his sponsor if he continued on the job. As will be demonstrated, it was fear of a contrary sentiment that prompted the broadcasting "blacklist." Only about a third would terminate their friendship with anyone who "had been a Communist until recently, although he says he is not now." A rather small minority would penalize anyone "whose loyalty has been questioned before a Congressional committee, but who swears under oath he has never been a Communist." The largest proportion who would support any unfavorable action against him was about one-fifth.[16] As will be seen, this is opposed to the stigma that frequently resulted from appearances before such committees.

Furthermore, one of the most publicized findings was that those defined as "community leaders" were, generally, more libertarian than the average. This turned out to be true for such varied people as local political officials, party leaders, presidents of both labor unions and the chambers of commerce, presidents of bar associations and woman's clubs, and even the local officials of the American Legion and the Daughters of the American Revolution. The opinions of leaders of the last two organizations, generally the least libertarian, are illustrative. Almost three-fourths of the American Legion commanders and DAR regents would permit a man with "socialist" ideas to speak; among a cross section of the population in the same cities, only 60 per cent would grant that right. Almost half the Legion commanders and 56 per cent of the DAR officials would allow an atheist to speak; only 39 per cent of the population sample in the same cities would do so. Almost half the Legion commanders and 36 per cent of the DAR regents would permit an admitted Communist to speak; 28 per cent of the population sample in the same cities would do so. Almost half of all the community leaders would fire a Communist radio singer, which can be considered a rather high proportion for this type of question. Still, it compares with the almost two-thirds of the population cross section in the same cities.[17]

Thus, the libertarianism of community leaders is generally greater than that of the general population, but it should not be exaggerated. About two-thirds favored revoking a Communist's citizenship, a figure significantly lower than the 80 per cent of the general sample in the same cities who had a similar opinion, but still conspicuous. Especially interesting is the fact that the comparative tolerance of the community leaders did not generally extend to the seemingly sensitive area of teaching. Thus, 71 per cent would not permit an atheist to teach in a college or university; the figure for the cross section in the same cities was 85 per cent. In discussing those with "socialist" ideas, 47 per cent of the community leaders would not allow them to teach as compared to 54 per cent of the general sample in the same cities.[18]

Other differences in attitudes noted in the study might be encouraging to libertarians. The proportion of "tolerant" responses increased with more education and decreased with age. The pattern is quite consistent. With younger and more educated people becoming numerically larger this could imply an enhancing of libertarian opinions. Density of population also varied directly with degree of "tolerance," libertarian attitudes more characteristic of metropolitan residents and least likely in rural areas.[19] The population trend again indicates a possible increase in general libertarian opinions.

Similarly, studies of university students, an increasing proportion of the population, also seemed to indicate more libertarian values. The investigation at Northwestern, even if it did produce some apprehension among libertarians, indicated that a decisive majority favored the principles of the First Amendment.[20] This was even more marked in a probe of the attitudes of students at the University of California at Berkeley in the late 1950's, which asked more specific questions related to the subject.[21] To give a few examples, only 6 per cent would bar Russian or Chinese newspapers from general circulation, 10 per cent would have legal restrictions against meetings of groups who "disagree with our form of government," and 13 per cent would fire a high school teacher who pleaded the Fifth Amendment before a congressional committee. Some of the support for what can be termed "restrictive policies" was a little higher, but still only a minority. Twenty-nine per cent thought it was proper for legislative committees to investigate the political beliefs of faculty members, 27 per cent would fire a teacher in a private university who was a former Communist party member who refused to reveal the names of other party members, and 30 per cent thought it was appropriate for government investigators to take pictures of people listening to a street-corner speech. Another finding, quite in line with all the others presented, was that tolerant opinions increased with length of time at the university and involvement in school activities.

What seems to emerge is a general interpretation of popular acceptance of some of the principles of freedom of expression and association, but support of many restrictive policies, often situationally induced. The degree of libertarianism tends to increase with greater knowledge as well as interest in and involvement with civic affairs, suggesting greater "tolerance" among opinion-leaders and decision-makers. The question of the meaning of these findings for a sociology of civil liberties has still to be determined.

SALIENCY OF ISSUE

Opinions, attitudes, values, and so on, that are directly related to First Amendment questions are not, by themselves, crucial determinants because they do not mean that much to most people. Similarly, other general issues that might directly affect libertarian or anti-libertarian positions are comparatively low in the priority of interests. In the Stouffer study, for instance, the respondents were asked "what kinds of things do you worry about most?" The proportion of the national sample mentioning either civil liberties or the threat of Communists in the United States was less than 1 per cent. Further probing raised the figure to 8 per cent. Even for community leaders, the original question yielded a figure of 5 per cent who worried about civil liberties or Communists, which is five times the proportion of the general population but still incredibly low. Further probing raised the figure to a fairly significant 17 per cent, of which 14 per cent mentioned the dangers from Communists.[22]

The relative existence or denial of civil liberties depends upon much more than "value consensus," the "voice of the people," or the "general will," even in America with a common abstract acceptance of the general principle. The issue, and related issues, has not occupied an important position among the personalized values that are dearly held. Accounts of the "ethos," the underlying predominant value system of American culture, buttress this interpretation. In Robert Lynd's study of Muncie, Indiana, in the mid-1930's, described in *Middletown in Transition,* the author sought to list the ingredients of the "Middletown Spirit." In his summary of the dominant beliefs of this midwestern community, which comprised an entire chapter, there is very little that can be considered relevant to libertarian or anti-libertarian attitudes.[23] The author himself once did a summary of the American ethos, as viewed by historians, travelers, social scientists, community analysts, and so on.[24] The dominant themes emphasized included such things as rational mastery of the environment, inventiveness and adventurousness, self-reliance and self-validation, friendliness, optimism, and so forth. But there was little reference to anything associated with civil liberties, particularly First Amendment freedoms. In his more composite account of American values, which he found relatively constant throughout history, Seymour Lipset found it appropriate to consider civil liberties only at the beginning of the Republic, when the nation's political leaders were openly ambivalent about the question.[25]

Other explanations of civil liberties as grounded entirely on opinions and values concentrate on special sectors of the populace, some undefined or specifically located "elite," as suggested in the introductory chapter.[26] These explanations can be as inadequate as the value consensus models. Whether this very cloudy term is meant to refer to the more cultivated, the more humanistic, or the more powerful, this type of analysis is at variance with the historical accounts presented, especially in the United States. Even among those for whom the issue is more salient, general libertarian beliefs do not necessarily produce appropriate behavior. Because of their "elite" positions in society, these people may sometimes be impelled to act in conflict with their values. The point is that for them, as for all others, opinions, and especially those on specific questions, are not a necessary index of what they will do or, equally important, what will result. The elaboration of these truisms becomes the appropriate corollary of our assessment of the function of opinions on civil liberties issues.

THE CONTEXT OF OPINIONS

General, abstract, or even causal acceptance of the rights of freedom of expression and association, and even more fervent adherence among the influential, is probably an essential ingredient for the existence of this type of civil liberty. They are not sufficient explanations, however, because of, to summarize crisply, two kinds of reasons: political-social decisions are not a mere composite of opinions and, to repeat, a discerned opinion does not necessarily determine behavior.[27] The first proviso will be dealt with at length in the following chapters. Initially, however, one feature of the "elite" formula should be noted. Everyone's opinions obviously do not have the same consequences. For instance, the opinions of Supreme Court justices, however derived, generally have greater significance than those of anybody else because they are called upon to make so many relevant decisions. As an overall formula, this is applicable to all government officials. Stouffer allays some of the prevailing pessimism from his findings with his accent on the apparent greater "tolerance" of community leaders, for, after all, they are the people most likely to influence others' ideas and to mobilize supporters.[28]

More immediately germane is the relation between opinion, particularly expressed opinion, and action. Even when the citizenry is called upon to make a decision on the basis of its opinions, as in elections and referenda, the connnections are complex and sometimes surprising, as observed in all voting analyses. To take an example directly related to our subject, about two-thirds of polled Australians were in favor of outlawing the Communist party. Yet a national referendum on the proposition, conducted about the same time, was defeated.[29]

As indicated earlier in this work, pro- and anti-libertarian values must be viewed in relation to other values.[30] Some bolster libertarian inclinations; for the immediate purpose, however, those values which may produce a conflict are more pertinent. To offer only the most prominent examples, adherence to the idea of freedom of expression and association may yield to such other strongly held values as patriotism, religious and political orthodoxies, desire for social stability and the maintenance of the social order. These and similar values are the essential bases for court decisions that balance First Amendment freedoms against other legal and, implicitly, value considerations.

The dimension of saliency must again be emphasized. How significant are libertarian or anti-libertarian values in a specific situational context? What is being asked is what will a person be motivated to do or not do to achieve or diminish any of these

values. The low priority of civil liberties within the value hier-
archy means that most Americans will do, and have done, very
little in most situations to defend them. Since there is a typical abstract adherence to those values, they will usually do little to
thwart them. There may be things that can make these questions
more salient, as will be later elaborated. For most people, the
motivation to act in some way is a product of some combination
of other values and/or some type of "self-interest." These values
and interests may, moreover, be quite tangential to questions of
civil liberties themselves. This was a basic theme that emerged
from historical surveys. So much of the development of freedom
of expression and association can be credited to the desire of
many groups to claim this right for themselves and thus, in so
many cases, to help engender a social-political system that extended them to many others. Even philosophical defenses of such
freedoms are frequently posed in terms of practicability, which
has been the motivation of many who have struggled for them.
The emphasis is on liberty as an instrumental value—it will
create more knowledge, a better society, make one a better
scientist, and so forth. An even more "tangential" possibility is
illustrated by the seeming paradox that, although, according to
some surveys, working-class respondents tend to have less libertarian opinions than others, their organizations have been among
the most important agencies for the development and maintenance of civil liberties.[31] These bodies simply could not grow or
function in the absence of such liberties in society. What we are
suggesting is the value of the concept of "latent function" as
originally devised by Robert Merton, which can be crudely summarized as the search for the behavioral consequences of social
action beyond what the actors consciously intended.[32]

Anti-libertarian attitudes can also be "tangential" to the suppressive behavior that follows or for which they lend support.
The attitudes may be irrelevant to the situation. In Stouffer's
material, the national sample was particularly adamant about
granting rights to atheists. Yet outspoken atheists were hardly
prominent at the time, and the generally uncontested religiosity

of America was a frequently observed phenomena. Perhaps the findings can be explained by the identification of irreligion and communism. When asked what "Communists believe in," about a quarter of both the national sample and the community leaders emphasized that they were "against religion." [33] Such attitudes may be one of the reasons for the new fundamentalist appeal of the "radical right" since the time of the study, resulting in a more general type of anti-libertarian intolerance. But, at that time, the contest between religion and atheism was not a significant public issue. The sentiments revealed helped justify suppressions that were based on quite other considerations.

Similarly, when asked about what aspect of communism they most feared, twice as many of the sample referred to something that could be codified as "conversion" or "spreading ideas" as those who mentioned items that could be classified as "espionage" or "sabotage." Within the group of community leaders, the findings were even more striking. More than three times as many considered "conversions and spreading ideas" as dangers as compared to those who stipulated "espionage" and "sabotage." [34] Yet, as will be further amplified, not only was the political impact of the Communist party reduced to a virtually nonexistent influence by that time but also the official anti-Communist spokesmen, ranging from those in government to intellectuals, accentuated the threat Communists posed as hidden "conspirators," and not as open propagandists. Those who were worried about communism in the study were thus worried for the wrong reason. The suppressions that did occur were rarely, and certainly not officially, because of anyone's "ideas," but were usually based upon potential behavior. Again, specific attitudes provided a bulwark for anti-libertarian acts that were, at best, "tangential" to those opinions.

In summary, the emphasis on public opinion as the basis for the existence or relative absence of civil liberties is even more limited than the emphasis on court rulings. In different ways, both are important. Court rulings involve actual binding decisions. Opinions, and their underlying value basis, are obviously part of the process by which decisions relevant to civil liberties are made, but they must be further elaborated in terms of such variables as relative significance of opinions of different people, relationship to other values, saliency of those opinions to the people who held them and the resulting motivation for behavior, and relevance to the situational context.[35] Another related element, which will be considered in more detail later, is the clarity of the opinions in the situational context.

Decisions about civil liberties are political decisions, whether made by government or private groups. With this statement as the basis of our orientation, the general model for our analytical scheme follows. Its formulation is based on a utilization of the original theoretical propositions, the historical summaries, the accounts of the role of government agencies and court decisions, the analysis of public opinion material, plus an anticipation of some of the data included in the specific analyses of post-World War II events that form the major body of this volume.

6

A working analytical model

THE SCHEME OF ANALYSIS

A scientific "model" is a conceptual tool, an intellectual mechanism for organizing ideas and data so as to provide a more meaningful explanation of any phenomena. The "grand models" of the physical sciences are abstract constructs, with enough resemblances to some aspects of the "real" universe that they lead to the most appropriately precise and testable propositions explaining at least that part of the reality. Some social scientific models may approach such requirements.

Our aim is more modest. We can hardly offer the desired precision or systematization. On the basis of what has already been said and some preliminary ideas about what is to follow, it is both possible and helpful to set up a scheme for locating the variables relevant to a sociology of civil liberties and to suggest some of their interrelations. The intellectual outlook is a multivariate "field" approach—the existence, extension, limitation, and defense of freedom of expression and association are a result of a constellation of specific types of factors. Since the subsequent material is mostly concerned with "threats," in the contemporary United States the emphasis is on the last two types of resultants, or "outputs"—limitations and maintenance of liberties. The most popular analyses in discussions of civil liberties, the legal-juridical and the crude "opinion" approaches, have been deemed as insufficient at best. Instead, we offer the following framework for investigation: the relative existence or curtailment of freedom of expression and association is viewed as a product of a series of choices and appropriate behavior of particular people, as affected by a set of *values*, specially involved *roles,* kinds of institutional *structures* and *processes,* and concrete *situational* factors. Since these elements are seen as forming a matrix, they will tend to overlap and have an effect on each other. Although devised for this particular area of interest, it is our belief that a similar scheme could be relevant for political sociology generally. In essence, it is an elaboration of "decision-making" analysis.

A hypothetical "pure" authoritarian complex society, which has probably existed, or a "pure" libertarian society, which may have occasionally been approached, would not be readily available to such analysis. There is an obvious assumption of "conflict." Somebody wants something, or does something, which can lead to the extension or retraction of somebody's freedom. The quest for the nature of the social *actors* involved, why and how they act as they do, and the possible consequences becomes the principal objective of inquiry.

From here on emphasis will be on problems in recent America. If this were a comparison of different societies, one would try to correlate the general degree of freedom of expression and association with the likelihood of particular values, roles, structures, and situations. Since the focus is on this country, one must begin with the given datum that, with all the limitations, restrictions, and crises described, such liberties have generally prevailed in America for the following reasons: many people value them somewhat and a few a great deal, and the legitimacy of the Constitution which formalizes them is generally accepted; there are people whose specific roles encourage their involvement in maintaining such liberties; there exist structures which facilitate their continuation, especially the courts; and there have been few situations seriously challenging legitimate power-wielders and the legitimate order.[1] Our major interest then becomes one of probing threats to such freedoms. This means, first of all, that the threats, themselves, must be clearly demarcated. Then one seeks to ascertain what factors produced those threats, what were the countervailing elements, and what were the varying results. The following elaboration of the analytical scheme is a guide suggesting what to search for, but it also includes several propositional statements about the foundations for maintenance or retraction of freedom of expression and association, some of them already indicated.

THE "ACTORS"

In analyzing the civil liberties decisions under review, three different types of people can be discerned: the actual *decision-makers,* the *influencers,* and the *affected.*

Decision-Makers

Decision-makers include all those whose acts permit or curtail someone's freedom of expression or association. The most obvious and publicized examples are government officials of all types, whose decisions carry the legitimate force of the state behind them and directly affirm or deny a particular right—a court trying or hearing appeals on a case, an executive enforcing a law, or a legislative representative considering the adoption of a law related to a civil liberties question, for example. Other government officials have more indirect effects—congressional committee investigators, department officials responsible for "loyalty and security" programs, and so forth. They do not determine what one can legally say or do, but the formal and informal sanctions available can have and apparently have had significant effects.

Other types of decision-makers can limit, maintain, or extend civil liberties by the type of sanctions available. They can frighten dissidents with threatened or actual expulsion, loss of job, damaged reputation, even physical violence, or refrain from doing any of those. Other decisions may not involve any serious individual deprivations. A book may be removed from a library, a magazine taken from a newsstand, a newspaper barred from the mails, or a group denied a meeting hall. Books and periodicals may still appear elsewhere and the organization may find another hall. But those who make the decisions are restricting expression and association. In fact, that is the conscious intent of some of those responsible for such decisions. Contrariwise, those who are, for various reasons, asked to make such decisions and refuse are thus deciding in favor of civil liberties.[2]

Influencers

The *influencers* try to affect the decision-makers, with devices ranging from a legal brief to some form of "pressure" politics. The pressure may vary from a test case before a court, to the various techniques used to sway legislatures, to campaigns to persuade librarians and booksellers to remove, or keep, particular books. The influencers include the myriad of individuals or groups making such efforts.

The "Affected"

The person or group affected, those whose freedoms are challenged, are not necessarily passive agents. Even in response to decisions by some branch of the state carrying inherent sanctions of force, there are options available, extending from the extreme of civil disobedience, to suits and legal appeals, to continued political campaigns, that is, pressure for changing the decision. For other types of decisions, the alternatives are more open. There may be quite different reactions to loyalty-security investigations, threat of job loss, and so on—yielding, ignoring, fighting back, or pressuring for change. For instance, a witness before a congressional committee who believes questions asked of him are violations of his civil liberty may answer them, plead the Fifth

Amendment, answer selectively and thus risk a contempt citation, challenge the committee openly, and so on, with varying possible consequences. An additional variable affecting the reaction of the affected "victim," and the possible impact on the ultimate decision, is the likelihood and nature of support from individuals or groups of influencers—legal assistance, pressure politics in his behalf or in favor of the principle he seeks to extol, and so forth.[3]

Values, roles, structures, and situations—interdependent and overlapping elements—motivate the actors and determine the nature of the actions of either the decision-makers, the influencers, or the affected, and thus contribute to actual decisions. As spelled out in the introduction and amplified at other points, the impulsion to act is frequently not directly related to a civil liberties question. (This almost simplistic statement about *latent functions* seems a truism by now; it is necessary to reiterate it because it has generally been ignored as an explicit formulation in analysis of the subject.) If the "decisions" that comprise the "dependent variable," the relative absence or presence of freedom of expression, are thus frequently motivated by latent factors, they may also have further latent consequences. For instance, the constraints resulting from government loyalty-security programs may have diminished the appeal of government employment. Such considerations are not an inherent part of the analytical design, but they obviously cannot be ignored.

Some examples of relevant values, roles, structures, and situations follow.

VALUES

Other supporting values enhance freedom of expression and association: legitimacy of government, especially the courts; individualism; civility; pluralism. Conflicting values may spur limitations of such freedoms: patriotism; orthodoxy; national security; public order; or "decency." For our purposes, the additional important variables are the *conflicts* among values, their respective *saliency* to different people, and their relative *clarity* or *ambiguity*.

Value Conflicts

Value conflicts are the substance of court decisions, usually stated in terms of legal norms—freedom of expression against the demands for mobilization of the armed forces in wartime, prevention of disorder in public parks, invasion of privacy at home, public morals and decency, or protection against "subversion." An interesting example of such conflict is revealed by differing attitudes of Supreme Court judges on whether the First Amendment occupies a "privileged position" among legal norms. Similarly, everyone else involved in the process of decision will emphasize one or more relevant values, pro- or anti-libertarian, whether in their own decisions, in attempts to influence the decisions, in striving to mobilize support, or in responding to decisions made. To use a complex example, in academic freedom cases, the "rights" of faculty members, administrators, students, or trustees may present a form of value conflict. The employment "rights" of a competent jobholder may thus be counterposed to the needs of protection against "disruptive" or "disloyal" employees. Another possible source of conflict is that between one's own values and the legitimacy of the decision-maker, who may decide contrary to those values. Thus anti-libertarian sentiments of possible influencers may be held in check by libertarian decisions of the courts, based on "constitutional values." On the other hand, an anti-libertarian decision of a government official poses the aforementioned choices for the affected, which includes the possibility of challenging its legitimacy.

Saliency

The relative importance of particular values has a great effect on what is decided or what is done to influence the decision. The decider's choice is frequently a weighing of the value options in favor of that which is most salient to the situation, as in court decisions. For the influencer, the saliency of the entire issue can determine not only the appeal used but also the amount of effort. Most disputes about literary censorship are joined only because there are a few people on either side who care about the question.[4] The intense motivation of a group avidly committed to civil liberties as a prime objective, as best exemplified by the American Civil Liberties Union, has undoubtedly had a tremendous effect.

In this respect, the notion of latent function, perhaps better defined operationally as "tangential motivation," is particularly significant, as already described. A group becomes a proponent of civil liberties to maintain or enhance its position in society. Book publishers fighting censorship may be motivated by libertarian attitudes, but they are also obviously stimulated by their commercial interests. Similarly, the general trade union support for libertarian measures in the larger society, despite the authoritarian attitudes of much of their membership and the frequently authoritarian internal operations, reflects the crucial importance of maintenance of civil liberties in the larger society for union functioning.[5] Similarly, those who perceive a threat to their positions of power may foster suppressive policies against those who constitute that threat, whatever the generic attitudes toward civil liberties.[6] To continue with the previous theme, this describes both anti-union employers and union officials fearful of organized opposition. To give one more example, freedom of expression is salient to universities not only because of a typical commitment to such a value per se but also because suppressive policies will repel scholars and produce a "poor" university.

Clarity and Ambiguity

The degree of knowledge and explicitness of attitudes have a bearing on the decider and, even more likely, on the influencers and the affected. Because of the typically low saliency of civil liberties disputes as public issues and in the vistas of much of the population, those who know and are more certain of their beliefs are more likely to act vigorously and, frequently, successfully. This is an important weapon of the avid libertarian, despite the many obstacles he must surmount. For instance, in his contests with the proponents of literary censorship he clearly knows what he wants and possesses the appropriate information to argue before a court and public. This is one of the reasons why his opponents, motivated more by vague indignation rather than by precise ideals and ideas, tend to avoid formal debates with him.[7]

Clarity, of both values and information, is particularly important in determining the behavior of the affected. Our point of departure is the psychological principle that perceptual, cognitive, and value ambiguity intensifies anxiety, increases the likelihood of submission to external controls, and, as an obvious corollary, reduces the possibility of autonomous behavior.[8] One is thus less prone to speak and act freely or to affirm the right to do so. Naturally, relative clarity will result in more assertion of autonomy and greater defense of libertarian values in the face of external pressures.

All of this is well illustrated by the varying McCarthyite phenomena later detailed. The general impact was so pervasive because so many were apprehensive about a general political atmosphere and accompanying processes that they could not understand. But the differing reactions were also based, in large measure, on the clarity-ambiguity dimension, as well as the somewhat related factor of saliency. "Resistance" was more likely among the knowledgeable and the committed.

ROLE

Requirements and Values in Role

Specific role requirements and expectations, as well as inherent value commitments, can determine both the degree of involvement in civil liberties decisions and the direction of attitude. A justice of the Supreme Court must make a decision on such questions. In recent times, the role has been further defined to emphasize guardianship of the First Amendment rights, so that many regard the Court as the most important single force in maintaining civil liberties. On the other side, a police chief may feel that his job demands that he satisfy the wishes of the local citizenry and remove certain publications from the newsstands. The federal executive involved in loyalty-security problems is faced with a value conflict between the demands of his security directives and the expectations of justice and "fairness" by many people, and he can be held accountable on both scores. The behavior of many of these government decision-makers, particularly judges, also makes them significant "influencers" because they tend to set the boundaries of legitimacy. As explained in the discussion of Supreme Court rulings, this not only defines the legally permissible but becomes a form of public "education" about values.

Lawyers tend to be concerned about civil liberties questions because these constitute an integral part of the legal value system upon which their profession is based. If all lawyers and bar associations are not always profoundly committed to defending such freedoms, there is no group which contains so many people contributing "free time" to efforts to maintain them. In essence, Alexis de Tocqueville's early nineteenth-century estimate of the importance of lawyers and judges in protecting freedom in America remains valid today.[9]

Perceptions of Role

Differing perceptions of one's role, whether it is associated with the position of decision-maker, influencer, or affected, can also determine attitudes and behavior on a civil liberties issue. Supreme Court justices differ on their estimates of their option for judicial review, the right to overturn acts of the legislature and executive, including decisions related to civil liberties questions. In one study, the likelihood of librarians' removing books upon the demand of organized groups was partly a product of their relative role security, that is, their estimate of their ability to resist such pressures without hurting their careers, and their commitments to their "professional ethic." [10] Similarly, "cosmopolite" professors were less likely than "local" professors to submit to pressures which would limit academic freedom. The former, with their wider orientations and wider reputations, were both less anxious about personal job threats and more committed to the chosen values of scholarly pursuits.[11]

STRUCTURES AND PROCEDURES

The formal scheme for decision-making and the actual process by which decisions are made have impact on the immediate decision and the general atmosphere. If we have disputed the overemphasis on legal stipulations and legal procedures, it is equally important to affirm that civil liberties require an appropriate foundation in law. The particular form and style may vary, but some definitive, and more or less legally binding statement of "rights," with mechanisms for maintaining those rights, is essential. A particularly crucial element is the provision for regularized, relatively comprehensible, and "fair" procedures for treatment of those charged with violation of laws—some element of judicial "due process." In the United States, the practice of judicial review has, at least in some instances, become a significant device for defending all types of civil liberties.

When the standards of judgment, methods for ascertaining "guilt," and meting out punishment are, in the language of court rulings, "vague," "overbroad," or, in our own language, quite capricious, the impact can be a serious diminution of freedoms. As described in connection with the subject of clarity and ambiguity, the more unclear the criteria and processes in decision-making on questions of civil liberties, the greater the apprehension and the resultant suppression. The police state is the extreme representation, but the idea is also applicable to many of the McCarthyite tendencies.

One other example of the structural and procedural variables comes from the study of library censorship. The fact that ultimate decisions were in the hands of boards and school superintendents helped determine an individual librarian's response. He was always concerned with the likely reaction of "superiors" and his personal professional security if he opposed them.[12] One other structural feature should be added, a feature of contemporary society rarely considered in discussion of civil liberties as such, but very conspicuous in contemporary sociological literature. *Bureaucratic* organizations, characterized by, among other things, an emphasis on administrative canons rather than substantive policies, behavioral conformity rather than expressions of divergence, and organizational loyalty as an operating imperative, present a constant danger to freedom of expression and association, both to those within the organization and those affected by its actions.[13]

SITUATION

National Security

The previous discussions have sufficiently emphasized the threat to civil liberties from external conflict, or from some form of mobilization for potential conflict. The values, the behavior of the people in specific roles, and the structure and operations of government can all be affected. In line with what has become the almost conventional appellation, we have included all such situations under the category of a "garrison society." This generic classification is apt, if one adds the cautionary proviso that it is not an unreserved stipulation, noting, of course, that other social variables are also involved.[14] To begin with the initial and quite obvious proposition, societies with a constant orientation toward external violence are not likely to permit much freedom of expression and association, whereas societies which are characteristically more pacifist will tend to have more civil liberties. More germane for our discussion, however, is what happens to a more or less "pacifist" society that becomes a garrison society. A further recapitulation of relevant American history reveals the complex variety of possibilities. The administration of Woodrow Wilson, in the period of World War I and shortly afterward, found men with general libertarian beliefs responsible for perhaps the most pervasive suppression in American history. World War II, however, which required a much greater involvement of natural resources in a much more extensive military operation witnessed few infringements of civil liberties, much less than the period of the cold war which followed. The Civil War was a more complex period. It is easy to document the suppressions. But it is also important to note the comparative absence of restraints in a situation of military defeats, wide and open dissension, and actual physical force utilized against attempts at conscription. In relation to genuine external danger, curtailment of civil liberties was greater in the period of the Alien and Sedition Acts.

All these situations may be better understood in terms of what is loosely defined as *ideological conflict*, especially challenges to the legitimacy of an existing government.

"Ideological" conflict

The belief that there is a serious threat to the legitimacy of a government or to the ongoing social order, held by various elements in the decision-making process, can produce the most widespread curtailment of civil liberties in a generally free society. Either jurists or laymen or both feel, whatever the justification, that there is a "clear and present" danger. To the Wilson administration, active dissenters were challenging the authority of government in a time of crisis. To others, they were exponents of dangerous "foreign ideas." Many Federalists apparently had a similar estimate of what they considered the Jacobin influence in some Jeffersonians. (The absence of serious dissent in World War II against prosecuting the war eliminated the pressures for suppression.)

Similarly, perceived threats to religious beliefs and "moral" values can lead to an abridgement of liberties. Shortly after World War I, the desire to suppress political radicalism dissipated because it was irrelevant. The need felt to defend challenged values, however, took on the form of religious fundamentalist efforts to prevent the teaching of biological evolution and nativist authoritarian attempts at suppression, even by physical means, of deviance of any sort. In the recent context, a complex of uneasiness about the cold war, rock and roll, beatniks and hippies, and publicity about sex and crime foster a reaction for preservation of established values by eliminating "obscene" literature.

What has further ensued in these situations illustrates the importance of counterpressures. The existence of many people with these deviant values, and appropriate roles and structures for expounding and maintaining them, can check the efforts of those who wish to suppress. If nothing else, "civil peace" may best be obtained by avoiding restraints at certain times. This is probably one of the explanations for what happened in the Civil War. The opposition was simply too large and included too many people in important roles and with powerful structures, especially so much of the leadership in the Democratic party, to permit any further clamping down in the midst of the strains of war. Conditions of severe political-social conflict obviously can lead to internal suppression, but so many people may be impelled to demand their freedoms that such suppressions will prove too costly.

The suppressions of the cold war, however, still require more explanation. In this instance, the garrison society was accompanied not by any large-scale opposition to established values and government legitimacy but by a state of general insecurity.

Insecurity

All situations of ideological conflict and external threat are usually accompanied by intense feelings of insecurity, and this insecurity has been the central feature of the mentality of the cold war. Accompanied by perceptual ambiguity, the insecurity engendered generic demands for suppression, extending to television actors. The impulse was rarely rational, that is, a means to a clearly sought end, but partook more of a classic frustration-aggression process.[15] One simply got mad at anyone whose activities at some time were, in the subjective feelings of the observer, associated with the idea of the "enemy," even though there was hardly any indication that they had any direct connection with that enemy. The cloak and dagger symbolism in which the cold war was portrayed further intensified insecurity and ambiguity and thus the demand for inclusive and capricious suppression. This will, of course, be further developed in the chapters that follow.

CONCLUSION

The analytical model we have sketched is not a comprehensive scheme for understanding the bases of freedom of expression and association in all societies, though it utilizes material from different societies and might, hopefully, contribute to the development of such general formulas. It is designed as a method for a better understanding of problems within recent American society, with its historical tradition, general legal and value commitments, appropriate structures, and so on, encouraging maintenance of such freedoms. In analyzing specific civil liberties problems against that background, they are seen as specific types of "political" disputes. Particular political *actors* are involved in particular ways, because of the particular values, roles, structures, and situations. Furthermore, the number of actors is generally rather small, much less than in many other political disputes, but with sufficient value support in many publics to permit a wide variety of decisions.[16]

There are still a few elements left out, or only touched upon implicitly. The motivation to express oneself or join with others, noted as a variable in the introduction and deemed pertinent in parts of the historical accounts, is not explicitly included. This is also true of the question of *channels of communication.* Other questions such as the general issue of psychological conformity or the possibility of positive inducements rather than negative restraints limiting expression and association might be added. If significant in particular analyses, this will be added to the scheme. As a final propositional statement, the notion of "indivisibility of freedom" has been an important guide to all discussions, but, as emphasized earlier, it defines only one variable. Essentially, it seems to be more applicable to extensions of freedom rather than its limitations. Thus, all limitations of freedom in American history, however general and serious their effects, have not, at least to now, so curtailed freedom as to upset the designation of the nation as, at all times, one of the "freest" societies known to man.

In the discussions that follow, predominantly about recent disputes, there is no attempt to follow the above scheme rigorously. Rather, it serves as a fundamental guide or intellectual orientation that directs our attention and, to some degree, structures our presentation. Furthermore, since the emphasis is on "threats" to liberty, a great deal of effort will be devoted to delineating the nature of those threats and even, to some extent, proving that they were actually threats. The descriptions and analyses should be viewed not as attempts at well-rounded social scientific monographs but as discursive essays, in which the content is molded by the demands of appropriate exposition more than by preformulated structural design.

Part Two

The McCarthy era and after

7

What was McCarthyism?

Our analysis of the McCarthy era comprises a major section of this book. What happened in the decade or so after World War II was both the most pervasive and most widely discussed series of threats to civil liberties in America since the early 1920's. The commentary includes the most usable research on such questions ever conducted. On the other hand, most "explanations" were misdirected and irrelevant.

One set of common misconceptions, particularly among those who were apprehensive, concerned the extent, and more importantly, the nature of the suppressions. Another failing was the inordinate attention to one type of government action, the legislative investigation, and, above all, to the role of one legislator, Senator Joseph McCarthy, as either the active or the symbolic progenitor of the most significant events. Finally, there was a characteristic contention that all of this was associated with a widespread "political movement" that both inspired and lived off the tactics of these principal protagonists.

With this type of orientation, much of the effort was directed at locating McCarthy's supporters, a term that was, operationally, usually applied quite literally. The typical findings were that McCarthy's popular support came from such sometimes overlapping categories as the status insecure; the former isolationist; the members of specific ethnic groups, either Germans or Catholics, according to the specific emphasis; the authoritarian-minded; and the "powerless." [1] The findings, themselves, have recently been reevaluated. For instance, Nelson Polsby has indicated that apparent approval of McCarthy was most clearly associated with traditional Republican voting.[2] Our own criticisms accentuate the general limitations of public opinion data which exclude the element of *saliency,* among other things.

At this point, this set of researches is viewed from another vantage point, namely, its relation to the intellectual-political orientation or one might even say the "ideology" prevalent among so many anti-McCarthyites. McCarthyism was seen as a kind of neo-Populist intervention of a mass political public into the province of political elites. In accord with such interpretations, as earlier outlined, the suppressions that occurred were a result of the authoritarian drives of the untutored and irresponsible mobs against those who were cultivated and responsible. As best summarized by Edward Shils in his "The Torment of Secrecy," the McCarthyite phenomenon was a manifestation of attempts to make public political issues of things that should best be left to the private province of decision-makers.[3] By bringing them out into the open and by ignoring the canons of secrecy and privacy, demagogic politicians had produced an atmosphere encouraging suppression. The obvious answer was to reassert the need for secrecy and the assumption of more "responsibility," that is, resistance to demands for public intervention.

Much of what follows is offered as a refutation of these and the other listed ideas about the McCarthy era, particularly its relevance for the subject of this volume, freedom of expression and association. Our own general description and analysis is the initial entry to the subject.

NATURE OF MC CARTHYISM

McCarthyism was not a monopoly of the McCarthyites. The term, which will be used euphemistically from now on, represents a type of political behavior and an accompanying type of thinking that were neither initiated by one man nor ended with his personal political fall, and were typical of many people, including some anti-McCarthyites. What Joe McCarthy, and those who might definitely be described as his close allies, did was simply the ultimate, bizarre, and thoroughly destructive variant—both a logical fulfillment and, to some extent, the antithesis of what more "responsible" people were doing.

The "rabble-rousing" congressmen, so widely feared, were thus not the only actors initiating and developing suppressions of freedoms and creating a suppressive atmosphere. Legislative investigations into subversion were a significant element but not the only type of government behavior, or probably even the most significant. The laws passed by Congress, beginning with the McCarran Act of 1950, were among the most potentially suppressive acts ever passed in this country, but, whatever their contribution to the general atmosphere, they were, and have remained, legally inoperative. The action of the executive branch of government, particularly the "loyalty" and "security" programs, had the greatest impact on most people. In essence, the "era" formally commenced with two actions of the executive branch under President Truman —the issuance of an executive order on "loyalty" of government employees in 1947 and the prosecution of the leaders of the Communist party under the Smith Act in 1948. These actions initiated the themes that were to be prevalent for at least a decade—a man's hidden record and his current associates could make him dangerous to the national security.

Many of those who approved these tendencies were fearful of subversive "propaganda." Those who opposed them because they feared the resulting pressures toward conformity in beliefs may have exhibited the proper libertarian concerns, but they failed to note the unique features of the times. In the much quoted terminology of Sidney Hook, "heresy" was rarely directly suppressed in the attempt to combat "conspiracy." [4] Naturally, there were incidents and tendencies, but dissident *ideas* were rarely the focus of attention. Fringe groups attacked particular books, and their complaints sometimes resulted in removal of the books by school boards and librarians. A congressional committee sought to direct the efforts of foundation grants. These maneuvers were rare, however, among official government acts or even among the pressures of politicians and private groups. The personal dossier rather than the index of forbidden works was the likely weapon. The detective rather than the political demagogue, the censor, or the vigilante was the major protagonist. Joe McCarthy ranted more about the promotion of a suspect army major than about anybody's "subversive" speeches or writings. His staff's investigation of USIS libraries abroad sought to locate the books of "suspect" writers, not to uncover "subversive propaganda." They were interested in the background of the writer, not in what he wrote.[5]

Radio and television blacklisting, an extreme extension of McCarthyism, eliminated actors and directors because of some previous activity or contacts, but there was little control of content. Postal regulations demanded that certain foreign publications be delivered only in accordance with a formal request, which was, again, a mechanism for "labeling" a reader of such material rather than preventing him from getting it. Except for the few cases of elimination of books from specific bookshelves and schools, there was little suppression of anyone's political writings. The penalties inflicted were also historically atypical. Very few, except the Communist leaders, were imprisoned. The most common "punishment" was loss of job or threat of loss, or mere public embarrassment, a special feature of those times for which traditional legal and philosophical concepts of civil liberties left many unprepared.

Public opinion studies revealed widespread fears about "Communist propaganda" and desires to put "subversives" in jail.[6] As already indicated, such attitudes had no direct relevance for the situation, although they provided the popular support for the various McCarthyite tendencies. Such a discrepancy between beliefs and the contextual reality was one of the reasons why both "Mc-Carthyism" and "anti-McCarthyism" were so nonpolitical.

The McCarthyites did not constitute a political movement, they had no "politics," and they presented no program—foreign or domestic, immediate or long range, realistic or fanciful. All they sought to do was to get rid of traitors and dupes.[7] Furthermore, the McCarthyites could not mobilize many of those who supported them verbally in response to a public opinion questionnaire. During the Senate debate on the motion to censure McCarthy, mass meetings to defend him were organized throughout the country. Almost automatically, his opponents were impressed by the turn-outs, but his sophisticated supporters were very disappointed.[8] The point is that even if one applauds a sleuth, one does not participate in a political campaign for him.

So many opponents were, therefore, upset by McCarthyism for the wrong reasons. The inordinate attention to the McCarthyites and the accompanying overemphasis on legislative activities led to a failure to appreciate the essential features—the nonpolitical atmosphere, the role of the executive branch, the search for the hidden "record" by the many types of ferrets, the loss of job as the most likely penalty, and the comparative absence of any type of censorship.[9] If the drive was to expose "secrets," the mechanism was primarily the "secretive" probing investigation.

The specific character of the McCarthy era might be more clearly appreciated by a comparison with the World War I period (and by a later comparison with the current situation). The suppressions of those earlier times consisted of mass imprisonments and deportations, denial of mailing privileges to publications, and refusal to seat elected Socialist legislatures. If the notion of "guilt by association" was prevalent, it was a contemporary, generally overt association with people who had pronounced views. Most of those prosecuted were tried for what they openly said, and were usually firm in admitting that they said it; they were not prosecuted for any hidden record or merely because of potential future behavior. They were in trouble because their proclaimed views were deemed immediate incitements, not because of fears of covert conspiracies. The very fact that so many were tried meant that there would be definite charges and some resemblance to procedures of due process, even if the behavior of prosecutors and judges was not always up to the best judicial standards.

The McCarthyite style consisted more of vague and frequently unformulated charges, so often based on comments of anonymous informants. The accused was guilty until proven innocent; the nature of his guilt and the method for proving his innocence were usually not too clear, except for possible agreement point by point with his accusers. The standards for judgment were likewise very cloudy. For example, one might be suspect not only because of past and present personal acquaintances and organizational associations, but also because of his tastes in music and films, as well as opposition by those who investigated him.

Which era posed more of a threat to civil liberties is not an immediately pertinent question nor can it be readily answered. In many ways, the World War I syndrome was more serious because it did limit the conscious political expression and action of highly motivated people. More important is the fact that they were so different. The contrast is between the forceful suppression of some types of political dissent and the frightening of countless casually political people. What happened in the earlier period resembled the actions of traditional authoritarian regimes, limiting the rights of political opposition. Obviously, we are referring to the *style* of suppression and not the extent or the impact. From this vantage point, the McCarthyite suppressions are akin to those of totalitarian systems, even though, and it must be repeated ad infinitum, the intensity and effect have been generally exaggerated. We hope we are not similarly chastised. Very few were imprisoned and not many directly silenced.[10] In many ways, America remained a more libertarian society than most of the world throughout the McCarthy era. But what many people faced was similar in form to what confronts citizens in totalitarian societies, particularly its Stalinist variant.

The common fear was the possibility of "guilt" as a result of some scarcely remembered or relatively trivial comment or action or personal association, reported by unknown sources, and judged by unseen figures or those who were uninterested in their defense. "Absolution" could come most easily from a complete identification with their accusers, especially by assisting them in locating other aspects. In both instances, the victim perceived an ambiguous setting and reacted with a generalized diffuse anxiety. The likely impact on freedom of expression and association should be apparent and will be further detailed. In essence, the many aspects of McCarthyism were nonpolitical suppressions that helped accentuate a nonpolitical era. The World War I suppressions were limitations on political protest that helped *create* a somewhat *less political* atmosphere.

BACKGROUND AND INTERPRETATION

The rock-bottom necessary condition for McCarthyism has been mentioned by many analysts only in passing—the existence of a "garrison" society in the context of the cold war.[11] The latter aspect is crucial. The thoroughly mobilized America of World War II witnessed very little suppression whereas World War I saw a different type of suppression. The indicated differences with World War I tendencies are readily explainable by the quite divergent situations; such explanations provide the basis for an understanding of the specific characteristics of the McCarthy era.

Hostility to American participation in World War I was sufficiently widespread, actually until its termination, to prompt concern among officials and many "patriotic" citizens. Opponents were vocal in their opposition and advocated specific acts that could be construed as inimical to the war effort—avoidance of military service, strikes, noncooperation with bond sales, and so on. The speeches of the more radical spokesmen could be interpreted as revolutionary proclamations. The impetus of the Russian Revolution and the accompanying revolutionary events throughout Europe stimulated both the intense zeal of American radicals and the fears of the defenders of the established order. The postwar strikes were typically intense struggles, even without the appeals of radical messages, for the labor movement was fighting for its right to legitimacy in many industries. Violence was, if frequently exaggerated and often perpetrated by the defenders of order, a definite reality. It was clearly a time of storm and stress. If the reactions went far beyond the "clear and present danger" formula, they were, at least, a response to a genuine internal crisis. The crisis was essentially over with the apparent success of the search for normalcy. Large-scale suppression ended with the coming of domestic prosperity and relative world peace, and the accompanying shattering of the radical movement.

Since there was so little opposition to the prosecution of World War II, there was no immediate historic groundwork for widespread opposition to the cold war policies that followed. What happened afterward was, furthermore, not a response to any conceivable internal threat. The transition to domestic normalcy was fairly quick and easy, despite immediate problems of severe inflation and a housing shortage. The economic boom, which has essentially continued to this day, soon made more Americans participants in an "affluent society" than had ever been known before. A strong labor movement sponsored a wave of national strikes, but, whatever the settlements, they were not fighting for their existence and came out with sufficient "victories" and organizational strength. Radicals of all variants from the 1930's had lost so much of their fervor for reasons which cannot be here detailed. The Communist party, which had obtained considerable influence during the wartime alliance with Russia, quickly dissipated as a significant force. When its last big effort, its prominent role in developing Henry Wallace's 1948 third-party campaign, ended in a fiasco, it began its descent to a marginal and pariah status. Nor were other hopes for "new political forms" viable after 1948. If there was political excitement in the immediate postwar years, there was no intense ideological clash or pervasive threat of violence.

The other side of the comparison with the post-World War I period explains what happened and why it happened. There was no peace in the world. The continuing "cold war" against a former ally had begun. And it was a strange enemy, not only with ideological agents everywhere but also with possible spies and those who presumably might, by infiltration in government circles, influence policy. Revelation followed revelation of espionage, in this and other countries. The Communists "took over" so many countries and were so powerful in others that, although America at the time was probably the most powerful nation in history, the conspiracy interpretation seemed a feasible explanation. We were "sold out" by hidden domestic traitors. Those who had long-standing grievances against the Democratic administrations had an opening for attacking the "disloyal elements." They could do little else, for general foreign policy differences were rare. The Democratic administration felt compelled to retort by its own actions against those considered "disloyal." [12]

The culmination was the Korean War, an endless bloody stalemate after the Communist Chinese entry. In varying degrees, it was an annoyance to most Americans, obviously more intense for those directly involved in the fighting or those with family members who were or could be involved. Very few opposed it, but even fewer were enthusiastic about it. There was almost no attempt at patriotic fervor. The most common orientation was to hope it would be over very soon and that everyone could continue with the delights of affluence without this annoyance. Such frustrations, in line with the classic psychological process, produced its attendent aggressions. For many, the favorite targets were those domestic "traitors" or "dupes" of traitors who got us there in the first place—by "selling us out" or by "tying our hands behind our backs." Major policy decisions were not simply wrong, they had to be a result of the machination of some Communist agent. This was the stock-in-trade of McCarthy and the various McCarthy types. More "responsible" politicians, generally Republican but including some Democrats, either reluctantly responded to such pressures or utilized these sentiments for their presumed political advantages, although it is debatable how much voter support they actually gained thereby.[13] The personal file replaced the policy debate as the mode of political conflict.

There was one other important contrast with the World War I period. Many "liberals," with genuine libertarian values, were in a dilemma. They might be against suppression in this country but they also feared the American representatives of the most suppressive power in the world, with its known record of operating through "fronts." They were thus at least as anti-Communist as anyone else and were aware that they were dealing with people who adopted different rules of the game. The world of the dossier and the secret informant was outside the liberal's traditional vista but could not be ignored. With appropriate reluctance and demand for avoidance of "excesses," as in their attitude toward McCarthy personally, many of them found themselves compelled to accept the loyalty-security drive.[14] Only a few went so far as to view the conviction of Alger Hiss as the "trial of a generation," encouraging a change in political values. It was all too nonpolitical. But the resultant ambiguity on a crucial civil liberties question intensified the murkiness of prevailing political ideas and political debate.

Political discussion continued, and the amount of fear in the American population, especially as expressed by foreign observers, was grossly overstated. The suppression was more subtle and so were the effects. McCarthyism, in all its forms, simply accentuated the existing political "blandness" and the avoidance of public political commitment of the mildly or potentially political, particularly if it involved formal or informal associations with active "suspect" politicals.[15] These were the times when commentators searched for the causes of "apathy" and "conformity." For those who could be classified as genuine "radicals" the results were more profound. Their counterparts were destroyed as a political force in the post-World War I period, but many maintained their political position, providing a continuing tradition that could be reactivated during the depression. The McCarthyite inroads further decimated the already disoriented radical remnants, producing the much discussed "lag in generations" with the newly emerging radicalism of the 1960's.

In summary, the McCarthy era meant a limited, unique, and,

to some, very profound suppression of the rights of freedom of expression and association. In contrast to earlier similar situations, the labor movement and the revived pacifist movements were hardly affected, nor was the growing civil rights movement.[16] The principal method was the exposure of some hitherto concealed personal information, particularly some associations, which might still remain specifically unknown after the assumed revelation. If the object was to uncover what was private and secretive, the mechanism might be equally secretive. The situational context was the cold war garrison society and the apolitical climate. The actors —influencers and decision-makers—were those who responded to these situational pressures for whatever reasons. In addition, they also included those who sought to make political mileage out of the prevalent frustrations, those whose roles demanded decisions in such matters, and those who made a career entirely out of their anti-subversive activities.

Much of this will be amplified and developed in the description and analysis of three principal manifestations of McCarthyism— legislative investigations of "subversion," loyalty-security programs, and "blacklisting" in the entertainment industry. All of these resulted in relatively "pervasive" suppressions, with a "profound" impact on many of those affected. One of the objectives will be simply to delineate how and why these suppressions were inimical to freedom of expression and association. It should then be possible to present a set of summary statements about the entire phenomenon.

Despite the end of the Korean War in 1953 many McCarthyite tendencies continued to prevail until the late 1950's. The McCarthy era, however, apparently did end. This section of the book will thus conclude with an appraisal of the possible evidence of and reasons for its termination.

8

Legislative committee investigations

Legislative committee investigations of "subversion," regarded as a particularly dangerous threat to First Amendment freedoms by many observers, had many earlier precedents; they have continued, in an abated and somewhat different form, to this date. This type of inquiry, however, used by both Congress and state legislatures, was specifically characteristic of the decade and a half after 1945. The state inquiries, most evident in the late 1940's, have occasionally existed to this date, especially in some southern states, but the congressional committees have been the most significant and most controversial.[1] Their special relation to problems of freedom of expression and association, detailed in so many commentaries on the subject, warrants an elaborate analysis.[2]

HISTORY AND PURPOSES

The House Committee on Un-American Activities has been the most continuous and most conspicuous of these committees. Its immediate precedent was a committee to investigate Nazi propaganda, under the chairmanship of the current Speaker of the House, John McCormack. (Its modest operations culminated in 1935 with a recommendation for a law requiring agents of foreign governments to register, which was passed a few years later.) Congressman Martin Dies then proposed a continuation of the committee under its new name. The publicity from the Dies Committee, which included attacks on the CIO, the WPA Theater project, the Boy Scouts, and Campfire Girls as dangerous organizations, and produced the well-remembered charge that Shirley Temple had been used by subversives, probably had some significant 'political impact. For instance, some observers have claimed that its activity was responsible for the defeat of several Democratic incumbents. But it was too ostensibly "political," with committee members avidly declaring their intent to expose the "New Deal." Its appeal was very partisan, which meant extreme hostility from all political opponents.[3]

In 1945, the committee received an historically unique status for such a body. Most investigating committees are set up, ad hoc, for specific purposes. The HUAC, as it has become familiarly known, instead became a regular, permanent committee of the House of Representatives. Most of the other congressional bodies probing "subversion" have assumed a similar stature, that is, they are associated with standing committees, which, by authorization of the chairman, assumes this specific function. Thus, the Senate Judiciary Committee set up its "Internal Security Subcommittee," which, under the chairmanships of Senators McCarran, Jenner, and Eastland, has frequently been a Senate counterpart of HUAC. Senator Joseph McCarthy used his position as Chairman of the Senate Permanent Subcommittee on Investigations of the Senate Committee on Government Operations for his inquiries. This type of formal classification gave the work of these committees a form of intrinsic, atypical legitimation. They were not created at a particular time for a particular purpose but always remain unless expressly abolished by Congress. Other special committees have been set up, such as a House committee organized to examine the possible "subversive" grants of tax-exempt foundations. Other regular congressional committees have sometimes participated in investigations of "loyalty" and "security" matters, as in the confirmation of executive appointees. The investigating committees have more of an omnibus scope.

Obviously, there have been a large number of other types of congressional investigating committees, according to some estimates, close to a thousand since the first use of the practice in 1792.[4] Some of what has been said, in support or criticism, about the anti-subversive investigations is also applicable in some ways to many of these other committees. But, as will be described, there were many conspicuous differences and none of the other committees was continuous. The major purposes of such committees, legally proper and politically appropriate, are to provide information for proper legislation and to act as a check on the executive and, sometimes, the judiciary. The defenders of anti-subversive investigations have, however, accented another type of function, the so-called "informing" function. This concept is usually credited to Woodrow Wilson, who explicitly described it as a mechanism for giving the public significant information about the executive branch of government.[5] Typically, it has also meant dissemination of the kind of knowledge that might facilitate public support of, or clamor for, the legislation that emerges from the hearings as well as occasional directives for executive action.

The "information" that anti-subversive investigators sought to spread, however, was primarily data about specific people as such, or, sometimes, the investigator's political line. A book written by supporters of HUAC, and edited by William Buckley, contains one chapter summarizing its entire history and another detailing the activities of one year, 1958.[6] The first emphasizes, above all, the revelations about specific individuals or groups, either in the hearings or in the publications of the committee. The review of the particular year is devoted mostly to listing similar disclosures about people as well as accounts of the testimony of those who had a particular political orientation, especially on foreign policy. Although foreign policy is obviously a pertinent subject for a congressional committee, there are other committees for that purpose. Placing political disputes within the domain of an anti-subversive investigation is an attempt to brand opponents as beyond the pale, and thus is an implicit suppression of freedom of expression.

In accord with the prevalent mode of the time, the more typical style was, at least to the late 1950's, to "name" those with "hidden records." The "informing" function thus becomes a public exposure of people and hoped-for action against them by some mechanism. Other investigative committees have, to some extent, operated similarly, as witness the treatment, and subsequent prosecution, of the racketeers who appeared before the Kefauver crime hearings, or the experience of Jimmy Hoffa before a similar committee under the chairmanship of Senator McClellan. But the investigations of "subversives" were associated with presumed political beliefs and activities, and are thus directly related to First Amendment freedoms.

A few examples reveal the dominant motifs, in contrast to the operating formulas of other congressional hearings on similar subjects. During the Korean War, several congressional committees conducted hearings to analyze what was widely regarded as the Far Eastern debacle. Expert witnesses on all sides were invited to give their testimony. Senator McCarran's subcommittee, on the other hand, devoted its efforts to exposing the role of one organization, the Institute of Pacific Relations, and spent considerable time on one individual, Owen Lattimore. A Senate Foreign Relations subcommittee sought to make a comprehensive study of the "Voice of America." Senator McCarthy's committee, instead, broadcast intraoffice disputes in which "friendly" witnesses defined their opponents as likely subversives and two "unfriendly" officials were castigated by the chairman. His two assistants, Roy Cohn and David Schine, toured the overseas libraries of the United States Information Service, removing books by authors they deemed "disloyal." [7] (Some were actually burned, an act with obvious symbolic connotations.)

DANGERS TO CIVIL LIBERTIES

Such branding and public embarrassment of individuals and organizations appears as an inherent threat to freedom of expression and association even if actual criminal penalties have not been too common. One likely consequence is extensive caution about stating one's opinion freely and joining with others, informally and in organized groups, if the result can readily be loss of job or reputation and official harassment, frequently in an unpredictable manner. The very act of appearing before a committee can become a stigma.[8] Accusations, by committee members, counsels, and other witnesses, become part of the public and publicized record. The possibility of refutation is limited by characteristic procedural methods of the committees. In addition, the official reports become government-sanctioned documents which "cite" individuals and groups without any considerations for due process. Such citations can then be utilized by all sorts of people, for instance, by those responsible for "blacklisting" in the entertainment industry and by administrators of the executive branch's loyalty-security programs. Association with organizations "listed" by the committees, both federal and state, was frequently part of the adverse record of someone under investigation on loyalty-security grounds.

The testimony and other releases of the committees become part of the readily available public files, described as "a hodge podge of information from *all kinds* of sources about an individual." [9] These may be particularly dangerous, for some reports utilizing such material do not check their sources or distort the implications. Thus, a person may be accused of being "listed" by HUAC, which merely means that he was named in a testimony or a document for some reason. To show how fantastic this can become, J. Edgar Hoover has, quite understandably, been listed frequently. All of this is available to a variety of people for many purposes, from the entertainment blacklisters to the investigating committees in southern states seeking to damage leaders of civil rights organizations. The quintessential feature is that anything that comes from a congressional committee is an official government document and thus carries an aura of legitimacy.

The potential dangers to civil liberties from such legislative investigating committees are, to some extent, inherent in the necessary conditions of their operation. To function properly, to gather the kind of information helpful to the legislative process, and to check on the other branches of government, these committees have found it essential to assume not only an official legitimacy, but also some strong legally sanctioned powers. They subpoena witnesses and records, place witnesses under oath, provide for punishment for those who refuse to answer questions or give false answers, and set up their own rules of procedures. On their side, the investigators are immune from legal restrictions in order to permit them to operate freely. Naturally, these essential requirements can be transformed into legal support for Star Chamber tactics or public pillorying. In their typical attempts to find some balance, the courts have ruled out inquiry into the "purely personal" and have stipulated that the relation between the questions asked and the stated purpose of the committee must be made explicit. Since investigations into subversion have been deemed a response to a "clear and present danger," however, these limitations have not been too decisive.

Since the major objective of the committees investigating subversion, that is, to brand individuals and groups by a legally empowered agency, carries with it the additional possibility of criminal penalties, the inquiries take on the character of a quasi-judicial proceeding, with the same people playing the roles of police, prosecution, and judge. Those being judged have few procedural protections. The typical ground rules of these inquiries further intensify the "inquisitorial" features. The witnesses can answer only the questions directly asked and are rarely permitted to qualify or elaborate their statements. (In this respect, the Kefauver crime investigation, which has also been frequently criticized for going beyond its legitimate purpose, was far less restrictive. No legislative investigation into subversion has ever included anything like the long, rambling testimony of former New York Mayor O'Dwyer before the Kefauver group.) The hearings of several committees in the late 1950's, which covered a somewhat similar area as the anti-subversive inquiries, the operation of the loyalty-security programs, furnish a dramatic contrast. To obtain the information considered appropriate for their purposes, witnesses were encouraged to speak freely and at length.[10] If the legislative anti-subversive investigations contain something like the restrictions of a court trial on the type of comments permitted by witnesses, the other side has few limitations. The investigators and "friendly" witnesses can make and have made any utterances they wish. For example, in Senator Joseph McCarthy's committee, the chairman's speeches ranged far and wide, chastising witnesses and others, sometimes in the most insulting manner, as in his widely publicized charge that General Zwicker was "not fit to wear that uniform." [11]

Hostility to the investigations, to people associated with them, or to activities that ensued from them could produce investigations of the critics and/or publicizing their "records." HUAC accused the leaders of the National Council of Churches of Christ of "Communist-front" affiliations, an action regarded as a "vendetta" against the council because of its frequent opposition to the committee. When the Fund for the Republic published its investigation of blacklisting in the entertainment industry, HUAC responded by chastising the author of the reports, John Cogley. One of the most extreme demonstrations of this sort of "retribution," and of the nature of committee hearings, occurred when James Wechsler, editor of the New York *Post,* was questioned by Senator McCarthy's committee. The ostensible reason was that books he had written were distributed by the United States Information Service, but it is certainly feasible to interpret the proceedings as a reaction to the *Post's* constant criticism of the senator.[12] One of the principal objectives of McCarthy's questioning was to imply that Wechsler's many published comments against Communism were actually written under the direction of the Communist party.

The implication of the documented record, noted by many observers, is that these committees were out to "get people"—those whose "subversive" activities or associations were already known or, in some cases, those who were actually uncovered by their proceedings. The legislative function has been, at most, very secondary. If possible, the best way to "get them" would be to put them in jail. After all, this would be in line with widespread popular opinion, for 51 per cent of the general public and 27 per cent of community leaders favored putting admitted Communists in jail in the 1954 national survey.[13] The specific item in the historical record of HUAC that its supporters, above all, use as a major defense of its work was the conviction of Alger Hiss as a result of perjured testimony before the committee. Similarly, some critics of Joseph McCarthy criticized him because "he didn't put a single Communist in jail." In other words, many of the supporters of these investigating committees have seen their functions as comprising some combination of the attributes of a detective agency and prosecuting attorney. The publicizing of "names" also made them de facto judges.

REACTIONS OF "VICTIMS"

Those affected by the actions of these legally empowered bodies have a few procedural protections, most of them defined by court decisions.[14] Included are requirements such as the "pertinency" of questions, the adherence to the committees' own rules, the right of counsel, the precision of questions, and the stipulation that the witness be clearly informed about the possible implications of refusals to answer. The device most used by witnesses to avoid interrogation, however, has been the refusal to answer because of fear of self-incrimination—"taking the Fifth Amendment." According to court rulings, this cannot be applied at will, but only at an early part of the testimony when the question of possible criminal prosecution would be relevant. One cannot, for instance, invoke the privilege in order to avoid testimony about other people. This is one obvious reason why some witnesses plead the "Fifth." Other motives are also likely—actual fear of revealing something about oneself that can result in prosecution, defiance of the committees, or concern about subsequent perjured testimony. In any case, the purpose is to stop the inquiry right there and to prevent further probing so that a subsequent refusal to answer would not prompt a contempt citation. Because of the prevailing informal norms, Congress has typically granted a committee's request for such a citation and the Justice Department has prosecuted.

The Fifth Amendment plea may thus be motivated by conscience or anxiety about legal harassment, but it does not prove an easy way out. In violation of the spirit of the constitutional provision, the stigma of likely "guilt" remains pervasive. To Joseph McCarthy, one became a "Fifth Amendment Communist." Many schools, including some prominent universities, automatically dismissed or suspended teachers who took the plea before legislative hearings, even though the Supreme Court ruled that this act, by and of itself, was not sufficient grounds for any discipline. A committee of the American Bar Association suggested that any lawyer who took the Fifth Amendment should be disbarred. Evaluations of those who invoked the plea were typically unfavorable, ranging from the popular notion that he "must have something to hide" to the more sophisticated political chastisement for lack of courage and forthrightness.[15]

This type of subpoenaed witness, called because of some "subversive record," frequently including membership in the Communist party at some time, obviously had other options. Some, despite their principled opposition to the practice and personal anguish, did, for various reasons, name names. Refusal to testify, either about oneself or others, without invoking the Fifth probably resulted in a more favorable image for the witness and, frequently, little subsequent harassment, for he had asserted a more courageous personal affirmation. In addition, many recalcitrant witnesses were not punished, even before the Supreme Court's *Watkins* decision in 1957, which formally stipulated the requirement that the witness be informed of the particular question's pertinence to the committee's authorized purpose. A large number of contempt citations, which issued from the three anti-subversive investigations, were lost somewhere in the judicial process—lack of indictment, acquittal by the trial court, or on appeal.[16] Those who thus challenged the committees, whose response to this type of threat to freedom of expression and association was a vigorous statement of their clearly understood values, did, by their definitive postures, thwart that threat, whereas those who took the "Fifth" were yielding to that threat in effect.

PROCESSES AND MOTIVATION

The committees' particular impact on freedom of expression and association is bound up with their operating methods. The fear, however vague, of being called to testify, of being somehow "named," or of joining an organization that might someday be cited, was an integral part of the impetus toward "caution" so characteristic of the McCarthy era. One could not argue against the "naming" of an organization since such a listing had no formal basis. Unlike the attorney general's list, for instance, they were not necessarily defined as "subversive." Someone somewhere had simply said something with some such implication, which was picked up either in testimony or in published reports. A witness could not answer freely; the interrogators were in complete control of the proceedings. Those personally named had the option of asking permission to reply at a hearing, but, again, only to the specific questions which the committee was interested in posing. To repeat, the proceedings have tended to have a unique judicial quality with few meaningful protections of due process, and many witnesses were assumed "guilty" until they proved themselves "innocent." Committee members and counsels have characteristically been out to "make a case" rather than to acquire any information. The material that has emanated from the committees has been used for a wide variety of suppressive activities or attempts at suppression by both public and private agencies.

The official emphasis has been so dominantly directed toward alleged present and former Communist party members that the large number of other types of people and groups affected has sometimes been ignored. A list of those "injured" by the committees, whose connection with anything associated with the Communist party was, at best, peripheral and farfetched, would be very copious. After all, despite the quasi-judicial characteristics, no test of "proof" was necessary. The "facts" might or might not be valid, but their implications, in headlines and reports, were usually too vague, however damaging, for legal challenge. Joseph McCarthy's targets were, of course, very inclusive, extending to Secretary of State Dean Acheson and General George Marshall, the leader of all American military forces in World War II. The other committees have publicized charges against civil rights and pacifist leaders, leading clergymen, and some prominent government officials—like those who were simply opponents of the committees—generally based on some past association, however tangential, with some persons or groups somehow defined as suspect.[17]

The structures and processes would obviously have had much less meaning in the absence of the situational context—the entire cold war complex. The pervasive value aspects, that is, the generic patriotism and hostility to and fear of Communism, were other self-evident ingredients. In addition, the work of the committees, and the suppressive atmosphere to which they contributed, was also affected by other readily apparent values and accompanying self-interest of those in specific roles. It is likely that most investigators were devoted patriots and as dedicated to public service as any other group of office holders, and one can assume this as a "given" and necessary condition. The existence of a more narrowly "political" motive has, however, also been accepted, by both critics and defenders. Uncovering "subversives" can be an effective technique for maligning political opposition, facilitating one's own political career, or, in some cases, punishing a personal opponent.

Despite the generally "issueless" character of the inquiries, the partisan motivation has been manifest. The members of these investigating committees have generally been Republicans or "conservative" Democrats, usually southerners. Many of the counsels can be similarly identified. Although open attacks on the philosophy of the New Deal and those who stemmed from that tradition were not as common in the investigations of the 1950's as in earlier times, the disclosure of "subversive names" and those who worked with them was so frequently directed at Democratic administrations and certain types of Democratic leaders as to make the intent self-evident. Few went so far as Joseph McCarthy in denouncing the "twenty years of treason" under the Democrats, or questioning the patriotism of General Marshall, coincidentally an incumbent of two cabinet positions in Democratic administrations. The revelations of "tainted individuals" in Democratic administrations, with even some alleged spies, and the claim that the Democratic officials did little to eliminate their influence was more than a check on the executive. It was obvious political capital.[18]

The political career of Joseph McCarthy offers the clearest illustration. Richard Rovere's biography describes the senator's assumption of the anti-Communist mantle as a response to frantic anxiety about his chances for reelection.[19] Whether he had any genuine further political ambitions is unknown, but his actions as chairman of his investigating committee were clearly those of a man bent on building a name for himself. The most conspicuous example of a political career engendered by this type of investigation was that of Richard Nixon, his climb to national prominence starting with his initiative, as a freshman member of HUAC, in pushing the inquiry that led to the conviction of Alger Hiss. Of course, as the supporters of the committees have retorted, none of this is unique in the history of congressional investigations. The Democrats continued to get political mileage from the Teapot Dome investigation for a long time. National political fame came to such committee chairmen as Senators Truman and Kefauver. That these countercharges are valid does not gainsay the significance of such motivations for the particular investigations under discussion. Note, we are interested only in what contributed to the behavior of the investigators and not whether they achieved their aims. Despite the many claims, especially by critics, the effects of the anti-subversive committees' exposés on voting is a matter for dispute at best. Furthermore, with the exception of Nixon, and, perhaps, Senator Karl Mundt, the subsequent political fortunes of both the investigating committee members and the counsels have not been very conspicuous. This point is irrelevant, however. The investigators did what they did at least partially to enhance their political images and, if nothing else, to provide a regularized niche for themselves in Congress by their specific roles. An explanation of the suppressive atmosphere that resulted must therefore include their personal political drives as significant variables.

The anti-subversive investigations have, in addition, included a special type of role, with rather unique career motivations—the paid experts, consultants, and informants, using a more neutral term for the last rather than the more derogatory "informer." Many of the informants were former members of the Communist party or some offshoot. The testimony of all has been very crucial for the committees. The information supplied by informants has been instrumental in much of the process of "naming names." A large proportion has been on regular salary, sometimes for many years. Some of the informants can also be described as "professionals" in their roles, with appropriate pay.[20] Their charges have often constituted the major bases for accusations against individuals and groups, who may reply before hearings but generally do not confront their accusers. Their statements are, furthermore, "privileged," that is, they are not subject to libel suits because of their testimony. They can only be prosecuted for perjury if there is evidence of a legally defined "lie." This has happened in a few cases. In fact, one prominent "professional informant," Harvey Matusow, amplifying his statement in a published book, admitted that he had made inaccurate statements.[21] In his case, partly because he had turned on his former associates, he was prosecuted and convicted of perjury. One can simply conclude, in the most objective appraisal and using the most circumspect language, that a significant number of people, whatever the complexity of their motivations, have had a considerable vested inter-

est in continuing these investigating committees with their direct
and implicit effects on freedom of expression and association.

SUMMARY ANALYSIS

The defenders of the committees, as indicated in the collection of
essays that vigorously praised the work of the House Un-American Activities Committee, point to such features as the seriousness
and clandestine nature of the Communist threat, the continuation
of a tradition of congressional investigations, the check on the
executive, the valuable function of providing public information,
the prosecution of Alger Hiss, the recalcitrance of witnesses, the
type of people who oppose them, the existence of procedural
safeguards, and the resulting legislation proposed and enacted.[22]
To the writer, the contentions of opponents are more credible.
In essence, the investigating committees into subversion have
acted as inquisitorial prosecutors rather than legislative inquiries.
Their actions have tended to be punitive rather than that of seeking information. When witnesses are asked about their current or
past affiliations, they are being instructed to testify under oath
about information already in the committees' files, which will
probably be released. The object is either to embarrass them or
to put them in a position by which they may be forced to name
other names, most of them already known. Despite the admonitions of the Supreme Court, the objective has been "exposure for
the sake of exposure." Most Fifth Amendment cases have already
refused to answer in executive session; adding a public session for
them is merely a mechanism for public branding. Furthermore, in
many of these situations the witnesses will balk at giving information about the past, but may be quite willing to discuss what they
know about the current situation, especially about actual or
suspected Communist party members. The prodding of the committees on this score is evidence that the primary interest was in
developing a dossier. The emphasis was on actual Communist
party memberships, at least to the later 1950's, but other types of
affiliations, and even political tendencies, were also under inquiry.

The varied effects on freedom of expression and association have already been described. The apolitical atmosphere of the period was further intensified.

The question of the relation between the investigations and political opinions demands more amplification. The original authorization of HUAC, for example, was almost entirely devoted to the probing of "un-American propaganda." For this reason, some opponents, including dissenting Supreme Court judges, declared the authorization itself unconstitutional because it covers the area of expression that is constitutionally protected by the First Amendment. Court decisions have avoided this stricture by some adaptation of the clear and present danger doctrine. Still the committees have been much less concerned with opinions, except those about the committees themselves. The most ready response to these, and other stated opinions, has not been to probe or attack the opinions themselves but to present data about some of those who express such opinions or belong to organizations which uphold them. This further intensified the mood of depoliticalization, of attacking and defending people instead of discussing issues. Any genuine discourse about communism, that is, the actual tenets of the Communist party and its fellow travelers, was made more difficult because it would automatically become shrouded in a context of personal penalizations. Many opponents of the Communists, for instance, would be reluctant to point out that a political spokesman was following the "Communist line" for fear of implicating the man in a variety of torturous experiences. One might feel that he would then be acting not as a political opponent but as an adjunct detective.

RECENT DEVELOPMENTS

During the 1960's the legislative investigations into subversion have become less important and have changed in character. The HUAC and, to some extent, the Senate Internal Security Subcommittee, as well as other congressional and state committees, continue their activities up to this point. But their style and that of the witnesses and opponents have meaningfully changed. The disclosure of hidden records has tended to give way to the publicizing of open beliefs and actions. Not that the former style has completely disappeared. Legislative investigators still seek to probe and expose hidden associations and affiliations. Recent inquiries, however, are generally directed at people with vigorous political stands, not at those who strive to avoid public revelations. Charges of "conspiracy" sound hollow when aimed at those who vociferously proclaim their "radical" views and activities. The earlier tactic is not gone; it has simply become less relevant in the new context, especially since so many of those involved in political dissent have very little of what could be called a "record." The objective now seems more to stigmatize beliefs than to dig into previous personal history.[23]

Opposition to the committees has become much more pronounced. Within Congress itself, an increasing number of representatives have voted against the HUAC budget.[24] The courts have been less willing to sustain contempt citations, and fewer citations have been voted by the committees, partly because they anticipate such decisions. From 1959 to 1964, for instance, HUAC did not attempt to cite anyone. Three were charged that year, and their convictions were set aside on appeal. As a result, at the beginning of 1966 there were no cases on the federal docket arising out of congressional investigations into subversion, a condition that had not prevailed for more than a decade.[25]

How the congressmen and judges behaved was partly responsible for the changed responses of many witnesses, although the latter may have also affected the former. More have refused to testify, in whole or part. Others have insisted on making full political statements. The Fifth Amendment defense has become less prominent. An ACLU lawyer openly protested the HUAC's action at a hearing and was forcefully ejected. Even the investigation of "unfriendly" Ku Klux Klan officials has been widely protested. In a famous incident in San Francisco in 1960, student demonstration against HUAC hearings resulted in a riot. The question of responsibility and the respective behaviors of all sides have been widely debated. Without taking sides in this dispute, the very fact that it occurred indicates a different tenor of the times from that which could have existed earlier.[26]

Finally, two suits have challenged HUAC's constitutionality. One resulted from the subpoenaing of a heart specialist of the Chicago Board of Health, Dr. Jeremiah Stamler. To show how the times have changed, his refusal to appear was supported by countless professional colleagues as well as those in other professions. Dr. Stamler is not only opposing his contempt citation, but also has presented a countersuit challenging the existence of HUAC, both cases handled by a legal staff led by a former president of the Illinois Bar Association. Finally, the ACLU has also instituted a suit declaring the committee's authorization in violation of the First Amendment.[27]

The legislative investigating committees into subversion were a particular manifestation of the McCarthy era. They are still in operation and trying to maintain their functions. But their impact has become less and less evident, especially as the response of those affected has altered and opposition has mounted. The more recent and current threats to freedom of expression come from other sources and take different forms. The role of these committees, then, becomes one of a subordinate adjunct of other forces, dramatically disseminating otherwise widely publicized information rather than uncovering clandestine records.

9

The loyalty-security programs

An historian would, on the basis of the commentaries of the times, readily assume that the legislative investigations were the most significant and influential features of McCarthyism. Actually, the loyalty-security programs of the executive branch had much wider scope and more profound effects, and were probably more symbolic of the characteristic style of the era. Interestingly enough, the amount of useful published data is very marked. But general analyses of the prevalent atmosphere did not emphasize these programs.

The basic rationale was not entirely new in America. Something similar was part of the idea of the Alien and Sedition Acts and some aspects of Attorney General Palmer's tactics after World War I. The approach, however, was not a central part of government procedures until after World War II. Earlier "loyalty testing" had consisted primarily of requirements for "positive" oaths of fealty, sometimes rather grandiose.[1] The later phenomena pertained mostly to possible evidence of potential "disloyalty" or dangers of breach of "security." In line with our earlier discussions of the period, the result was most likely to be loss of a job.

Legislators were involved, by their prodding and by several statutes which provided the framework of the programs. The federal programs formally began with several congressional acts in the late 1930's and early 1940's and have, to some extent, been further mandated in appropriations since. Nevertheless, executives have been the principal actors, both administering the programs and setting up the ground rules. For instance, the list of "subversive organizations" was instituted by the attorney general under President Truman's directive in 1947, and the extension of the "security" criteria resulted from President Eisenhower's executive order in 1953.[2]

The programs were far-reaching. Most federal employees were included at some time. Many states and municipalities instituted "disclaimer oaths" for employees. The Atomic Energy Commission and the Defense Department developed programs for "clearance" of employees of contractors with any access to specified "classified" material. The Coast Guard had to furnish "security clearance" for all seamen and those handling restrictive cargo on shore. Inductees in the armed forces were required to fill out a questionnaire, including data about possible subversive memberships, personal conduct, and so forth, with appropriate investigation if any "derogatory information" was disclosed by any means. For volunteers and reservists, such charges might prevent induction. For conscripts, it could mean a "less than honorable discharge," either after completing the allotted time of service or sometimes earlier. For a while, the National Institute of Health withheld research grants from those whose loyalty was in doubt. Lawyers could officially be denied admission to state bars, or even disbarred, for subversive affiliations or beliefs. Some doctors were excluded from local medical societies, and a few from hospitals because of alleged subversive connections. The ultimate extreme was that of the Indiana Athletic Commission, which required loyalty oaths from boxers and wrestlers.[3]

There were other examples, too numerous to mention. The process, for instance, became applicable to entertainment personnel, a unique manifestation that requires its own chapter. In the most detailed summary of the programs, published in 1958, Ralph Brown estimated that about 13,500,000 employees, around one out of five people in the labor force at that time, had, as a condition of employment, "taken a test oath, or completed a loyalty statement, or achieved official security clearance, or survived some undefined private scrutiny." [4] Obviously, very many people were affected in some way, a far greater number than those who appeared or were named in legislative hearings. How they may have been affected is implicit in the structure and mechanisms of the federal programs—the procedures used and the standards applied.

PROCEDURES AND STANDARDS

The precise process varied with particular programs. The ultimate decision was up to the head of the particular federal agency of the employee, or those responsible for government contracts, and so on. Various other lower-rung personnel, however, were usually involved, with appeals from their decisions possible. Ultimately, one had the option of appealing any decisions to the courts.

The typical beginning was an employee's receipt of a written statement of charges.[5] He would then be requested to submit a reply in writing and/or be granted a hearing, usually before an agency's "security officer," where he would generally be the only witness. Rarely would he be able to confront those who had supplied the "derogatory" information against him. The employee had a right to counsel and to present witnesses in his behalf, who were "character witnesses" in effect, but he had no right to subpoena them, and no travel expenses were provided. As a result there was great reliance on affidavits, which were frequently discounted because they were not subject to cross examination. Other legal formulas were generally absent, such as "rules of evidence."

Nor was the employee informed of the grounds for the decision in his case. Similarly, the precise nature of the "evidence" against him might not be revealed, or, in most instances, the names of people who had supplied it. The use of material from unnamed "undercover agents" or unspecified and usually unchecked private informants was, of course, one of the most common criticisms of the program. Another conspicuous complaint was that, as revealed in several cases, "clearance" did not end the matter. The entire process could be repeated, in some instances many times, either on the basis of new material or, more significantly, as result of a reassessment of what was previously known.[6] In essence, the accused had to prove his "innocence"; then he might be subject to reaccusation under the same charge—an obvious example of what, in judicial procedures, would be termed "double jeopardy."

The procedures were thus arbitrary and ambiguous, a thwarting of substantive and due-process rights and a stimulant for the diffuse anxiety so inimical to freedom of expression and association. The apparent standards of judgment intensified the process. Although the security formula included many items unrelated to loyalty, the evidence from cases which have been made public indicates that the former meant a less stringent application of the latter criterion. The "security risk" appeared to be a "potential subversive," whose potential was less marked than that of the "disloyal," although the distinction does not seem too clear-cut.[7]

Many sources reveal the types of allegations made against suspect employees, although it is difficult to ascertain how they affected the actual decisions. They include several statistical summaries and accounts of individual cases, some of which were widely publicized whereas many were anonymous individuals whose "record" was available to researchers.[8] Of course, these cases are not necessarily representative, for they were generally contested cases with available information, which is not necessarily an accurate sample of the total. Since our purpose is to indicate the kinds of criteria that may have been relevant, however, and not to attempt any statistical summaries, this defect is not too serious. Most concern government employment, but some refer to military contractors and the armed services.

A sizable number was charged with membership, current or

former, in the Communist party or the Young Communist League. Many were accused of only "sympathetic association," which might include everything from actual concordant political beliefs to some personal contact with a member. In some instances this would mean a family relation with no implication of one's own political leanings. Another significant proportion of charges covered participation in, or views sympathetic to, or personal relations with a member of some other "subversive" organization. A codified systematic study of more than three hundred cases disclosed that, whatever the other charges, 36 per cent were accused of some type of association with other organizations on the attorney general's list and 20 per cent with organizations on some legislative committee's list.[9]

Additional allegations in other cases included membership in unions considered under Communist control, some connection with the American Labor party or the Progressive party, or, in a few instances, extended to affiliation with such groups as the Federation of American Scientists or the American Veterans Committee. Other items might be added, either in the original statement to the employee or in subsequent hearings. Prominent were those referring to reading, subscribing to, or collecting literature regarded as "suspect." Even such things as records listened to, films preferred, or opinions on segregation of blood banks might be covered. Some dossiers even contained allegations such as "going around in a nude state" or "sleeping on a bed board." In the publicized cases of several State Department officials, a negative appraisal of Chiang Kai-shek's government was regarded as symptomatic of possible "disloyalty."

A few individual case histories are further revealing. A landlord accused his tenant of having "Communist" literature because he had found the name of "Karl Marx" in one book. In one of the rare instances of cross-examination procedures, his charges were mitigated by the admission that it might well be an "anti-Communist" book. An employee with a defense contractor was denied security clearance because he was accused of being a former Communist who "might still be one." Eleven witnesses testified that he could not have been a Communist at the time alleged because he had fought against what the Communists favored.[10]

It is difficult to surmise the actual effect of these allegations, especially because of the typical anonymity of those who supplied the information. In fact, this ambiguity must be again accented as an essential feature of the loyalty-security programs. Nevertheless, what is available does emphatically support our general interpretation of all McCarthyite phenomena. Although the investigating authorities were obviously interested in people's ideas, and these were probably very important in decisions about those in relative positions of making policy, the greatest emphasis in most cases was on associations, both personal and organizational. Attention was particularly directed at some connection with organizations on the attorney general's list, or on the even less carefully drawn lists of legislative committees.

The attorney general's list was especially important. Eighty-two organizations were included in 1948, 197 in 1950, over 300 by 1959.[11] Most of them were no longer in existence, a large proportion for more than ten years. No formal procedures for establishing the list existed, unlike, for instance, the process of listing organizations under the 1950 McCarran Act or under the New York Feinberg Law. After 1953, organizations were permitted to contest their inclusion with the Department of Justice, which made up the list in the first place. Some organizations availed themselves of this opportunity, as will be later described. It should be obvious that it would be almost impossible for all but specialists to know the list. The result was a likely caution about joining any organization, as will be later shown, especially since organizations not included, the completely "innocent" as well as those on a legislative list, were sometimes mentioned in a dossier.

Since there were no clear-cut standards in the procedures, decisions as to the nature of involvement varied with the particular agencies and personnel examining and deciding. The stipulation of "knowing the purpose of the organization," which the

Supreme Court deemed applicable in criminal proceedings against Communist party members and in disclaimer loyalty oaths, was not a conspicuous element of most of the cases reported. As one examines some of the names on the omnibus list, it is easy to surmise the difficulty of assuming much from personal affiliation. Some of the organizations named were officially directed toward specific, limited purposes and all but the very politically sophisticated would ignore, for instance, their possible direction by Communist party members, especially when so many were reluctant to yield to what they considered "red-baiting attacks." Other groups were actually "non-Communist" or even "anti-Communist." The Trotskyite Socialist Workers party, although claiming to be revolutionary and officially so proclaimed by the conviction of its leaders under the Smith Act in the early 1940's, could hardly be considered part of the Communist "conspiratorial" apparatus. Yet, in one of the most dramatized cases, a legless World War II veteran member was dismissed from his position as a clerk with the Veterans Administration and even his veteran's pension rights were in doubt.[12]

An offshoot of the SWP, the Workers party (later changed to the Independent Socialist League) was one of the few organizations that went through most of the appeals procedure and was, ultimately, taken off the list.[13] What is immediately important is the type of standard used by the Justice Department to defend the organization's listing. The WP and ISL were not only anti-Communist in this country but also were very hostile to the contemporary Russian system. Furthermore, there was no evidence that the organizations upheld any program of "force and violence" for the United States. As it developed at the hearing, the Justice Department's case rested on the idea that the WP and ISL accepted Lenin as an ideological spokesman and Lenin advocated "force and violence." Apparently, this argument was ultimately considered insufficient by some department official, or was refuted by the testimony, because the organizations were subsequently removed from the list. But the precise basis for the judgment and its possible applicability to other organizations were still in doubt, for the decision was communicated without any explanation.

Usually, when accused of some type of alleged association with organizations or peoples deemed suspect, the person investigated was asked to defend himself against the charges. He might choose the option of ending the matter right there by resigning and avoiding further embarrassment. If he did appeal, he would be impelled, according to Ralph Brown, to make a "complete point by point refutation," or meet several of the following conditions: he is genuinely anti-Communist; he will avoid the associations that are the bases of the charges (sometimes extending to avoiding relatives); support the loyalty-security system itself; or be consistent in his testimony.[14] He would have to satisfy his "judges" in hearings that typically had no legal safeguards and where the grounds for the decision were unspecified. Further appeals would generally mean only more of the same procedures and might involve further inquiries on quite tangential questions not included in the original charges. The process would generally last for a considerable time.

In the study of some three hundred cases, almost 60 per cent took at least six months and more than a quarter over a year. Most of them, meanwhile, were suspended from government employment. Many were assisted by outside "help." The use of a lawyer could provide some legal protection, but this could add to the onerous burden. In the above study, the cost of counsel, for those who, in the majority, were now without government jobs, was at least $100 for almost two-thirds of the sample, and ran to $500 or more for more than a fourth.

Meanwhile, the judicial safeguards remained minimal.[15] Even with legal counsel, it was generally a long, expensive procedure during which the employee had to prove his "innocence" against a variety of accusations, some specific and some very vague and seemingly irrelevant, much of it based upon testimony from sources unavailable for direct refutation. Some of this could be circumvented by ultimately appealing to the courts, an even more expensive and time-consuming process in which the results were also uncertain because of the varying nature of the decisions case by case.

Two other types of assistance could be very helpful. Intervention by some organization of colleagues from work meant a potentially strong advocate in one's corner. Naturally, trade unions best fulfilled this requirement, and some unions did intervene, primarily in behalf of employees of Defense Department contractors.[16] The "victims" would then have significant resources for their defense. The other possibility was a widespread public campaign in the "victim's" behalf, in effect making the case a a political issue. For instance, in two fairly prominent cases "exposés" by the mass media resulted in vindication. A professional from the Department of the Navy was dismissed on the basis of anonymous testimony and presumed association with suspect individuals. A series of articles in the *Washington Daily News* initiated a campaign for a rehearing, culminating in his reinstatement with back pay. An air force reservist was asked to resign his commission because of his father's and sister's possible "subversive" activities. His story also became a publicized issue, especially after it became the subject of Edward R. Murrow's national television program. The secretary of the navy ultimately granted him his commission.[17] These situations were exceptional, at variance with the secretive, vague, complex, and commonly incomprehensible processes and standards of most loyalty-security investigations.

IMPACT

What does the available evidence indicate about the possible effects? An estimate of all those dismissed under the government programs by 1956 was a little less than one-twentieth of those involved. Studies of contested cases revealed that from two-thirds to 90 per cent were cleared.[18] If a comparatively small percentage was thus dismissed, this still adds up to a large number of people, and says little about the impact on those who were "cleared" after hearings and appeals or those who were merely apprehensive. What happened to those who lost their jobs has additional significance. Besides the obvious stigma attached to their names, for many their subsequent positions were in jobs that were lower paying and had lower status, and sometimes outside their professions. According to reports of psychotherapists, a severe psychic disturbance and family dislocation could be an accompanying result.[19] Military personnel with less than honorable discharges would also find difficulties in finding suitable jobs, especially if there was any element of "security" involved.[20]

The basis of decision, as already emphasized, was unclear and sometimes seemed capricious. A worker in the Government Printing Office, having minimal contact with classified material, was dismissed largely because of anonymous and vague accusations of "pro-Communist statements" and "Communist associations" and a subscription to *Consumer Reports.* An employee with direct access to material labeled "secret," however, was kept on the job despite admitted membership in an organization on the attorney general's list and accusations that his father and uncle were Communists.[21] With the process of clearance frequently taking a long time, with job suspensions meanwhile a likely concomitant, and with the accusations themselves constituting a form of branding, it is understandable why so many were so apprehensive.

The best published evidence comes from a series of depth interviews of federal employees in Washington, D.C., reported in a study by Marie Jahoda and Stuart Cook.[22] The need for "caution" was the most widespread reaction to the loyalty-security program, as might be expected. Respondents admitted that, as a result of their generalized fears, they would avoid such comments as open criticisms of the American Legion, discussions about atomic energy, or the admission of Communist China to the United Nations. One reported that he had decided to buy the *Nation* on newsstands rather than subscribe. The most complete admission was: "If Communists like apple pie and I do, I see no reason why I should stop eating it. But I would." [23] The most pervasive concern was, in line with the theme of the times, about associations. "Suspect" people were defined as among other things, "natural joiners," "those who actively work in elections," and "people with many friends and acquaintances." Their own acquaintances were, accordingly, to be guarded. Some avoided participation in organizations which could somehow be placed on the attorney general's list. One used this as a basis for withdrawal from the American Veterans Committee, an organization whose leadership had been engaged in a successful struggle against influences of the Communist party from the beginning. One respondent flatly declared that a federal employee should join only the "Knights of Columbus and perhaps the Masons." [24] Avoidance of association could become more extensive, including informal contacts—unwillingness to meet some people or to attend large parties.

This apprehension is more understandable in terms of what the respondents thought might, and sometimes believed did happen, to those under suspicion. Some believed they would gain little support from colleagues if unjustly accused of disloyalty, although others did expect more help. Generally, there was a feeling that their superiors would remain aloof, the approach being primarily to protect the reputation of the agency. The bureaucratic mode was considered at the bottom of likely responses. Thus, there was the report that one department avoided trouble by appointing only "conservative" people, with the philosophy of "let's not take a chance." Several believed that a person cleared might not be trusted because he had been investigated by the FBI, even though only 1½ per cent of all loyalty forms over a four-year period actually resulted in a full inquiry by the FBI. Others claimed that they would be "left with a black mark," and sometimes added the conjecture that "where there is smoke, there's fire." [25]

The report is clear in pointing out that these were not necessarily the responses of most or even a majority of those interviewed. In fact, all statistical analyses were avoided because of the smallness of the sample and the nonsystematic method of selection. What is reported does, however, indicate a significant type of response applicable to many people. Other types, however, were noted. Most important were those people whose attitudes were classified as "disliking the program, but not fearing it." Inclusion in this category was likely to be related to the following factors. 1. A favorable work situation—intimacy in climate of work group, confidence in fair practices in agency, or possible support from administrative superior. 2. Awareness of and belief in traditional American values. 3. Contact with those who took a stand. The last was not too frequent. The first two factors indicate the importance of clarity of values and favorable structural and situational milieus for maintaining one's freedom of expression and association in the midst of this suppressive atmosphere.

For the employees, or those whose current status required some form of clearance, the general tendency appeared to be an apprehension about associations, personal or formal, and some caution about expressing opinions. If the position had some relation to policy, although officially an administrative position, the observed tendency was to be safe, conservative, and conform to the ideas of superiors, an obvious latent result of loyalty-security suppressions. The possible influence on those who were potential recruits to positions requiring clearance has been the subject of comment, although there seems no definitive evidence. The supposition is that anything demanding such strains would be avoided, including the vast amount of scientific research with classified material. One is led to believe that this was a "likely" consequence, but no definitive statement can be made in the absence of any significant data.[26]

GENERAL INTERPRETATION

The structure and process of decision-making made the loyalty and security programs the most extensive and profound threats to freedom of expression and association of all McCarthyite phenomena. The details varied among agencies and programs. In some cases, the procedures were relatively "fair." [27] The "cases" of prominent individuals that were widely and openly discussed— J. Robert Oppenheimer, Bureau of Standards Director Conden, or even the attempt to thwart Senate confirmation of presidential appointees on loyalty or security grounds—were also "fairer," as indicated by the results. Either the intended "victim" was vindicated, and got or kept his job, or he continued in his previous career in some other position with relatively equal status.[28] The prevailing pattern, however, indicated unsubstantiated, frequently vague, and seemingly irrelevant charges, a lack of standards for judgment and inability to meet the charges point by point, absence of procedural safeguards, absence of statements about the basis for decisions, frequent anonymity of decision-making, the possibility of later revision of a "favorable" decision, or apparent capriciousness of the decision itself. At issue, although there was no precise indication, could be a wide range of possible expressed opinions and, more importantly, a variety of possible associations. The apprehension that was thus created was, understandably, far more extensive than the number of people who directly lost jobs or other "rights." The casual comment by involved government officials and some commentators that, since only jobs were affected this did not constitute a genuine civil liberties issue, can be readily dismissed. Anything that could frighten so many is very relevant to discussions of freedom.

Although the objective of investigations was to delve into "privacy," the "secrecy" of the process made the programs so dangerous. This is, perhaps, the central theme of this chapter, in direct refutation of the emphasis of analysts of McCarthyism like Edward Shils. A useful summary statement about the effects is supplied by John Schaar, in one of the most probing attempts to understand the programs.[29] He cogently points out that these efforts to enforce "loyalty" actually tended to destroy the "loyalties" essential to a free society—loyalty to associates, to beliefs, and freely given loyalty to one's community.

Schaar's account of why this happened provides a springboard for our own attempt at inclusive analysis. Like so many others, he finds a basic explanation in the drive toward "conformity," spurred by the fear of diversity characteristic of the developing "mass democracy." His presentation of this hypothesis is more valid than most similar expositions, especially since he does not counter with any "elitist" program. All McCarthyite phenomena were inimical to and, to some extent, countered by pluralistic features of society. Nevertheless, his interpretation still contains the typical implication of an ideological foundation. Although we have stressed the similarity in "style" of McCarthyite tendencies and totalitarian inquisitions, they were vastly different in many ways. The latter demands enthusiastic adherence to the ruling regime and its ruling symbols. The demands of McCarthyite pressures were more "negative," that is, to refrain from doing certain things, particularly associating with specific people and groups. The conformity expected was that of noninvolvement in public affairs, except along approved lines, a stricture more typical of traditional authoritarian rather than totalitarian societies. More importantly, Schaar does not, in accord with so many others, sufficiently dwell upon the most quintessential situational factor, the *unique* frustrations of the cold war, nor does he give enough attention to the other types of factors we found important in our analyses. Generic values were less important in stimulating this type of suppression than not only the specified situational context but also the relevant structures and roles.

Enough has already been said about the structures and processes, but one underlying ingredient has not been explicitly emphasized. The programs were administered by bureaucratic agencies. If the procedures did not fit the canons of a "pure" bureaucratic type, that is, they were hardly impersonal, efficient, concerned only with job performance, and so on, they were in line with observed operations of many "real" bureaucracies. In fact, the loyalty-security programs intensified the many prevalent features of typical bureaucracies which deviate from the classic model. The "personal" elements were very important, especially those that were outside the sphere of "office" life, including personal associates and even family connections. Other "loyalties" were thus, as Schaar emphasized, to be completely subordinate to organization loyalty, as defined in the programs. The affected were, themselves, predominantly bureaucratic employees. The decision-makers and influencers included many who could not readily be classified as bureaucrats—congressmen and other politicians encouraging the programs, mass-media spokesmen and pressure-group leaders behind them, the policy-making heads of agencies, judges, and so on. But those who usually made the decisions and those who had the most immediate impact on them, the government investigators, were, by definition of role as well as structural setting, bureaucrats.

Much of what has been described can be meaningfully explained by this significant feature of contemporary society. The jobs and careers of many people could be dependent on how they handled loyalty and security personnel problems. In the government bureaucracies, their "judges" could include a myriad of varied people—their superiors, "higher" bodies in the executive branch, or the investigating agencies such as the FBI, Congress, and elements of the political public. The tendency was probably to "play it safe," to bend over backwards in defining "risks," in other words, to "overconform." This is why the number officially notified of suspicions against them was so much greater than the number actually dismissed and why the charges could be so inclusive and tangential. Those with a more specific role assignment, agency security officers and members of hearing boards, and so on, had the defined task of weeding out suspects.[30] The likely result was that, in the absence of some explicit influence to the contrary, they would make every effort at extreme enforcement of the programs. Others inspired the programs and created some of the observed evils, but the bureaucrats made them rampant.

Similarly, for the affected, the typical diffuse anxieties engendered by McCarthyism were compounded by the ambiguities of the bureaucratic settings of their jobs, or, for those who were not bureaucrats themselves, by the bureaucracies they confronted. The former, as bureaucrats, were trained not to act independently and to be oriented to their careers above all else. The overreacting submission to vaguely potential threats, as illustrated by the Cook-Jahoda study, was an obvious corollary. Their relations to and evaluations of their bureaucratic milieus, supervisors, and, to some extent, colleagues helped determine their reactions to the perceived threats. It is probable that those who were subject to bureaucratic controls but not themselves in bureaucratic roles, particularly industrial workers in private industry, were more likely to resist the encompassing threats to freedom of expression and association.

To maintain one's right to freedom of expression and association in the face of the diffusely perceived dangers required, above all, some form of psychological resistance, the realization that the greatest fear was, indeed, of fear itself. As has been demonstrated, this was more likely among those with more precise knowledge and greater value commitments. But, for both actual and potential victims, it was also associated with the possibility of support if under suspicion. One would thus be less likely to accept the suppressions from the loyalty-security programs when there was some means of defense or even of opposition. The point is that active intervention rather than passive acceptance was, in varying ways, a method for combating the dangers of the programs. To be effective, however, this meant some support from influencers —lawyers acting in behalf of those charged, and sometimes larger groups both supplying the legal counsels as well as sometimes providing a mechanism for political criticisms. This is the major reason why industrial workers in private employment seemed to have a better chance of defending themselves than those in most public employment. Both were working for essentially bureaucratic organizations. But in that period the workers for private companies had one important countervailing power on their side not as typical of public employees—their trade unions. In confronting the seemingly faceless and monolithic bureaucracy, they were not anonymous entities of a mass society but members of a continuing, organized body on which they could lean for support. They possessed a collective, pluralistic power potential that could act as a counter-force against arbitrary treatment.

The role of unions in relation to these programs has not received sufficient attention. Official hostility to "Communists," buttressed by the beliefs of members, was at least as prevalent in unions as anywhere else at this time. Many unions had their own "loyalty oaths." A poll of six hundred union leaders disclosed "intolerant" attitudes not too different from cross sections of the population.[31] This same study, however, saw 90 per cent of the sample in favor of the right of confrontation and cross examination in loyalty-security hearings. Apparently, their own experience had made them very sensitive to the need for due process in job situations, and the protection of "innocent" members was a method for defending job rights. It was simply another type of grievance, an intrinsic part of collective bargaining. There were thus many reported instances of different unions involved in lengthy and complex litigation, which was often successful, for those suspended from their jobs on security grounds. Sometimes, this was part of the regular process of collective bargaining, and sometimes it meant a court suit or an appeal to administrative agencies. Among the most prominent unions were the United Automobile Workers and the United Steel Workers, with publicly identified anti-Communist leadership, which vigorously defended the job rights of ex-Communists and even those who had taken the Fifth Amendment before legislative hearings.[32]

The dangers from the loyalty-security programs were thus, to some extent, countered by some kind of opposition—the "silent" opposition of those who refused to be afraid; the lawyers who took up the defense of those accused, among whom a few lawyers and law firms were particularly prominent; the organizations and their allies who defended themselves against the strictures imposed upon them, like the Socialist Workers party in the Kutcher case, and the Workers party and Independent Socialist League in their effort to be removed from the subversive list; and such defenders of employees' rights as unions. The courts did have some role in limiting the "security" criteria to "sensitive" agencies, in offering some procedural safeguards, and in the frequent admonitions against abuses that were inserted in decisions and minority opinions. Other types of political criticism may also have had some effect. Three senatorial subcommittees held hearings in which criticisms of the programs were very common, and an official federal government commission suggested some changes. Meanwhile, the New York Bar Association presented an elaborate critique and stipulated some alterations in the direction of "fairness." [33] Because of the bureaucratic and secretive nature of the process, the actual impact cannot be validated. One can only surmise that the insecure and sensitive administrators of the programs were probably stimulated to more careful procedures by these pressures. It is our further contention that the ultimate result was a contribution to the gradual dissipation of the entire process.

THE END OF THE LOYALTY-SECURITY PROGRAMS

Schaar's appraisal of the current situation, in a book published in 1957, was as follows:

> The problem of what to do about the disloyal in our ranks has troubled Americans for some time. Nor is concern with it on the wane. Each week press and periodicals register new expressions of opinion on the subject. Nor can it be said that the problem is near solution; indeed the more it is considered, the more remote a solution seems to become.[34]

In an article published two years later, Alan Westin commented: "talk about loyalty programs stirs the blood only of Legionnaires and Civil Liberties Union buffs." [35] If one adds the qualification that most "loyalty" programs were defined as "security" programs by then, the implication is that the impact of all we have described was no longer significant by the end of the 1950's. The programs have become even less apparent since.

The concrete evidence is very minuscule, and most of it is very inferential. There were even attempts to extend the idea to other spheres—"disclaimer" affidavits for Medicare patients, and so forth, all of them widely resisted and, through various mechanisms, becoming inoperative.[36] Perhaps the best indication of the effective termination of the programs is the very lack of comment itself. It probably stopped being a public issue because very few people were any longer affected.

Westin has recently suggested that, on the one hand, the programs have become less necessary because "they ran out of victims," and the lack of publicity may be a result of the fact that they have become so "institutionalized" and casually accepted.[37] It is very difficult to argue these points without any substantial data. The best retort to the latter contention is that efforts at extending the programs were, as indicated, more vigorously resisted than ever before. The more significant idea, that there were so few suspected employees or prospective employees around, hardly permits a genuine test. Some type of rebuttal, however, is possible. First of all, in face of the numerical importance of employment in government and in industries with security requirements, the amount of vigorous dissent, some with a "radical" stance, has obviously become more widespread in the 1960's. It seems likely that the lack of apprehension was, for so many people, a concomitant of complete indifference about possible effect on employment. The reality of the situation, that people were no longer being hurt in unforeseen ways by such activities and affiliations, was a likely motivation for the absence of the earlier restraints, however dimly perceived. Although there is no available indication of the number of government employees among the various types of dissidents, there is likewise no report of the earlier anxiety. For one type of government workers, school teachers, involvement in political protest has been conspicuous. Finally, investigators, in legislative as well as executive branches of government, always did and still could find suspect people if so motivated. It is interesting that, in a case decided by the Supreme Court in 1967, a member of ten years standing in the Communist party was found to be employed in a shipyard under security regulations. The decision reversed his conviction under a revision of the McCarran Act, but what is most pertinent is that he had been working in the shipyard all throughout the years of the security program.[38] There may be many others like him.

There is one other type of oblique evidence. During the serious crises of the cold war in the early 1960's, the response was rarely a search for disloyals or dupes. Some did try to blame the Castro victory in Cuba on the mistakes of State Department personnel. But this was not followed by any grandiose campaign for internal housecleaning of suspect people, as followed the Communist take-over in China. This was no longer the accepted mode of operation. Although scarcely noted by anyone, the loyalty-security programs, most of them still existent on paper, had simply "faded away" as a significant feature of American life.

Why did they become largely inoperative? Among the few who have commented on the subject, the most ready explanation is the easing of the cold war, with the resulting change in political climate. Undoubtedly, this was a relevant situational factor, but it is not a complete explanation. For one thing, it does not explain why the programs did not become prevalent again when relations with Russia "hottened up." Our own additional analysis is implicit in the early discussion. Particular social actors were responsible for the programs. Particular actors sometimes opposed and thwarted their excesses. These same people and these same actions became the instrumentalities by which the changed general situation produced the de facto end of most of the programs. Every successful case of defense of a suspect employee, every court ruling that altered procedural requirements, and every public criticism was part of the cumulative process. The administering bureaucrats were either legally compelled or informally pressured to limit the scope or modify the nature of their programs. Sometimes the formal administrative stipulations were altered, but it was mostly a casual withdrawal from previous tactics.

To repeat, genuine documentation is lacking. Only a few concrete items are available. For instance, one year after the *Cole vs. Young* decision in 1956, which limited the security criteria to sensitive agencies, a Justice Department official reported that investigations into the "loyalty" of employees in such agencies, permitted under the Supreme Court ruling, had just about ceased.[39] This was an obvious example of the bureaucratic overreaction to legitimized pressure. After a 1960 court decision posed the dangers from lack of confrontation, a presidential order strongly advised increased use of this procedural safeguard if there were no definitive question of national security. Although this did not become mandatory policy, at least one agency, and one of the most "sensitive" at that, the Atomic Energy Commission, made it a requirement.[40]

Other fragmentary indications are available. When public campaigns, particularly those initiated in the media, resulted in the reversal of decisions not to grant reserve commissions to those with "suspect" relatives, this type of "punishment" became rare. The use of the "subversive list" was less evident after the Workers party and Independent Socialist League had their names removed. The Supreme Court's voiding of loyalty oaths resulted in an apparent decline in their application, even before the final culmination in the New York Feinberg Law case in 1967. The criticisms in Congressional hearings on the programs, and the proposals of the New York Bar Association for revision did not appear to have produced any formal changes. But it can also be surmised that these stimulated a caution against too forceful an administration. Even the more general public attacks, including those that emerged from reported studies, may have had some impact.

In this cumulative process, no one group of actors was singularly responsible. The courts did have some effect, mostly by their stipulations about procedures, encouraging and permitting some of the affected to resist, and by the influence from their role as legitimate "educators" in their nonlegally binding comments. The affected, their counsels, their organizations, congressional groups, legal bodies, other political spokesmen, media personnel, and so on, were all partly responsible. But ultimately it was up to the decision-makers, the harrowed bureaucrats, who simply changed their ways in unannounced, unformalized, and usually unnoticed fashion.[41]

As a final situational explanation, all of this occurred in the context of a "repoliticalization" of the nation. As part of the decline of McCarthyism in general, the loyalty-security programs lost their sting when the process of open conflict began to replace the operations of the investigating agency as the *modus vivendi* of so much of American political behavior.

10

Blacklisting

The "blacklisting" phenomenon in the entertainment industries was probably the most extreme, bizarre manifestation of the Mc-Carthy era. Nevertheless, it is possible to question the inclusion of such a subject in a volume concerned with freedom of expression and association, especially since, as will be indicated, the actual effect on media content was minimal at best. Freedom of expression, aside from what was put into the media, was to some extent involved, that is, what one said in public, or even in private, could be curtailed. Above all, freedom of association was a crucial issue, and the problems of procedural liberties, so often emphasized as a necessary foundation for substantive freedoms, were very germane. Finally, the atmosphere of diffuse anxiety engendered, a concomitant of all "McCarthyite" tendencies, is so patently inimical to the existence of genuine civil liberties.

The analysis of blacklisting in the radio-television and the movie industries is separated, for the phenomena were quite distinct. The differences between what occurred in the respective worlds of broadcasting and Hollywood constitute, in fact, an important feature of our discussion.[1]

BLACKLISTING IN THE BROADCASTING MEDIA

Even more than the government loyalty-security programs, the blacklisting process in radio-television resembled the themes of Franz Kafka's novels, the torment of individuals confronted by anonymous forces and serious, but unspecified, charges. Perhaps a more timely analogy would be that of the Theatre of the Absurd, appropriately popular at about the same time. The crucial decision-makers—network officials, officers of large corporations, and advertising agency executives—performed suppressive acts that they did not like, and frequently thought were ridiculous. Most importantly, they always denied that they ever made those decisions. The victims were immersed in a situation of chaotic uncertainty, rarely informed that they were actually blacklisted, and had little notion of why they were no longer getting jobs or how to reinstate themselves. Naturally, many others were apprehensive that they might be the next victims. For both decision-makers and victims it was thus a thoroughly irrational world in which they had little autonomy, a situation inherently inimical to civil liberties.

Only the "influencers" were both autonomous and, in some measure, rational. More than in any of the other areas under investigation, they constituted the sole active force responsible for suppression. There were actually very few of them, and it was easy to locate them. Particularly important were the publishers and editors of *Red Channels* and *Counterattack,* a book and a periodical newsletter, respectively. Both were devoted primarily to naming specific entertainment personnel as possible subversives because of membership in organizations, personal associations, appearances at meetings, and so on. The single most influential individual may have been Vincent Hartnett, a consultant to *Counterattack,* who served as a liaison with the other forces involved in the blacklisting pressures. Furthermore, Hartnett would "investigate" anyone for a specific fee, to be paid either by employers who wanted to know more or by the entertainers who wanted to be "cleared."

There were other allies. Most conspicuous was the owner of

four Syracuse supermarkets, Laurence Johnson, who worked through the organization he set up called the "Veterans Action Committee of Syracuse Supermarkets," and, to some extent, through the Syracuse American Legion Post. Among entertainers, an organization called "AWARE" supported the activities of people like Hartnett; at one time it included many of the officials of the New York Local of AFTRA, The American Federation of Television and Radio Artists. Further support came from prominent newspaper columnists. Hartnett's liaison with the House Un-American Activities Committee was very close, and they would help him by "investigating" recalcitrants. Some leaders of veterans' organizations would occasionally be involved, but only peripherally, by such acts as letters to producers and agencies, and so on. Even threats to mobilize the membership of these organizations were rare. On the face of it, the combined forces of these influencers hardly commanded sufficient resources to compel the powerful in the media, corporate, and advertising worlds to make their embarrassing decisions.

The overt pressure was usually very mild—a few phone calls, several letters, a communication from Hartnett, a visit from Johnson, or an item in a newspaper column. Then the process would vary from case to case. "Someone" would decide that a particular entertainer was "unemployable." Rarely was he told about the decision—what it was or who made it. To repeat, all those making the decisions steadily denied that they were "blacklisting" anyone. Public accusations were avoided, partly out of fear of possible law suits. Broadcasting personnel simply found that they were no longer getting jobs, although, to make the setup even more confusing, some might receive certain types of assignments but not others.

By a series of circuitous inquiries, they might then learn about the "charges" against them, In most of the reported cases, the "guilty" people did not have any significant "subversive" records.[2] An actress publicly spoke in favor of Henry Wallace's candidacy in 1948, and had difficulty getting any television parts as a result. Some were in trouble for being on the "suspect" slate in an election in an entertainment union. One appeared in off-Broadway plays with blacklisted people whereas several were accused of appearing at benefits sponsored by "disloyal" organizations. Many of those affected were not even listed in *Red Channels*. Sometimes names and identities were mistaken. As typical in all McCarthyite tenets, there was scarcely any reference to anything "subversive" in what appeared in the media.

By the same circuitous information channels, the blacklisted entertainer might be offered some methods of "clearance." The suggested procedures were complex and the results appropriately uncertain. He could hire special consultants to assist him, which might further involve him with the very people who made the original accusation. He could be told, informally, to contact Hartnett with his story, convince particular columnists who might write an absolving article, and get affidavits from prominent anti-Communists. He could write an explanatory letter of his "dereliction," sometimes with help of a lawyer, and might pay for a newspaper ad. Under the detailed guidance of men like Hartnett, he could make some appropriate public statement on some political issue or appear at some "anti-Communist" activity. One of the most poignant stories was that of actress Kim Hunter, who testified under oath that she had been pressured to take a particular position in an interunion dispute in order to be "cleared." [3]

But there was no assurance that any of this would work, since no definite decisions were disclosed. The mechanisms for absolving oneself could be insufficient for another reason. The appellation applied to those affected, whenever any official comment was made, was not "subversive" but "controversial." Clearance need not end the "controversial" status. This is best revealed in the most publicized continuous blacklisting case, that of actress Jean Muir. Although officially cleared, she was, and apparently still is, denied employment because she had become a "bruised apple," as explained by one television executive.[4]

Although the standards for judgment were very vague and the process secretive and unclear, the blacklisting procedures were institutionalized. Investigations have readily disclosed that the decision-makers and their modes of operation were often well structured, whatever the official denials and the planned ignorance of both the affected personnel and the outside world. Among the sponsors, the leading officials of large corporations might be directly involved. Advertising agencies and networks assigned particular individuals to a "screening" role, which they typically refused to affirm. Those who had to carry out the decision would, at best, briefly sketch some of the processes under the repeated prodding of questioners, possibly to ease their guilt. For instance, one network executive, initially asserted that "(I) do not feel free to discuss" the subject, and then elaborated that "(it) bothers me" to "have to placate big sponsors." [5] A radio-television producer, on the other hand, freely described how he had to call a particular extension at his network to ask if a performer were "available," all of which he described as "misguided" and "screwy." [6]

The general impact on entertainment personnel can only be surmised. Only a small portion of the effect has probably been publicly revealed. The careers of several people were destroyed because of previous "records," even leading to suicide.[7] This can be considered an ex post facto denial of freedom of association. If there is little indication of any curtailment of freedom of expression over the airwaves themselves, it was partly because the blacklisted were, predominantly, those with little influence on content, such as actors and directors. Their freedom of expression and association as citizens, however, was undoubtedly limited. Intensive interviews with broadcasting personnel revealed that several were now reluctant about being engaged in politics, about being seen with certain books and periodicals, about seeming "too intellectual," or even about living in Greenwich Village.[8] The suit of one famous blacklisted entertainer, John Henry Faulk, against Hartnett and Laurence Johnson disclosed how his professional life was all but terminated because of a position he took in an interunion dispute and because he decided to go to court in protest.[9]

Even within the general McCarthyite context of the times, how could all this happen? Why did those who were part of or adjuncts to the "power elite" yield to comparatively mild pressures from a few individuals, appropriately classified as rather marginal? Why did so many broadcasting personnel, some of them glamorous names and very close to the powerful, respond with submissive fear rather than protest? The initial answer is that the issue was more salient to the influencers, the blacklisters, that they were the only ones definitive in their methods and objectives, and that their behavior was appropriate to the random, irrational suppressions of McCarthyism. If most of the influencers were motivated by their own definitions of patriotism, to some, like Hartnett, black-listing constituted their major professional roles and practically their ways of life. On the other hand, the powerful decision-makers generally did not try to combat this monomania because of the nature of their businesses. In the few instances where they did take a stand in opposition to these pressures, they were usually successful.[10] In effect, they discovered that the "emperor had no clothes." But such postures were rare. Usually, sponsors, agencies, and networks did as asked because of diffuse fears about possible loss of sales and sponsorships. From this perspective, marketing was regarded as a "political" act.[11] The supposition was that a customer might not buy the product of a company that sponsored programs which used "subversive" or "controversial" performers. That this ever occurred has not been proven. The number of protests might be minuscule and those who defied them generally unhurt, but the safest course was still to avoid risks. Johnson actually threatened to place stickers next to products of companies that sponsored programs which used "disloyal entertainers," branding them as employers of subversives. Yet there is little evidence that any sales declined as a result. In one situation, during the Jean Muir controversy, General Foods hired the Gallup agency to survey public attitudes. Few people questioned ever heard about the situation, and even fewer cared.[12] Nevertheless, Miss Muir, as already indicated, was not rehired despite official "clearance."

The decision-makers were in a unique kind of business, with tremendous profit returns but with an accompanying rampant insecurity. Any "potential" loss of customers, clients, or audience was deemed disastrous. In the words of one producer, "Big corporations scare easily, they're afraid of publicity." [13] A radio-television executive in Syracuse, who refused to be pressured by Laurence Johnson, declared, "I don't know what's the matter with people in New York. Maybe they're so big they have to be stupid." [14] Perhaps, bigness did not produce "stupidity" as much as the vague fear of what could result from testing Johnson's strength, and such a contest was regarded as quite unnecessary. After all, those who might be hurt were mostly actors, directors, and producers—easily replaceable and hardly known. If employment of "controversial" persons had little effect on viewers, their dismissals produced few ripples in much of the audience. Similarly, publicity about dismissals was also to be avoided because this, too, could conceivably mean market losses, as well as possible law suits.

When the decision-makers did resist and exercised the power inherent in their roles and their available resources, it was usually because the person under attack represented something salient, that is, something significant to their own interests and/or values. For instance, almost nothing happened to prominent newscasters under attack by the blacklisting forces, even though, ironically, their "subversive" tendencies would be presumed to have more serious consequences. Apparently, the network officials conceived of news departments as sacred areas, where any interference from the outside would vitiate their necessary competence and responsibility.[15] Besides, freedom of expression was so clearly an issue, and previous experience in resisting similar pressures in that area made the situation much less ambiguous. Some personnel claimed that particularly popular entertainers would be protected, for obvious business reasons. As explained by one interviewed actor, anyone who was needed would somehow be cleared.[16] One possible illustration was the fairly casual public rehabilitation of Lucille Ball, one of the biggest "properties" in television, after her admission to the House Un-American Activities Committee that she had distributed petitions for Communist party candidates in the 1930's.[17]

Obviously, these situations were exceptional. Most threatened personnel were faced with a structure and a process that prevented any precise understanding of what happened and why and were immersed in the generic McCarthyite anxieties. There seemed little choice but to be fearful and acquiescent. Furthermore, many accepted the blacklist as little more than an extension of the industry's prevailing patterns. Major decisions were always so difficult to comprehend, competition for jobs so severe, and employment insecurity so endemic that another annoyance hardly seemed to make much difference. The ambiguity of everything in their special world militated against resistance from these victims of suppression.

But some did resist and at best, were generally no worse off for their efforts. Ultimately, resistance in a somewhat organized form may have been partly responsible, along with the general decline of McCarthyism and the extensive publicity, for the gradual disappearance of radio-television blacklisting as a regular, ongoing *institutionalized* practice. In 1954, a faction in the New York local of AFTRA began a campaign against the blacklist. Its arguments were those of trade unionists concerned with the job situation rather than those of civil libertarians per se. Blacklisting was an obvious ingredient of the job situation, and many members charged that the leadership of the union, closely associated with AWARE, had become so involved in combating "subversives" that it had failed to fulfill its collective bargaining functions. A resolution attacking blacklisting was passed, and the next year the supporters of that position were elected to local offices.[18]

Their stand did not end blacklisting as such, especially since the supporters of AWARE returned to office in a subsequent election. Furthermore John Henry Faulk's troubles started after his election on the anti-blacklisting slate and, in fact, because of it. Still, although there is little significant published data, there were few new reported rampant cases thereafter. Of course, some of those already damaged never got jobs. Several, with more clear-cut "subversive" identifications than was typical, have only very recently been permitted to work for the networks. But whatever blacklisting continued to occur was sporadic rather than systematic.[19]

What happened to John Henry Faulk was unique. He was initially subjected to the pressures of the blacklisting forces as a response to his stand in the union. He might have kept his job, or gotten other jobs, if he had kept quiet, utilized the traditional channels of "clearance," or continued his campaign along the previous lines. By suing his accusers he threatened to put the entire picture in the official public record. He was, therefore, by a variety of devices, kept out of all possible radio or television jobs for more than six years. In other words, he was completely blacklisted for this forceful opposition to the blacklist at a time when it was no longer very prevalent. But his victory in court, which utilized the testimony of many entertainment people and resulted in an incredible judgment of several million dollars, probably prevented any new blacklisting in the radio and television industries.[20] Thus, a few motivated and activated people—indignant entertainment personnel and lawyers dedicated both to the welfare of their clients and their perceptions of justice—were responsible for the ultimate removal of all but a few remnants of this particular barrier to civil liberties.

This analysis must conclude with a special postscript. One of the more emphasized social evils resulting from curtailment of freedom of expression and association is, of course, the likely diminution of meaningful communication, however defined. Whatever the indictments against blacklisting in broadcasting on civil libertarian grounds, this charge is not applicable because it had so little apparent effect on content. History reveals an even more ironic twist. The time of the full-blown blacklist, roughly the early and middle 1950's, is currently referred to as the "Golden Era of Television." It is not our task at this point either to evaluate or to explain the basis for this contention. It is sufficient to point out that, to many critical observers, television became more of a "wasteland" after the end of the blacklist.

MOVIES

The movie industry also practiced blacklisting, but, in many ways, it was quite different from that prevailing in the broadcasting media. For one thing, the details were more open and available, much of it widely publicized, and the entire process was more "rational." [21] Who was blacklisted and why they were blacklisted was generally known. The decision-makers could usually be located, and studio executives admitted their crucial roles. The method of "clearance" was usually spelled out. The injured or suspect performers were subject to arbitrary power, but the power-wielders were in view and the methods for satisfying them fairly apparent and regularized.

The charges were, in many cases, more definite and damaging than in the radio-television world. A significant number of those affected were named as Communist party members at some time. The political atmosphere was more directly relevant in Hollywood. A volatile atmosphere of political conflict in and around the movie industry had been prevalent for some time, in which the issue of "communism," accurately or inaccurately applied, was a pervasive element. In general, Hollywood blacklisting was not a duplicate of the Kafkaesque phantasmagoria of the networks. Whatever one's view of the process, and a genuine libertarian would have to be critical on principle, a sizable section of those affected were in difficulty because of their definitive political stands or affiliations, now or in the past.

If the decision-makers as well as the justification for their decisions could be located readily, so also were the names and tactics of the influencers, who represented actual and not vaguely potential power. The pressures did not come from a handful of phone calls, a visit from someone like Laurence Johnson, or from Vincent Hartnett's communications. Names and facts were, privately or publicly, presented by federal or state legislative committees, national officials of the American Legion, the leaders of the movie technicians' unions, or an organization of Hollywood notables called the "Motion Picture Alliance for the Preservation of American Ideals." The path to "clearance" was also readily apparent. It involved some form of public "penance," with the assistance of some of the influencers, or the utilization of one specific lawyer named Martin Gang. Unlike what was typical in the broadcasting media, this tactic usually worked. Since so many were actually "guilty," that is, had clear-cut records of some "subversive" connections, there was a readily available way of getting their jobs back—name names of others. In other cases, a public recitation of "anti-subversive" views would be sufficient, which was rare in the broadcasting world. The difference was, to some extent, a reflection of the existence of more "hot property" to protect in the movies and the fact that sometimes the Hollywood powerful themselves were under attack.[22]

The precise history of the Hollywood blacklist was also more definitely patterned, and much of what happened was associated with concrete events. A wave of firings would follow several publicized hearings of the House Un-American Activities Committee. Others would result from high-level meetings between national officials of the American Legion and studio executives. The basis for the policy was publicly stated by the movie companies in a famous communiqué at the very initiation of the process in 1947.[23] Despite some connection between the movie and network blacklists, they were not identically observed. Being named in *Red Channels* or *Counterattack* did not prompt any automatic actions by the studio executives.

Movie blacklisting was thus a precisely directed and limited process, with little evidence of the inclusive and ambiguous methods of the networks. The most painful experience was not diffuse fear but the agony of the testimony required for public rehabilitation. For those who were never actually Communists, the tactic might not be considered too onerous because merely a statement of their beliefs, as has been explained, could prove sufficient. If they were ever Communists, the choice could be painful, for they would probably be called to testify before the House Un-American Activities Committee or name names before other groups. In an extreme version of what was typical of witnesses before such bodies, any decision would result in personal branding. They would either remain suspect or become publicly identified as "informers." What is somewhat surprising was the comparative lack of vehemence that those who chose either tack showed toward each other. As one "noncooperating" witness said about one of his "informing" colleagues: "Who appointed me his judge? He's as much a victim as the rest of us." [24] Despite the typical mutual recriminations, the entire experience sometimes produced a generic tolerance, a reaction against the whole pattern of accusation on all sides. Friendships were sometimes maintained or restored and collaboration was possible.[25] In essence, the Hollywood story was characterized by pathos, especially the dilemma of those who had been caught up in an exciting melee of Communist-led activism, which had been very respectable in their immediate circles and which they now thought was a mistake. Although wanting to continue their productive artistic careers, but being "decent" human beings, any behavior chosen was fraught with severe internal conflict. But, it was up to them to do something in one form or other. The network blacklisting represented a typical McCarthyite absurdity rather than pathos, the wholesale passive victimization of all kinds of people rather than the moral turmoil of those who had, at some time, made a conscious political choice.

The "anti-Communist" Hollywood activities, in line with a more rational perspective, were, at least initially, directed at the movie content which the "subversives" might "sneak in." The House Un-American Activities Committee hearings in 1947, which initiated the entire campaign, began with such an intent, and were thus openly feared and opposed by much of the industry, right up to Motion Picture Association President Eric Johnston, who saw the hearings as an attempt to control film fare. The efforts to detect "suspect" material, however, proved to be a fiasco. About the only significant "evidence" that cropped up concerned the World War II films about Russia, some of which were obviously "slanted." The inquiries thus turned toward individual affiliations, in the characteristic mode of the times. The industry no longer envisaged a direct threat to its control over films, and its opposition to the hearings collapsed. But the element of content was always implicit. Note that, unlike the broadcasting situation, those fired included, from the beginning and throughout, a large proportion of writers, people whose possible relation to what appeared in the media was very obvious. After the industry had decided to "cooperate," it could take more concrete steps besides firing the suspected. It could take better pains to see that there were even fewer possible claims of "subversive themes," something network executives did not have to do and probably could not do.

The ironic result was that Hollywood movies, then in a desperate and defensive struggle against television, decreased their proportion of "socially realistic" pictures and went in for "safe themes," as indicated in a "content analysis" report that accompanied an account of movie blacklisting.[26] Television, meanwhile, merely looking for material for an ever expanding audience, went in for "socially realistic" drama at a pace rare in American mass media. It had no themes to "clean up," for few had made any accusations against television on that score. The fact is, however, that the suspect Hollywood writers had been responsible for little suspect content. The content analysis reveals that films written by admitted and alleged Communist party members were, in general, little different from typical Hollywood fare. Only a few examples of movies about "social problems" could be found. As the author of the study points out, the structure of decision-making in Hollywood, with so many people involved, would prevent insertion of any "party-line" material. These writers might show more people of humble means struggling against adversity, but this too has been a theme common enough in Hollywood. Perhaps the most striking twist was the blacklisted writers' greater devotion to patriotic emphasis during the wartime alliance with Russia. Their greatest influence may have been in preventing anti-Russian and anti-Communist films.

Some of the differences between the practices in the two media can be explained by the difference in structures. The movie business, for all its internal turmoil and anxieties, does have a more definitive index of success—receipts at the box office. It has only one clientele, the customer, rather than the bevy of sponsors, ad agencies, and so on. Any serious effects of employing the "wrong people" can thus be easily measured. Each film is, furthermore, an independent commercial entity, with little of the "halo" effect of each wireless program on a station or channel's total audience. The "star" system is more pervasive in movies, resulting in more "hot property" not readily replaceable for the fans. More leading figures were thus "protected." In television, the story of Lucille Ball was unique. The nature of the industry, tied in with the type of open and understood pressures and the more "rational" method of clearance, made the movie suppressions more comprehensible and, by and large, less pervasive. For instance, since the accusations usually involved affiliation with something more clearly and accurately defined as "Communist," the effect on freedom of association seems to have been less than in radio-television.[27] The possible effect on film content was slight and short range. Socially realistic films have always appeared. Soon the competition from foreign films and the wide dispersal of production companies actually made movies much "freer" than they have ever been. Independent producers even began to violate the industry "code" of "objectionable material." The easing of blacklisting was, for quite tangential reasons, accompanied by "better" movies and "worse" television.

A more dramatic difference between the two media was in the respective ways the blacklist, more or less, ended. The final end of the era did not come in the networks until the last "sideswipe" led to the Faulk suit. Essentially, it ceased to be an overall practice in broadcasting because of concrete *external pressures*. In the movie industry, on the other hand, the initiative to end the policy came, to a great extent, *within the industry itself,* when producers began to try to employ the blacklisted. Probably the most famous example was that of the writer Dalton Trumbo, one of the earliest blacklisted Hollywood luminaries, who had also served a prison sentence for his refusal to answer questions of the House Un-American Activities Committee. His "rehabilitation" ultimately led to his assignment of the scenario for "Exodus" and the greatest

financial success of his career. A comparison between his fate and
that of the "bruised apple" in broadcasting, Jean Muir, is the comprehensive comment on the difference between blacklisting in
movies and broadcasting. In the one case, a man was openly denied employment for what he had publicly done. One could readily
try and make amends by hiring him again and seeing what happened. In the other case, a woman was secretly denied employment with very few charges against her. It would be very unseemly
to admit that this had actually happened by reemploying her sud-
denly after all this time.[28]

11

The McCarthy era: an overview

The term McCarthyism was, itself, a misnomer. The personal role of the controversial Wisconsin senator was minimal. We have explicitly referred to him in these discussions only as one of the congressional investigators into subversion, whose antics produced the most random effects but whose impact was nowhere as pervasive and continuing as, for instance, the relatively anonymous members of the House Committee on Un-American Activities. His name is merely used as a conventionalized symbol of a series of phenomena in a period of American history associated with suppressions of freedom of expression and association. The most prevalent methods of suppression have been described—legislative inquiries and loyalty-security programs as well as a peculiar offshoot of these methods, blacklisting in the entertainment media. There were other aspects, of course—denial of passports, the impact on academia (which is largely left for later special consideration), and so on. The three modes described were the most significant and the most symptomatic. The legislative inquiry provided a legally sanctioned forum for pillorying people who had little opportunity for defense. The loyalty-security programs and blacklisting, especially in the wireless media, confronted individuals with what seemed like a secretive inquisition by anonymous people with, likewise, little opportunity for defense. Liberties were thus curtailed in the manner sketched, and open confrontation was rarely the mode. When there was opportunity for actual public contest, whether by genuine debate, a formal trial, or other "adversary" contests, or widespread publicity to a case, the affected "victim" generally fared better, either by official exoneration or in terms of his subsequent career. The problem of actual "Communists" was minor, despite the wide attention given to this presumed basic ingredient. The most common "penalty" was loss of job or damage to reputation and career.

The specific historical frustrations of the cold war, magnified during the Korean War, provided the situational setting. The decline of vigorous political dissent, particularly of a more "radical" type, was both cause and a further result of McCarthyism. Particular people, however, were responsible in different ways—a variety of decision-makers, influencers, and some of the affected themselves: legislative investigators, other politicians out to make political capital from anti-subversive crusades, members of the executive branch of government devising or enforcing loyalty-security programs, courts upholding some of these restrictive acts of some branch of government, the various business officials responsible for decision-making in blacklisting situations, individuals who made a career out of anti-communism, and so on. The affected victim was frequently a contributor to the general atmosphere by his "yielding" to the varying diffuse suppressive pressures, frequently in a manner above and beyond the actual explicit strictures. The context was essentially nonpolitical, even though some hoped to use it for political advantage. Dissident ideas were less important as a target than presumed clandestine activities and personal associations, formal and informal.

We have deemphasized the influence of specific public opinions, both generic and organized. Of course, the prevalent insecurities about the world situation and the desire to thwart subversion were the necessary foundations for the behavior of the crucial social actors. But they only supplied a supporting public, and not a mobilized movement spurring the suppressive actions. The issues were simply not very salient for many people, and the perceptions of the situation were frequently so alien to the reality that whatever widespread pro-"McCarthyite" sentiment existed represented only that of an applauding audience rather than a pressuring public.

The opposition to McCarthyite tactics also rested on some widely held popular values, whose saliency was also typically not too high for most people—civil liberties per se, fairness, and sympathy for the personalities or the ideas of some of the affected. Perhaps the most instrumental value encouraging opposition was the growing adherence to the need for job protection. The specific actors were, again, all important: decision-makers who administered some programs with caution, congressmen who criticized or actively opposed such things as the anti-subversive investigations or the loyalty-security programs, courts which stifled some of the suppressive behavior or released victims, the myriad of the affected and their allies who "resisted" in some fashion, those who publicly attacked one or more aspect, and so on. These actors, in the changed situational context, ultimately ended McCarthyism.

SOCIAL SCIENTISTS AND MC CARTHYISM

Much of what has been said constitutes a dialogue with the views of many social scientists.[1] Their prevailing orientations and our dispute with them thus demand more elaboration. A comprehensive study, considered later in the chapter on "Academic Freedom," reveals that many teachers of social science courses in colleges and universities were "apprehensive" and "cautious" during that period. This, however, was less true of academic "notables," whose reputations and relative job security made them more immune to suppressive pressures. Most of those who wrote on the subject of McCarthyism could be identified as notables, and here our critique is directed toward published material.

The commentaries of most social scientists on McCarthyism,

both scholarly and casual, avoided two extremes more common to other kinds of intellectuals; they neither submitted to any of its tenets nor exaggerated its significance. Hostility to all brands of totalitarianism did not prompt any noticeable concessions even to the more "moderate" suppressive actions under the principle of thwarting "conspiratorial" tactics. Most social scientists exhibited apparent hostility to all aspects of the phenomenon and serious concern about its impact, as indicated by their widespread attention. Likewise, as scholars dedicated to empirical observation, most avoided flamboyant claims about any resultant complete "loss of freedom" in America.

The most common defects were those of direction of interest, the type of analysis, and the accompanying stated or implicit program for improvement. The previous chapters indicate how much any analyst of McCarthyism is indebted to social scientists for the research conducted in the 1950's. Yet even in this area the misplaced focus meant that not only was insufficient research done but also much of the research potential was concentrated on one specific feature of the problem—the nature of the supporters of Joseph McCarthy, either those who were active participants in his personal political public or those who merely expressed some approval of the man in response to a questionnaire. Our theoretical opposition to this emphasis has been sufficiently explained, and our qualifications of the actual findings have been stated. As an overall assessment, such a concentration of interest meant an inordinate attention to McCarthyites rather than McCarthyism, to one particular, if extreme, manifestation rather than the phenomenon itself. Hence, many viewed the acts of the congressional anti-subversive investigators as aberrations, strains in the ongoing social-political system which could be attributed to the deviant malcontents, instead of seeing them as one aspect of the total system in a specific historical situation. In fact, the very existence of the cold war as the essential and necessary condition for all that happened was mentioned by several analysts only in passing. The loyalty-security programs, the most pervasive aspect of "McCarthyism," were deemphasized or ignored by many social scientists, especially sociologists, or merely considered another response to pressures from assumed McCarthyite publics.

Their typical stance has recently been critically examined by Michael Rogin, who sees their vantage point as a concomitant of a particular ideology, which can be summarized as an adherence to the doctrine of self-contained, autonomous, and elite plural- ism.[2] Our own formulation is expressed in our continuing dis- pute with the leading exponent of the prevailing analysis of McCarthyism, Edward Shils, and most of the authors included in the two editions of *The Radical Right*.[3] To them, McCarthyism represented an intervention of the "mass society," especially its most alienated representatives, into the private provinces of elites. The result was a politicalizing of issues that should best be left to gentlemanly discourse, that is, of bringing into the public arena what should be kept within the elite "clubs." The antidote was an assumption and an assertion by the elites of their right to function without external annoyance. In essence, they feared open, vigorous political contest as an unfortunate disturbance in an otherwise fairly harmonious social-political order. The perceived dangers seemed to come from those who made too many waves. Interest- ingly, most of this was written during a period of profound na- tional depoliticalization.

The 1954 censure of Joseph McCarthy by the "elite" senators, including many traditional "conservatives," was hailed as both a verification of their analysis and a specimen of the type of counter- tactics advocated. Exaggerated estimate of the impact of this event was one of the most common misconceptions of the times. It may have had a long-range implication for the gradual dissipa- tion of the political weight of the most blatant McCarthyites, but the McCarthyite modes of operation described in the previous chapters were hardly altered for some time. The characteristic suppressions of the era were countered by, as has been sufficiently described, some form of "political" opposition, even if we include lawsuits within this category of purposeful citizen action. Neither the defense of victims nor the alteration of practices could be left to strategically placed elites. Ultimately, McCarthyism lost its sting through an accumulation of such political acts in a changed context, within which the return to forceful and widespread political struggle was a significant constituent feature.

The concerned social scientists were so conspicuously remiss in analyzing McCarthyism because of an intellectual-ideological bias —a fear of political clashes. At the same time, contemporary sociological ideas, some of them pervading popular literature, suggested several seminal interpretations which were largely ignored in these analyses, even those written by scholars responsible for these potential insights.

FURTHER INTERPRETATIONS

Analysts of McCarthyism have rarely included any explicit reference to the concept of the "garrison society." Even by implication, it appears at best as a peripheral part of their explanations. The cold war has brought a permanently more or less mobilized America, with a special type of "enemy." Whatever else this means, it involves some type of regular official orientation toward the requirements of external combat, which in some manner affects the opinions and values of much of the population. The demands for "loyalty" bear some resemblance to the expected cohesion of a military unit. The notion of "security," a purely military canon, becomes applicable to so many spheres of national life. "Communists" and other "subversives" are literally perceived as active agents of the enemy, especially because the mode of Communist operation has been so typically "secretive."

Naturally, this is a crude summary of the "garrison" interpretation, one of the underlying conditions for the McCarthyite tendencies, but, as should be apparent by now, hardly the complete explanation. America remained a garrison society through the 1960's, but whatever else one can say about the subsequent period it has not been McCarthyite, as will be further elaborated. The specific features of the cold war atmosphere in the McCarthy period have been sufficiently detailed. Similarly, the fact that Mc-

Carthyite suppressions were related to the operation of particular structures and behavior in especially relevant roles, much of it succinctly revealed in research by social scientists although infrequently utilized in general analysis, has been frequently described in the previous material. These formulations are akin to the many valuable sociological insights that were otherwise so prevalent in the literature.

One of the most popular phrases used to describe the times was "political apathy." The two most prominent sociologists to the lay public, C. Wright Mills and David Riesman, began their influential dissections of contemporary America to determine the causes of the assumed apathy. Both, with all the major differences between them, ignored their own central orientations in their comments on any aspect of McCarthyism, and most other commentators have been similarly lax.[4] Political apathy is probably a less apt description than our own concept of "political blandness," Enough people were politically involved, but they directed their attention at peripheral questions and lacked the passion that encourages sufficient resistance to suppressive pressures.

Another slogan of the day was "conformity," which was utilized in many analyses of McCarthyism. The emphasis in such instances, however, was also misdirected and the term, itself, unclear. Marie Jahoda, who has written some of the most useful statements about McCarthyism, as well as conducted some of the most valuable research, has made a significant distinction among the apparently similar processes of "conformance," "consentience" (conviction), and "compliance" (coercion).[5] Most discussions slur over the differences. The McCarthyite tendencies were primarily "coercive" —one refrained from having certain associates or sometimes saying certain things because of fear of particular sanctions, particularly those associated with one's job. Unlike the image created in Orwell's *1984*, few were *convinced* by those who suppressed them. More importantly, little "conformity" was demanded, for this implies following prescribed behavior. McCarthyism was more "negative." One was merely stimulated to refrain from certain actions. In other words, the suppressions were not designed to obtain political assent to any creed but only to limit political dissent or, in other words, to accentuate political blandness.

The suppressive attempts took their characteristic form and had so much impact because of the commonly accentuated feature of all contemporary society—*bureaucratization*. The many-faceted observations of social scientists on this subject had thoroughly pervaded popular culture, as well illustrated by William Whyte's best-selling *The Organization Man*.[6] The loyalty-security programs and, to some extent, entertainment blacklisting cannot be understood without considering the bureaucratic elements. Whyte pinpointed one essential aspect of American bureaucracies during this period more decisively than most of the scholarly writers. The mammoth bureaucracies are very seductive settings to their employees. They seem to represent the ultimate "welfare state." Since the major penalty from McCarthyite actions was the loss of a job, or difficulty in finding a subsequent job, especially in a bureaucracy, the feared eventuality was a possible loss of the rewards of the current "affluent" society. The McCarthyite strictures thus meant more of a withdrawal of the "carrot" than the implementation of the "stick." With the political setting offering so little motivation for vigorous political dissent, the "internal migration" to doing one's job quietly and enjoying the fruits of consumption from that endeavor seemed a much more salient choice. Put in slightly different language, McCarthyite suppressions were primarily a result of anxiety about the withdrawal of positive inducements rather than the imposition of severe negative restraints.

The vast amount of psychological literature on the relation between free, autonomous behavior and the clarity-ambiguity dimension should also have sensitized social scientists to its relevance to McCarthyism, although literary figures were apt to note the "Kafka" analogy. The bureaucratic organizations and their method of operation, in the concrete historic settings, did not produce the rational, predictable, and clearly understood actions assumed in classical formulas.[7] What happened was exactly the opposite, resulting in the diffuse anxiety that made submission to McCarthyite suppressions so pervasive, except among those who, in general or at a particular time, had clearer perceptions, clearer values, and/or meaningful allies.

Sociologically, the impact of McCarthyism did illustrate one possible manifestation of "mass society" with its bureaucratic underpinnings. The fearful, isolated individual submitted to suppressions of his freedoms because his isolation made him fearful. Furthermore, the result of the strictures imposed upon him, and, to some extent, their actual objective was to make him avoid particular associations, in effect to make him more isolated. Those who showed less fear and were less isolated, and the two states had reciprocal effects on each other, were more capable of resisting and opposing the suppressions. Pluralistic associations provided a mechanism for combating the "evils" of the bureaucratized mass society.

THE END OF MC CARTHYISM AND ITS LEGACY

In each of the previous chapters, the "end" of McCarthyism has been sketched. In essence, the earlier method of operation became inoperative because, within the changed situational context, particular people became more "political" in their opposition to the "McCarthyite" methods, and decision-makers, in whatever way or for whatever reasons, responded accordingly. The methods of the 1950's never completely disappeared, but they became relatively unimportant.

Open, vigorous debate returned to the fore as the style of political contest, replacing the search for the secret dossier. On the political "extremes," a genuine "radical right movement" became very successful in the early 1960's, and effectively captured the national Republican party in 1964, whereas the "new left" became a prominent part of the scene by the middle of the 1960's. The campaigns for civil rights resulted in large-scale political mobilizations on a dimension rarely seen in this country. New crises in the cold war did not prompt any far-reaching search for "traitors" and "dupes," even during the most serious moment in all of post–World War II international relations, the Cuban missile crisis in 1962. When the nation got into a hot war again in Vietnam, the reaction was vastly different from that of the Korean War. The opposition to American policy was open, sizable, organized, and vigorous. It represented many stances and many tactics, ranging from the clearly stated opposing views of political notables, like the chairman of the Senate Foreign Relations Committee and three aspirants for the Democratic presidential nomination in 1968, to the significant number of Americans ready for some form of civil disobedience. The "silent generation" of the 1950's, with a few bohemian "beats" and "hipsters" as the only publicized deviants, was succeeded by the mass of youth in some form of revolt against the "establishment." Apparently, the McCarthyite suppressions, and the corollary features of American society on which they were based, did not ultimately stifle dissent in America.

Why, then, did the nation recover so readily from the McCarthy suppressions and what, if anything, was the resulting legacy? One of the most striking observations is that general public opinion apparently changed very little, either in substantive political attitudes or in those directly related to civil liberties. Despite the blithe remarks of many journalists, the basis for vote choice, for instance, exhibited an amazing similarity in the 1960's to what prevailed in the middle 1930's.[8] Whatever change has been manifested, McCarthyism had little to do with it, primarily because it was so nonpolitical and stimulated withdrawal from politics rather than new political convictions. Most importantly, generic democratic values, however interpreted and whatever the saliency for most people, did not seem to decline. Similarly, the motivation to express strongly dissenting opinions and to organize for their implementation was never squelched; the return to a situation which made this both meaningful and more permissible was all that was required.

Other features of American society that permit or encourage free expression and association remained intact. Those features of the governmental structures which fostered libertarianism, such as the Bill of Rights itself and the operations of the courts under its provisions, were never seriously altered, however occasionally modified. The pluralistic tendencies, which suffered so much under the McCarthyite drives, remained viable enough to permit an appropriate arena for organized dissent afterward. McCarthyism actually produced few fundamental changes, and, when the appropriate actors, in the changed context, brought about the effective termination of the suppressions, America became "free" again fairly easily. The spread of freedom may be indivisible, but its curtailment need not spread far if sufficient underlying conditions for its maintenance remain.

One of the reasons that the suppressions had less of an impact than feared is that they were not very severe, even if they were rather pervasive. Above all, criminal penalties were rare, and political "censorship" was, in the literal sense, almost completely absent. A major reason was that the suppressions, in this non-political atmosphere, were not a forceful response to counter-legitimacies, which historically has been the principal spur to the most serious suppressions. The social-economic-political order was in no way threatened by organized opposition, including that of any "downtrodden" sector of society. In the absence of widespread criminal sanctions against dissidence, what might be crudely termed "radical" criticism was openly published at all times.

All this would imply that McCarthyism was merely an annoying episode that passed with little lasting effect. This was hardly the case. The scars remained, many of them too subtle to detect without more thorough probing. Perhaps the most obvious impact was on the nature of subsequent "radical" protest, the much-discussed "generation gap" in this sphere. "Radicals" may have been free to publish, but the McCarthyite suppressions, within the nonpolitical context, helped to reduce the audience and the adherents to a minuscule number. The "new radicalism" of the 1960's rested on two political movements relatively unaffected by McCarthyism: civil rights and pacifism. Both tended to have, however, a "nonpolitical" character. Civil rights represented an elementary demand for equal citizenship with nonsubstantive political content, and pacifism meant, for a long time, a campaign for preventing the worst eventualities from international tensions without any implication of a foreign policy program. The "new leftists" of various types thus come on the scene in the absence of much continuity with the messages of earlier "radicalisms," including their emphases on substantive policy. What they picked up from the two "movements" was mostly a sense of moral dedication, including an intense outrage at the "immorality" of their opponents. The political blandness of the previous era, intensified by McCarthyite suppressions, had made them, to use the language applied by Arthur Koestler in another connection, veritable political "Neanderthal men." [9]

Political dispute has been as sharp and extensive in the mid-1960's as ever in the nation's history. The McCarthy era is thus well behind us. But new dangers to freedom of expression and association have arisen. To speak of the possibility of a new McCarthyism is to submit to word-mongering rather than to seek any meaningful understanding. The threats are entirely different, as the following chapter will illustrate. Nevertheless, the above-mentioned McCarthyite legacy has helped create the immediate civil liberties problems.

12

The problems of the mid-1960's: the crisis of legitimacy

By the early 1960's, the McCarthy atmosphere was primarily a subject for historians. Yet the mid-1960's present another series of crises for freedom of expression and association. Referring to them as a possible manifestation of a new McCarthyism misses the specific characteristics of each era. Of course McCarthyite tendencies remained. Loyalty and security criteria have continued to show up in strange places, such as demands for oaths of non-affiliation with subversive organizations of recipients of Medicare. But such efforts stand out by their very strangeness, that is, they are not a major pattern of American life. Furthermore, they have frequently been removed by public pressures, as in the elimination of "disclaimer oaths" for recipients of national scholarships. Congressional investigating committees into subversion have continued their activities, but their roles have become less important and both the type of inquiry and response have changed. The "torment of secrecy," however viewed, has been a serious issue in only one situation, the actual attempts of some form of government censorship of certain types of information on grounds of "national security." It is interesting that this most structurally rooted type of suppression of a "garrison society" was so rare in the 1950's, and, although relevant in the 1960's, it was so sub-sidiary a phenomenon that, in the interest of thematic structure, it is best excluded from immediate discussion and left for a later perusal of more peripheral issues.

To recapitulate briefly, the suppressions of the McCarthy era were mostly a matter of exposure of the hidden politics or per-sonal backgrounds of specific individuals or organizations. The most common penalty was loss of a specific job, or type of job, and attendant loss of reputation. All of this occurred in an atmosphere of absence of sharp political divergencies. The civil liberties problems in the current period have been connected with open and avowed political conflict, not with anything concealed. The prison sentence has again become the feared penalty. In-volved are the sometimes interconnected tensions engendered by Negro protest, the war in Vietnam, the "revolt of youth," and, to some extent, the existence of a set of genuine "radical right" political movements. Unlike the 1950's, participation in these various kinds of dissidence do not automatically mark one as a suspect. All cover a range of participants and activities from those generally defined as quite respectable and responsible to those frequently considered beyond the pale of tolerance. (Where the line shall be drawn is one of the most persistent dilemmas.) The typical "nuisance" threats to freedom of expression and association, such as the contest between the rights of assembly and the need to protect public order, again pose sharply divergent and relatively pervasive legal, political, and value disputes. In its ultimate expression, the nature of some contemporary political contests presents the most serious of all challenges to the mainte-nance of civil liberties, a "crisis of legitimacy," a series of agoniz-ing decisions about which actions of people against government and which acts of government against people are permissible.

The amount of suppression has not been as pervasive, or even as profound, as that of the McCarthy era, and may not become any more conspicuous. But the situational context offers a potential for very severe restrictions. Meanwhile, American society has changed very little, except for those aspects directly related to the above-mentioned political and quasi-political tendencies. The relevant structures and roles have remained essentially intact, as have the *fundamental* values. But the sharply divergent specific values associated with these movements, all resting on some feature of the traditional American ethos, have produced the type of internal conflict that, if widespread and long enough, is very inimical to civil liberties. Whereas the McCarthyite strictures were enmeshed in a nonpolitical atmosphere, the current problems are a reflection of intense involvement in politics. Since so many people are participating in some manner, and since so many perceive of themselves as directly affected, the number of social actors affecting decisions has become much larger and the opinions of so many people, even those in relatively passive publics, have become more significant. In other words, the pertinent issues are salient to a large sector of the populace.

CIVIL RIGHTS MOVEMENT: THE NEGRO PROTEST

At the outset, it may be again necessary to explain that substantive "civil rights" questions are outside our immediate domain. The interest is only in the problems associated with the type of expression and collective action of those who proclaim those rights.

The initial civil liberties aspect was the test of the legitimate right of civil rights organizations to exist and function in the South. The legal harassment, by local and state governments, of the National Association for the Advancement of Colored People, has already been described, for it resulted in several significant court test cases, generally resulting in legal protections for the NAACP.[1] More complex were the physical abuses—legal, semi-legal, and extralegal—of those involved in what were clearly legal activities. The extreme manifestations, actual murders and attempted murders, have been sufficiently publicized. In such situations, the civil liberties demands consisted of requests for protection by government, essentially the federal government, from private suppression, rather than a call for freedom from government. In other situations, as in the use of police dogs and water hoses against demonstrators in Birmingham, the demand was for protection against the policies of local government. In both circumstances, federal law enforcement officials were asked to become, and frequently did become, the most important caretakers of freedom of expression and association, a role which they have rarely been assigned in analyses of civil liberties. This could take the form of police protection by United States marshals, investigation by the Department of Justice, or prosecution by United States attorneys, in which their actions were based on constitutional as well as statutory provisions, some of them newly passed by Congress. In the specific context, with civil rights both a popular value and a political tenet to which national leaders had to respond, such behavior by federal officials was readily predictable. The federal courts, of course, assume a crucial function in curtailing the suppressive acts of local and state officials.

Then, the civil liberties issues became more complex, the legal questions more perplexing, and the passions of the participants more profound as civil rights activities assumed more of the character of some type of "nonviolent resistance." The boycott mechanism, the essence of the campaign against bus desegregation in Montgomery, Alabama, which was the spark for the more vigorous activities that followed, was a purely "political" question, with little civil liberties implication. When the protests took the form of "freedom rides," sit-ins, and so on, the problems became more pertinent to this discussion. In a literal sense, all such manifestations of free expression and association were "illegal acts," violating local or state ordinances or constituting some form of trespass. Such a simple formulation, however, conceals the more pertinent issues. Those who favored the curtailment of these acts were generally using legal arguments to bolster the legitimacy of the segregation system itself. The supporters of "the movement" either insisted that "higher" considerations transcended the apparent legal restrictions or explained that, since segregation was itself illegal under the Constitution, actions in defiance were implicitly legal. In essence, this was one of the bases of the several Supreme Court decisions that uphold the right of such activities. The legitimacy of such behavior and, in fact, the entire question of legal segregation were more or less settled when both court decisions and federal legislation made the practice illegal.

When civil rights actions changed from militant mass-pressure demonstrations and defiance of "illegitimate" laws to what were, deliberately or unintentionally, "disruptive" acts, the value and legal disputes became more serious. This was evident in court cases involving demonstrations at government buildings, including courthouses, beginning in the early 1960's. The issues became more profound when the objective of actions was to upset the functioning of social life, either to dramatize a specific set of proposals or merely to protest existing conditions, codified by some ideologists as the doctrine of "creative disorder." The range of possible behavior extends from deliberate and specific single-issue actions, for example, preventing construction of a building because no Negro labor was employed, to the largely spontaneous and amorphous ghetto outbursts of the past few years. Among other things, these actions posed the type of value conflicts that can make "nuisance" suppressions become "pervasive."

Obviously, the events grouped under this heading are quite varied. Some have been led by purely "respectable" people in civil rights organizations, and others by those who have become publicly identified as "dangerous agitators," whereas the ghetto disturbances have been essentially leaderless riots. What they do have in common is the forcefulness of the protests and the fearful reactions to them, which together produce the kind of clash of fundamental values that tends to produce a serious threat to the maintenance of civil liberties.

As seen by Negro protestors, they are fighting for elementary justice, so long denied, with whatever means present themselves. It is unimportant for our purpose to determine the relative significance of the victories already won or the lack of significant change for so many Negroes in prompting these tactics. Whatever the reasons for this type of behavior, always thoroughly dramatized by the media, and the vast differences among different acts, typically ignored by casual exposure to media communication, they do scare many other people. The latter's response is also grounded on morally sanctioned values—defense of family, property, safety of public thoroughfares, and so on.

As many Negro leaders proclaimed the slogan of "black power" and assumed a militant rhetoric, the pressure for constraint, even among those who might be considered "sympathetic" to their aims, was very widespread. The language used did often contain apparent incitements to illegal and forceful actions and, occasionally, to actual violence, though such declarations were very ambiguous. But, as is common in such situations, the reactions have been above and beyond the genuine dangers. Few commentators, for instance, attempt to analyze the actual content of "black power" programs, which can in many ways be interpreted as a very "conservative" approach, a retreat from struggle for national equality to the protection hoped for from a separatist enclave. It is therefore understandable why so much of the public responds in terms of diffuse anxieties and some clamor for restraint of "agitators." The ghetto disorders are casually accepted as evidence of a clear and present danger from their activities. The fact that the "National Commission on Civil Disorders," which investigated the riots, concluded that there was no conspiracy and that "agitators" had little to do with prompting the disturbances does not seem to have allayed the widespread fears, especially since so many, particularly the police, still insist on a conspiracy interpretation.

One result was congressional inclusion of penalties for those who travel between states to foment riots as a bizarre rider to the Civil Rights Law of 1968. More serious is the prosecution and trial of particular Negro spokesmen who have assumed the image of dangerous public enemies. The details vary from situation to situation. Whether each or any is guilty of the crimes charged is not, for our purpose, the relevant issue, although in some cases the magnification of possible petty offense seems obvious. More important is the fact that they tend to be judged in a "lynch" atmosphere which makes it all but impossible for an outsider to determine the facts without considerable probing. In the minds of much of the apprehensive public, they are clearly guilty until proven innocent. The trepidations of so many about the Poor People's Encampment in Washington in the spring of 1968, an experience which, considering the circumstances, was very peaceful and law-abiding, attests to the widespread, unclearly defined general pattern of fearful concern.

The reaction becomes more serious because it is associated with the problem of "crime in the streets," which, among other things, was a prominent issue in the 1968 election campaign. That individual crimes and black protest are different phenomena, even if based upon similar social conditions, is inconsequential. The question of personal safety is assumed to be involved in both, and, similarly, the role of the police is evident in both. Those who proclaim the slogan "support your local police" are asking for more forceful action against those accused of personal criminal acts as well as "cracking down" on protesters. As a supplement, private vigilante groups have organized as an auxiliary police force, presumably to "protect" neighborhoods against Negro rioters. Their opponents are pilloried as defenders of rioters, including the American Civil Liberties Union. For instance, a meeting of the New Jersey ACLU was picketed by members of one such group, accompanied by the arrest of several of the organization's officials by an off-duty policeman who was on the picket line.[2]

The previously orderly and, apparently, somewhat successful "Negro revolution," has, for whatever reasons, reached an impasse. Many Negroes and Negro organizations have thus felt compelled to call for, and sometimes pursue, more drastic actions. Furthermore, ideas and behavior have frequently consisted of confused and generalized romantic appeals and chaotic outbursts. The result has been a set of poorly defined fears, misunderstandings of both motives and objects, and demands for some type of suppression of "dangerous" elements. Civil liberties are threatened by an historically unique manifestation of the tendency for suppression to follow the failure to realize the aspirations of the downtrodden.

The impact should not be misinterpreted. There has been very little direct suppression of freedom of expression and association. In fact, never have so many spokesmen of all kinds of views been given so much of a public forum, including network television. The danger has been the personal and legal harassment of particular types of spokesmen, which involves the possible branding of their organizations as beyond the pale. Those affected may then react in an even more dramatic fashion, resulting in calls for more drastic efforts against them. The tenuous "legitimacy" of what they ask for and do makes demands for more vigorous suppression, both legal and extralegal, more popular, and public opinion on these salient questions is very hostile to the tactics of the protesters.[3] The governmental decision-makers and political influentials, ready to implement these attitudes, are very available; the suppressions may then be directed against the more "legitimate," as is typically the case. In the absence of a more thorough solution of Negro problems and/or general political movements that both defend their rights and make serious efforts to solve those problems, this represents an always present danger to civil liberties in contemporary America.

THE VIETNAM WAR

Obviously, another serious threat to freedom of expression and association in the current setting is the war in Vietnam. There is no available method for determining the precise degree of seriousness, actual or potential. In line with the theme of this book, it is more meaningful to delineate the nature of, and reasons for, the threat, from which it may be possible to determine the likelihood, given specific political trends, of continuing or more encompassing dangers. Nevertheless, it is important to initiate the discussion with the observation that, despite the tremendous national strain accompanying this frustrating war and the many types of suppressive actions to be reported, the unprecedented amount of public discourse and militant demonstration of position has, until the point of this writing, attested to the existence of a generally "free" society in the civil libertarian's meaning of the term.

The contrast with the reactions to the Korean War is amazing for events only about a decade apart. Occurring in the heyday of McCarthyism, American entry into the Korean conflict evoked little opposition. The only significant dispute was about military-political strategy—whether to bomb Communist China's territory, use of nuclear weapons, and so forth. The response was only that of indignation toward the respective targets who were blamed for the three-year debacle. A survey of student attitudes, for instance, revealed almost no opinions about the war itself, but merely an avid concern about the possibility of personal involvement.[4]

It should be unnecessary to emphasize the manifold types of large-scale opposition to America's position in the war in Vietnam, with students, significantly, probably the most conspicuous dissident sector of the population. The more "respectable" opponents include representatives from a variety of political publics, and include many prominent political spokesmen. A sizable proportion of congressmen are in opposition, and the issue received an unprecedented floor debate at the 1968 Democratic National Convention. The effect of such opposition in that election—including the primary victories of Eugene McCarthy and Robert Kennedy and President Johnson's decision not to seek reelection—is sufficiently known.

This opposition would not be likely to pose any threat to civil liberties by itself, because this type of opponent is not fostering a "legitimacy crisis." The danger flows from the more "radical" opponents, especially those who freely admit their sympathies with the enemy, the Vietcong. Some of them have engaged in activities that pose a clear challenge to the legitimacy of government or an attack on the symbols of government—from refusals to be drafted to burning draft cards. Other tactics, with varying degrees of possible illegality, include such things as anti-war propaganda in the armed forces, attempts to disrupt draft activities by demonstrations in front of draft boards, civil disobedience to prevent movement of troop trains, counseling others to avoid the draft, an actual "confrontation" at the Pentagon, burning American flags, and so on. The most likely potential penalty has been not loss of a job, but a prison sentence. Some servicemen, and those who are about to be conscripted, avoid this contingency by voluntary expatriation to another country. None of this was characteristic of the McCarthy era. The resemblance is more to the World War I period, with all the differences that can be noted.

The current anti-war posture, which is occurring at the same time as the challenge posed by militant Negro rhetoric and action and which represents the disaffection from established social forms of many students and other young people, can and has been viewed as a threat to social and political order and the legitimacy of government. Some anti-war activists have, consciously or implicitly, proclaimed that this is their goal.[5] Government agencies as well as some private individuals react as though this were the case in more situations than is justified. The legal and moral issues are very thorny, the passions on both sides very intense, and the possibility of a schism within American political society perhaps as wide as any in our history, creating the typical threat to civil liberties of such profound divisions. Sometimes, the problems have resulted from the nature of demonstrations, the conflict between right of assembly and public order, the maintenance of street traffic, and even the security of the Pentagon. The fervor of the demonstrators, including a large proportion of those involved in the generic "revolt of youth," tends to extol the "rightness" of their objectives over all other considerations. This leads to a sentiment for suppression of more approvable demonstrations, though, because of the legal and value tenets of enough of the public and many government decision-makers, as well as the strength of the "opposition," this has rarely occurred.

The most serious tensions, however, involve the most crucial aspect of a nation engaged in war, behavior in regard to the armed forces, which also provided the most dramatic issue of World War I. The similarity is symbolized by the fact that the attention of the American Civil Liberties Union is, to a great extent, directed at situations which, with all the uniqueness of each period, are reminiscent of the kinds of issues that prompted the formation of the original organization. The most pervasive disputes involve the behavior of men in service and actions in relation to conscription, for they symbolize the traditional conflict between the rights of citizens and the permissible option of the state as a war-maker, even in a generally democratic society. They also symbolize the specific perils to civil liberties in this particular garrison society at this time. Among servicemen, the reported incidents are related to the very unsettled question of the extent of applicability of civil liberties, including First Amendment freedoms, to miiltary personnel.[6]

As is so often true, however, civil liberties issues are intertwined with other questions particularly with the problem of "insubordination" in military life. Several servicemen have been penalized for refusing to do anything connected with the war in Vietnam, such as training personnel; this is another type of dispute which, by and of itself, is outside the scope of this volume. But formal charges arising out of such alleged behavior is readily associated with, and may actually have arisen from, a serviceman's expression of dissent. In one case, a court martial conviction for disobeying a "lawful order" included subsidiary indictments such as "promoting disloyalty and disaffection," "making statements prejudicial to good order and discipline," and "trying to promote 'disloyalty and disaffection' by making intemperate and disloyal statements." [7] In other words, the issue of free expression was relevant. Such incidents have not been conspicuous in the United States in any of the other three armed conflicts of the twentieth century. The degree and type of disaffection with American policy thus produces a unique dilemma for civil liberties in these times.

Reactions to conscription have involved more people, have been much more dramatized, and contain more complex value and legal issues. The varied aspects of the question of "conscientious objection" to service is a civil liberties issue, but not directly germane to expression and association. The acts of those who dispose of their draft cards have been widely publicized. A favorite tactic is a public burning, which has been declared a crime by congressional statute, despite the protestations of those who insisted it was a First Amendment freedom because it represented "symbolic speech." [8] Freedom of expression and association becomes more relevant when efforts are made to counsel others to evade the draft, as in the trial of Doctor Benjamin Spock, Yale Chaplain William Sloane Coffin, Jr., and three other defendants. Four of the five were convicted of "conspiring" to hinder the operation of the conscription system by counseling others to evade service, a felony under the 1940 Selective Service Act. The defense case rested on other considerations besides the First Amendment—the doctrine of the Nuremberg trials, the illegality of the war itself, and so on. These issues are irrelevant to our discussion, except for the serious challenge to government legitimacy indicated. The First Amendment claim was based upon the lack of "clear and present danger," which, it should be remembered, Justice Holmes defined as primarily applying to those acts committed during a time of war, which is not the officially defined state of the United States during the Vietnam conflict.[9]

The legal dispute should not overshadow the more significant aspects of these events. They are a vivid portrayal of the fact that many "respectable" Americans are challenging the legitimacy of the government in certain areas, in some ways a more dramatic disaffection than those of radicals and others in World War I. For our analysis, the basic dilemma can be posed in this way: either many otherwise responsible Americans are demanding the right to expressions that are impermissable legally or the government is illegally preventing such expressions. Whatever one's stand, the conflict poses a threat to the maintenance of a libertarian society.

Another serious type of situation has presented a more clear-cut issue for civil libertarians—sanctions against those who par-

ticipate in demonstrations against conscription or military recruitment. The possibility of criminal penalties for those engaged in
illegal acts is not the most pressing problem. What is unique to
these times is the use of conscription, itself, as a penalty, a technique scarcely noticeable even in World War I. The major source
of this threat has been one particular role incumbent, former
Selective Service Director Hershey. His directives to local draft
boards, a nonbinding type of influential communication, have
included the stipulation that such protestors should lose their
deferments. (Whether many local boards actually followed this
advice, or what effect his announcement had on anti-conscription
activities is not too evident.) [10]

The possible "illegality" of some demonstrations is a more
perplexing issue. Since many anti-war activists have proclaimed
their intent to utilize all techniques, usually short of violence,
many acts are probably in violation of ordinances and in conflict
with the values of public order, right of access, and so on. But,
as is also typical, the behavior of police, in capricious arrests
and in their own extralegal actions, including unnecessary force, is
of concern to civil libertarians. Large-scale demonstrations are
typically followed by reports of police violence against orderly
participants, even bystanders and observing journalists, of crowds
attacked by police after the demonstration was over, and of
arrests of the victims or those who commented on the actions.[11]
It does not seem too likely, in the absence of evidence, that this
type of freedom of expression and association has been appreciably curtailed by police behavior. Nevertheless, it is safe to
conjecture that an intensification of this atmosphere presents an
obvious stimulant for both caution by some potential participants
and even more vigorous use of force by the police, which, accompanied by some other possible developments, could lead to a
small-scale, but meaningful, mood of terror.

The political passions and the moral fervor on either side are
so profound that each hardly recognizes the legitimacy of the
other's claim, and in fact may relegate his opponent to a sub-
human status. The demonstrators are unpatriotic, disruptive riff-

raff to some law enforcement officials and their defenders, whereas the representatives of officialdom are symbols of a basically immoral order engaged in an indefensible "criminal" war to some demonstrators. Some demonstrators have codified their approach in the doctrines of the "Resistance," a self-identified group of organizations and unorganized individuals, for whom *all* forms of opposition to the war are a categorical imperative. Such deep schisms in the values of so many Americans are the type of phenomena that can encourage severe suppressions, even though they have not yet been anywhere as extensive as, for instance, in World War I, and may not get any worse.

In fact, what is noteworthy about the Vietnam War atmosphere is that it has not been accompanied by any widespread drive for ideological mobilization and a possible corollary suppression of dissent. President Johnson has referred to opponents as "nervous Nellies" and General Westmoreland has publicly charged that the opposition assists the enemy, but there have been few allegations of lack of patriotism; the "doves" are too numerous and include too many of the most respectable and responsible citizens for such claims to be offered or accepted. Governor Reagan of California, whose political bent can be considered as touching that of the "radical right," is unique among prominent political figures in his advocacy of strict "wartime" rules to prevent demonstrations which he believes are "giving aid and comfort to the enemy." [12] Even the extreme and conceivably illegitimate type of opposition, for example, those who openly favor the Vietcong, has not been seriously harassed. In 1965, when Governor Hughes of New Jersey was running for reelection, he refused to intervene when Rutgers University did nothing to penalize a faculty member who openly declared he was for a Vietcong victory.[13] Whether a similar result would follow in more recent times is a moot question. In any case, except for such possible atypical examples, mere opposition, whether verbal or active, to the war itself has rarely resulted in any penalizations.

A few other episodes of suppression might be mentioned, some of them involving lasting penalizations. School boards have been rent by violent disputes about whether to permit Dr. Spock to speak at a meeting on school grounds, and some have denied him permission. Members of particular unions have denied janitorial service when anti-war meetings are held, have refused to transport people to demonstrations, and some longshoremen even assaulted demonstrators. Such incidents have not been too prevalent, however. The tensions that threaten civil liberties are more directly concerned with the clash of legitimacies of the type found in confrontation demonstrations, actions against conscription, and in the armed services.

YOUTH MOVEMENTS, STUDENTS, THE "NEW LEFT"

Reactions to the war in Vietnam could not, by themselves, have produced the kinds of attitudes and behavior described on all sides, except for the presence of other accompanying contemporary features. The situation of Negroes is one other such element. The somewhat interrelated youth and student "revolts" and the existence of the "new left" political movements are other relevant characteristics of the day. Many aspects of the so-called "youth culture" are not directly relevant. The right to live the "hippie" life and even the right of students to come to school with long hair may be civil liberties problems. So also may the question of drug use and the severe sanctions meted out to those who possess legally defined narcotics. These problems do not, however, directly pose issues involving freedom of expression and association, except for the possible inclusion of "freedom of religion" as a defense for those who utilize such things as the peyote cactus. These problems may indirectly, however, become relevant to our discussion because of some counterattitudes that develop.

The turmoil on the campuses, however, does pose some definitive value and legal issues closely associated with freedom of expression and association. The "student rebellion" of these times is a special manifestation, intimately related to other unique aspects of the era—the Negro revolt, the youth culture, the war in Vietnam, and the "new left." The "silent generation" of the

1950's was succeeded by the contemporary student activists, assuming a style formerly most characteristic of Latin American and Asian countries, and, more recently, of Western Europe. The "incidents" have become daily fare for consumers of news media. The specific disputes vary with the situation, but the most common ingredients consist of one or more of the following factors: demands for student rights and/or "student power," restructuring of universities, some concern about Negro problems, and a posture in connection with the war in Vietnam.

Some indication of the typical underlying, latent features may be gleaned from a close examination of probably the two most publicized events, the confrontations at the University of California at Berkeley in 1964 and at Columbia University in 1968. At Berkeley, it started as a student demand for the right to make speeches and engage in other political activity on a strip of sidewalk which had traditionally been used for such purposes. Symbolically, the ad hoc student groups organizing the protest formed the "Free Speech Movement." The original problem was more or less satisfactorily resolved, but by then the dispute had escalated into weeks of turmoil, including vigorous police action, arrests of students, a sit-in demonstration at the administration building, a student strike, and varieties of actions by faculty, administration, and the Board of Regents. The "free speech" issue was hardly the sole or even the basic explanation for all these events. One pair of prominent faculty members saw them, at least in part, as reflections of a "totally moral solution to issues of racial discrimination, and foreign policy," and then worried that the "indifference to legality shown by serious students can threaten the foundations of democratic order." [14] Two other faculty members, while emphasizing the general atmosphere of "alienation," explained that "these students broke the rules and the law in an agonizing effort to compel an administration that, by its unwillingness to listen to their just claims and to treat them as participating members of a community of the intellectuals, inevitably brought about its own moral downfall and forfeited its claim to willing obedience." [15] Both analyses, despite their different evaluations, agreed that the students were acting "illegitimately" out of moral passions, and that acts against them were stimulated by the intent of the administration and the state to defend their legitimate right to govern, even if the acts sometimes extended to "illegal" police tactics.

At Columbia, the issues of dispute were more clearly joined— the construction of a gymnasium in a Harlem park and the university's association with a planning institute for war policy. The student protesters occupied several campus buildings, including administrative offices, until they were removed by the police upon instructions of the president of the university. Subsequent accounts described physical destruction, including the scholarly material of one professor, with differing accounts assessing the blame on the occupying students and the police. The process of evacuation was orderly in some buildings whereas police "brutality" was reported in others, even against innocents and some supporters of the administration. Other events followed, including a student strike, but the building sit-ins were the most crucial aspect of the dispute. One other specific feature was, however, very pertinent to our analysis. The occupying students apparently were ready to leave the buildings voluntarily if the administration would accede to one demand—no disciplinary action against them. The students themselves avowed that they were specifically challenging the legitimacy of the administration in this area. The administration, in turn, would not yield and refused the demand.[16]

The student rebels are, as has been mentioned often enough, a minority, but a fairly sizable and vigorous minority with sufficient support, including that of faculty members. A large part of the academic community, both faculty and students, agrees with the aims if not with the tactics. Furthermore, the rebels tend to appear so "likable" as individuals that those with personal contact find it difficult to be genuinely hostile. Nevertheless, the various acts of "disruption" have tended to make these students, especially in the eyes of those outside academia, social pariahs entitled to few rights.[17]

In more complex ways, this has also been the case with those who participate in "black student" revolts. The demands for more black students and professors and black-oriented courses are accepted among many academic personnel, and various efforts are made to realize them. Whether the achievements of the administration, from the perspective of the student activists, are sufficient is not immediately relevant. The more divisive issue is the insistence that the students set the conditions and make the relevant decisions, which may, among other things, vitiate academic standards. What they are then attacking is the legitimacy of any type of academic governing body. In essence they are fighting for their brand of "student power," a guiding slogan behind so much of the student protest. This, too, is a type of demand to which the administration and faculty can yield and have yielded. What causes the more serious clash is the protesters' claim to sole legitimacy, expressed in the frequent implication, or sometimes outright assertion, that what they proclaim as their rights is "non-negotiable." The maintenance of any "rights" on either side is thus in grievous peril.

The danger is also symbolized by the campus anti-military actions, such as the sit-ins to prevent recruitment by military representatives as well as officials of the Dow Chemical Company, one of whom was locked in a room at Harvard. All of these actions involve the question of "civil disobedience," a perilous question for both civil libertarians and members of an academic community. Can such action be included under civil liberties protection? This will be probed in the summary discussion of the contemporary era. More immediately relevant is the question of punishment for those who participate, which can so readily extend to those who engage in more clearly legal demonstrations. One reaction against all campus demonstrations is the adoption of laws, both national and state, denying government scholarships and other financial assistance to those who participate. Such legislation, grounded in attitudes laden with emotion, becomes a threat to all student freedom of expression and association and reveals some of the inherent dangers of the current situation.[18]

The philosophy and organization of the "new left" are not only an integral part of student insurgence but also intimately associated with the Vietnam protests, the Negro revolution, and, to some extent, with the "youth culture." This is hardly the place for a thorough analysis of this special contemporary American radicalism, which is primarily confined to young people, especially students. Our purpose is to point out that the orientation and mode of activism of those who can be included under this heading correspond to the emphases of the protest actions already described. An overriding sense of moral indignation prevails. The student activists believe that the society run by the "establishment" is basically corrupt, and the major effort must be toward opposing it by all means available, generally excluding outright violence. Alternative programs are less important than the appropriate existential stance of the moment. They believe that one simply defies and "resists," which includes defining many officially proclaimed modes and rules as "illegitimate" and, therefore, not binding on them. Besides, one has his own counterclaims of legitimacy, the belief that one is acting in accord with the inclinations, if not always the decisions, of a genuine "participatory democracy," a slogan made popular by the Students for a Democratic Society, the best known and probably most influential of the groups of the "new left." The resulting posture can resemble the declamation made to the Columbia administration by Mark Rudd, SDS chapter chairman during the 1968 disturbances: "Your power is directly threatened since we have to destroy that power before we take over." [19] Whatever the interpretation and evaluation of such sentiments, they as well as the reality of the events themselves inevitably stimulate calls for suppression of freedom of association, beginning with groups like the SDS and very likely extending to others who did not proclaim the same ends.

A more extreme version prompts fright even in the usually sympathetic. A man named Jerry Rubin, regarded as a caricature even by many new leftists, wrote these lines, which have been reproduced in college newspapers under the auspices of the "Liberation Press": "I think the thing to do is to get a travelling guerrilla theatre band roaring through college campuses burning books, burning degrees and exams, burning school records, busting up classrooms and freeing our brothers from the prison of the university." He then adds this plaintive note: "We'll probably get beat up and arrested, because physical force is the final protector of law and authority in the classroom." [20] If such attitudes become very prevalent, the resultant response would find little room for First Amendment freedoms. The unknown reader may, in any case, easily identify these remarks with current student protests in general. The expected counterpressures, which are so inimical to civil liberties, can be surmised.

THE RADICAL RIGHT

What are the threats to civil liberties from, to use the conventional political topology, the other extreme—the "radical right"? Most commentators saw this tendency at the bottom of most suppressive efforts in the 1950's. This type of analysis has been assessed as very limited at best, because there was no genuine "radical right" political movement at that time. By the 1960's, however, there was a significant set of organizations, policy formulations, quasi-ideologies, and so forth, which could be meaningfully classified as part of the "radical right." Adherents were actively involved and even mobilized; they did not confine their support to applauding heroes.

It is a varied conglomeration, which is discussed in detail by several analysts.[21] The common elements, with all the variations in emphasis and intensity, include some of the following factors: a forceful posture in international affairs; decrease in government intervention in economic life, which also implies lower taxes; an enhancement of the role of state and local governments vis-a-vis the federal government; and the demand for vigorous law enforcement and accompanying opposition to "permissiveness." With their slogans so often extolling the virtues of "freedom," the last might seem paradoxical to those who do not appreciate the underlying encompassing values. The adherence to a nineteenth-century laissez-faire economic program is not accompanied by the typical libertarianism of the "liberalism" of those days, as exemplified, for instance, in the philosophy of Herbert Spencer. The adherence of the "radical right" to a "militant" stance in foreign policy is obviously in conflict with early liberalism. Often characterized as "pseudo-conservatives," the proponents and supporters of the "radical right" have been shown to be authoritarian in their approach, with a characteristic orientation toward strength and conventionality. A significant number, furthermore, are religious fundamentalists, favoring suppression of deviances (including what they define as "obscene" literature), and many are "racists." Obviously, the general heading includes many types, but most of the above are elements of the prevalent values that must be listed. Those who favor such political orientations have had a major political impact in the nomination of Barry Goldwater in 1964 and in the political strength of Ronald Reagan and George Wallace.

What does this all mean for First Amendment freedoms? Understandably, some have sought to suppress the "fringe" of the radical right, which is generally disowned by most libertarians. Actual official actions against them have been rare and typically opposed by civil libertarians—denial of meeting permits to American Nazi leader Rockwell and legislative inquiries of the Ku Klux Klan which demanded presentation of organization records. Potentially more dangerous is the conceivable "radical right" demand for curtailing dissent, as symbolized in proposals for preventing action against the war in Vietnam and, above all, the call for more forceful police action with fewer procedural protections. In essence, the threat of the "radical right" to freedom of expression and association is its part in fomenting an atmosphere that can encourage suppression. Its system of belief, to recapitulate briefly, comprises aggressive military actions against Communists everywhere, fear of deviance, a reformulation of the McCarthyite anxiety about domestic traitors (usually much more in the open in these days), and a generic acceptance of force as a means of solving all of these problems, as well as those of urban disorders. The translation of these beliefs into official governmental action has been slight up to now, except that of the police, and may not become any more evident. The Chicago events of 1968, however, suggest dangerous possibilities. Furthermore, the "radical right" has helped stimulate the creation of vigilante groups.

GENERAL INTERPRETATION

The current threats to freedom of expression and association flow from an intense and open political conflict, quite different from the situation in the 1950's when the dangers were part of a milieu of relative political quietude and the respective desires either to keep beliefs and activities private or to expose them. Efforts to uncover "conspiracies" are, of course, again very popular. "Radical" groups, in turn, try to maintain their own "security" systems, as exemplified by the barring of newsmen by the SDS from their 1969 national convention. Such reactions are a reflection of the fear of possible prosecutions and anxiety about "distortion" of the proceedings. They may also indicate that what is almost a functional equivalent of job fears in the McCarthy era, the potential loss of scholarships and loans, may have some impact. The existence of open political contest, with the major contestants generally known, however, remains the crucial feature of the current setting. Actual formulation of the positions in conflict has frequently been imprecise and nonrational and has often assumed the form of moral posturing rather than programmatic statements. This has only made the contemporary conflicts more intense, leading to the possible ascription of inherent legitimacy to one's own side, regardless of the methods used, and the denial of legitimacy to opponents. In many instances, the contest has been between some branch of government and those who oppose it, although the rivals have sometimes been private individuals and groups on both sides.

The denial of legitimacy to at least some of the opponents is related partly to interpretations of specific events, but also to a set of general beliefs that values which are dearly held are being placed in jeopardy. With all the differences among some of those in the overlapping categories, black militants, anti-war resisters, student protesters, rebellious youths, and the "new left" perceive that their desires for "liberation," "creativity," "controlling their lives," and so on, are thwarted by the "establishment" or the "power structure." The intense opposition at, to use the usual cliché, the other extreme conceives of its task as the maintenance of home, country, public safety, morality, decency, and so forth, against the tactics of the unclean, unkempt, licentious, lazy, animal, and traitorous. Both sides can readily make these classifications very inclusive. The resulting dangers to civil liberties have been sketched.

The actions and attitudes of the protesters and demonstrators of all types engender fears about personal safety itself. "Crime in the streets" became the important appeal of political candidates in 1968, typically Republicans trying to unseat Democrats, further intensified in the campaign of George Wallace. The police (not the detectives this time, but rather the uniformed personnel with weapons) are the leading villains of the protesters and the heroes of their contenders. The slogan "support your local police" became a popular symbol on automobile stickers. In every contest with police, undoubtedly the police are "provoked," but enough observers insist that their response is inordinate. The right of assembly, a simple form of association, becomes threatened. Individual violence, and the consequent organization of private vigilante groups, intensifies the atmosphere, further marked by a series of political assassinations on a scale previously unknown in this country.

What happened in Chicago during the 1968 Democratic National Convention offers a composite picture of the entire situation, with one exception—the surprising absence of "black militants." [22] Many people came to the city for some demonstration against the national Democratic leadership, centering, of course, on the war. As is typical, the participants were varied—those openly stating their intent to disrupt the convention, supporters of Senator Eugene McCarthy, those interested only in vigorously proclaiming their dissent from current national policy, and so on. Fearful of what might ensue, and always anxious about the possibility of political assassination, Mayor Daley and the police, bolstered by National Guardsmen and army troops in readiness, set up a veritable state of martial law. Personal movement in and around the convention hall itself, as well as other parts of the city where there were actual or potential demonstrations, was severely restricted. (The fact that Mayor Daley may have hoped to assist the nomination of his "candidate" for president was, of course, another possible motivation.) The characteristic dialectic of action and counteraction ensued, all widely publicized—verbal and physical abuse of the police, attempts to hold "illegal" marches and demonstrations, mass arrests, assaults by police (sometimes against the innocent), riots, and harassment of convention delegates and newsmen.

Meanwhile, the convention carried on its business in a manner that almost denied the existence of strains in the city and even what was transpiring directly outside, as exemplified by the free and sharp floor debates. Nevertheless, the events symbolized the deep schism in the nation and obviously stimulated anxiety about the future of freedom of expression and association in the face of police power, prodded by the purposes and the fears of prominent public officials. After all, this did happen at the national gathering of a major party. The sequel included a series of verbal clashes between Mayor Daley, his supporters, and the personnel and officials of the news media, prompting further concerns about freedom of expression. Some of this anxiety was alleviated when the campaign, itself, produced few incidents, but the emphasis on the theme of "law and order" indicated that the scars were still present.

CONCLUSION

The people directly involved, the relevant actors whose attitudes and actions are responsible for potential widespread suppressions (and one must emphasize that it is still only potential, without the widespread suppressions of the World War I period or the special type of difficulty of the McCarthy era), have been identified mostly by motivation. Only for "black militants" are the social backgrounds available, and the findings are rather complex. The "rioters" seem to be concentrated among the ghetto residents who are not the most "disadvantaged," but whose economic and social positions remain very insecure.[23] The members of organized "black power" movements appear to be primarily intellectuals and students. What seems common, then, to these varied Negro "activists," responsible for an important aspect of the "legitimacy crisis," is that they represent the somewhat "achieving" downtrodden whose demands for "more" are not being granted and, because of the nonprogrammatic and "nonrational" nature of the demands, probably cannot be granted.

With the realization that very little "hard data" are available, the other "protesters" can probably be said to be relatively "advantaged." [24] The economically downtrodden are not conspicuous, and there is probably a wide distribution of many ethnic groups. What is so historically unique is that so few seem to be blue-collar workers, who, if anything, seem to be more evident among the "suppressors." Other militant "protesters," who also pose a clash of legitimacies, can be viewed as children of the "organization men," growing up in a post-affluent society. Their values and behavior are a form of defiance against the perceived evils coming from a bureaucratized world and its accompanying consumer gratifications, plus, of course, the more patent evils of racial suppression and the war in Vietnam. Frequently, their stance is a moralistic challenge, also tending to be nonprogrammatic and nonrational. The influencers among the "suppressors" (who often become "decision-makers") contain a large number of those who have "arrived" in status in fairly recent times.[25] The status factor, often emphasized in analyses of Joseph McCarthy's supporters, may be even more important now, although now it is not dismay about status lost or still to be won but of status to be defended. It is a commonplace observation that those most hostile to Negro aspirations are those who climbed out of a similar situation most recently. More importantly, threats of disruptions are seen as a challenge to their comparatively new stability and security, which was difficult to win. Protesting young people are judged as pampered "brats" who do not know how good things are for them. The desire to slap them down helps to create the climate for suppressions.

Of course, the range of people on both sides covers many types, all in different ways affecting events and being subject to the results. The majority of those who emphasize "law and order" as a political issue are probably also sincerely committed to the maintenance of civil liberties, including freedom of expression and association. Nevertheless, they provide the large audience and implicit popular bulwark for those favoring suppression. On the other side, the majority of the protesters are probably not in favor of disruption, and some of those who participate in "confrontations" are quite willing to accept legal penalties. This majority covers the large periphery of sympathizers without which the conscious disrupters would have little impact. Even the supporters of Eugene McCarthy could be classified among such sympathizers, and some did join those seeking a "confrontation" with the police during the events of the Democratic convention. More importantly for our purpose, they may be similarly suppressed, although it must be pointed out that the results of the primaries and, to a degree, of the convention itself hardly indicated any serious curtailment of their rights of expression and association up to this writing.

The vast number who passionately oppose the war in Vietnam and, to some extent, many of those who have intense feelings about the Negro plight are immersed in a resulting value dilemma, a replica of the clash of the entire society. The most profound manifestation is the dispute, and internal conflict, among many libertarians about the idea of "resistance." The essential element of this posture is that "unjust" policies must not only be opposed but one must, in good conscience, also refuse to obey laws which flow from them, and, in fact, one should dramatically flaunt one's refusal and encourage and assist others to do likewise. Whether this constitutes an appropriate political tactic is, of course, not our immediate concern. More relevant is the question whether or not these tactics constitute "protected" actions, whose suppression should be fought on libertarian grounds. The case of Spock and his associates represents one example of this conflict in legal form. It has become a divisive issue in the deliberations of the American Civil Liberties Union.[26]

Those who defend the rights of "resistance" explain that, among other things, what they do may be the only viable form of expression in a situation when the major legitimate channels of communication are not available, at least in a form suitable to the moral fervor of their positions. On the other hand, many may agree with the formulation, but add that a corollary should be a willingness to accept the consequences, an orientation so prominent in the tradition from which "resistance" stems, as characterized by the relevant ideas of Thoreau, Gandhi, and Martin Luther King. The dilemma and conflict continue as long as the situations that produce them remain. That they do exist for so many people further reveals the strains that the current historical context presents for the maintenance of orderly civil liberties.

The major danger to the maintenance of freedom of expression and association in contemporary America is the severe clash of political values, associated with many other strongly held values, which can lead and has led to the denial of the legitimacy of their opponents, including the "legal" government. As yet, the resulting suppressions have been episodic rather than steady or systematic. What are the likely prospects at this writing? An attempt at any detailed prognosis would require a thorough political-social analysis —a meaningful and challenging demand, but not appropriate for this volume. One can only surmise that, unles the clashes become more common and include more people, things will probably not get much worse. The end of the war in Vietnam, unless followed by some other similar or more serious international conflict, would undoubtedly ease the strains, as would the proposed termination of conscription. The problems of black America are not likely to be solved immediately, and this offers the most serious threat to both stability and the maintenance of civil liberties of all types. A large number of "alienated" youth, especially students, will probably remain part of the national picture for the coming period, although whether activist political radicalisms of the current type will continue to be part of the pattern is debatable. In fact, militant student protest actions seem to be getting less student support than before. In any case, these actions only produce persistent annoyances, and not the dread that can foster pervasive suppressions.

Too many factors militate against extensive suppressions. More people may be profoundly committed to civil libertarian doctrines than at any other time in our history, as exhibited by the increasing membership rolls of the ACLU.[27] More government officials are concerned about maintaining freedoms than was typical, for instance, in the McCarthy era, and the courts are far more likely to exercise the power of judicial review to void suppressive government acts than was true in the World War I period. Other elements of the historical situation also encourage some optimism for libertarians: the size and influential positions of the Vietnam "doves"; the appreciation of and support for many of the demands of rebelling students, especially from many faculty members and faculty organizations; and the widespread sympathy for those who participate in urban riots, even while condemning them.[28] All these factors indicate the existence of many powerful forces providing a serious opposition to any possible widespread suppressions.

Only a genuine "revolutionary" type of situation would prompt severe suppression, even to the extent of the suppression prevalent during World War I. This is very unlikely because the messages of "rebellion" are potentially meaningful only to a small part of the population who, except for the ghetto residents, have no strategic position in society. Among the Negroes, the riots actually indicated that, unless mobilized by some yet nonexistent political force, they are not prepared for "revolution," only for the expression of despair by nonrational outbursts. There is nothing similar to the fears of the post-World War I period that radicals might, as happened in so much of Europe, arouse a significant part of the very large and strategically placed industrial working class to revolutionary action. The current rebelliousness is a serious harassment to many people, and attendant "nuisance" suppressions that are not quite "pervasive" will be, and have already been, one result. Only a further breakdown of the social order, with greater agony over the war in Vietnam, or a similar conflict, or a possible severe economic crisis, would produce the atmosphere of potentially extensive militant protest and possibly accompanying more pervasive suppressions. (If the prevailing atmosphere again becomes "depoliticalized," for whatever reasons, we will then be in a new era, prompting a different kind of analysis.)

Part Three

Continuing problems

13

Censorship

Much of the history of civil liberties disputes is a chronicle of struggles over the right to publish freely versus the right of authorities of various types, or groups of citizens, to prevent or alter such publications beforehand, or under Anglo-Saxon law since the seventeenth century, to prosecute afterward. The usual basis for such restraints, prior censorship or post facto penalties, has been the fear of dangerous doctrines—either purported religious and political heresies or material embarassing to the powerful. Certainly this type of suppression remains a pressing problem throughout much of the world, most dramatically behind the iron curtain. To mention only the recent example that stirred the world, the most definitive demand of the Russian occupiers of Czechoslovakia was the reinstitution of prior censorship. A survey of "new states" listed seven distinct methods of official control over press content as well as a variety of other kinds of formal and informal pressures. The active role of the government of contemporary France, a generally "free" society, in fostering and limiting particular types of dissident communication, in print and on the airwaves, has become a leading political issue.[1]

In recent American history, the various suppressive actions include little direct control of communication, in print or the newer media. The overt strains of the current period have been accompanied by an unusually extensive public presentation, in all channels, of contesting positions. Of all the McCarthyite actions, only the conviction of the Communist leaders under the Smith Act can be construed as some form of *direct* curtailment of public expression. In other words, censorship of divergent views, whatever the mechanism used, has not been a crucial civil liberties issue.

The major recent threats to First Amendment freedoms in the realm of political ideas have been more complex. Perhaps the only exception involves textbooks and libraries, as depicted later in this chapter. Other problems associated with the right of free expression in the public media are apparent, such as the conflict between "freedom of information" and subtle government restraints to withhold such data, the many organizational limitations within the media, the issue of libel and slander, and so on. Some of these problems will be considered in a "miscellaneous" chapter. None was continuing, pervasive, or pressing. The entire "censorship" question has been, for some time, almost entirely identified with the question of "obscenity," in print and in motion pictures.

CENSORSHIP OF "OBSCENITY" IN PRINTED MATERIAL—
A BRIEF HISTORY AND EXPLANATION

Within the range of possibly "objectionable" printed material, the bizarre emphasis on the "obscene" is, in universal historical terms, fairly recent.[2] Ironically, the issue has probably been most serious in this country and Great Britain, two nations with viable continuing traditions of freedom of expression. This is not meant to imply that such concerns have been absent in other places. It may come as a shock to learn of apparent prissiness in supposedly libertine France. The Anglo-Saxon countries, however, have been unique in the continuing and usually exclusive attention to this type of literary content as the kind which should be forbidden.

This has prompted a rather facile explanation for its prevalence in England and the United States, that is, the common "Puritan" tradition. Yet no one was convicted of publishing anything obscene in England until 1725, and the first conviction in the United States, in Massachusetts, occurred in 1821 for the publication, interestingly enough, of *Fanny Hill*. Both of these cases were tried under "common law." The first statutory regulation in England was contained in an 1824 vagrancy law. The first state law in this country was passed in Vermont in 1821. The initial federal regulation, dealing with imports, was enacted in 1842.[3] Puritan-minded early America did not seem obsessed with the need to prevent dissemination of literature of a sexual content. Perhaps there was too little of it to worry about, although no less a prominent citizen than Benjamin Franklin openly published such items as "Advice to a Young Man in Choosing a Mistress." Laws against "profanity" were prevalent, but this was generally identified with impiety. Puritanism could have had an indirect effect, for it "bequeathed a heritage of squeamishness of speech and action" that influenced the later censors.[4]

But other historical developments also inspired the desire to "cleanse" literature. One was the development of the mass reading market, which might include the uncultured, the impressionable, and the oversensitive. A British judge once justified his negative decision about one work with the assertion that "it would never do to let members of the working class read this." [5] Today, pro-censorship groups strive to prevent the circulation of paperback editions of books almost exclusively. Many emphasize the fear that the suspect literature will be read by young people. The underlying rationale is, obviously, the belief that such material is "bad" for young people and that exposure will produce some particular or unspecified evils. Contemporary arguments commonly concentrate on the possible connection between obscene literature and juvenile delinquency, family disorganization, and even the appeal of "subversive" political doctrines. Such attitudes are apparently summarized in the allegation of the man whose name has become a symbol of such censorship, Anthony Comstock, who claimed that the literature he suppressed "breeds lust, lust defiles the body, debauches the imagination, corrupts the mind, deadens the will, sears the conscience, destroys the memory, hardens the heart and damns the soul." [6] Court decisions, to this day, refer to the dangers from material that appeals to "prurient interest."

The basic assumption is a simplistic and casually accepted analysis of the communication process—widespread distribution of literature with "indecent" content will produce, among some sections of the public, immoral values and behavior. The second historical underpinning of this type of censorship is, similarly, grounded on what to many is a self-evident truism. "Bad reading" is inimical to "good reading," and if the former results in evil the latter encourages virtue. The nineteenth-century evangelical and uplift movements sought to encourage reading with a moral purpose.[7] Contemporary court decisions also reflect this orientation in their search for the "redeeming social importance" of otherwise suspect works. Of course, the criteria of censoring groups is generally much more narrow—anything with "unclean" passages cannot be good for people. But this quest for a calculus of likely "good" and "bad" effects is a major theme of disputes on the question, whether in public debates or judicial decisions.

The corollary observation that emerges is that the various "bluenoses" have been moral and sometimes social reformers. On their side are the values which appeal to all men of good will. They have not always been, in the language of contemporary liberal rhetoric, "reactionaries," out to suppress the populace's legitimate interests. At least in earlier days, they were frequently men and women of profound social conscience; like the advocates of temperance, their cohort included people who also supported the Progressive movement. It is of some interest that a New York judge, who wrote one of the most restrictive decisions on literary expression, was the man whose name is on more social legislation than any other legislator in American history, Robert Wagner, Sr. His reasoning was roughly similar to that given for such legislation, the idea that the "fostering of the health of women and children is one of grave concern." [8] The American Civil Liberties Union was not, in its earliest days, committed to the defense of writings considered obscene, because of the attitude of the many religious pacifists prominent among its founders.[9]

Among the items barred have been any open discussions of sex, no matter how cold-blooded, circumspect, or moralistic the presentation. As late as 1930, a woman in New York was convicted for mailing a factual pamphlet on human sex, originally designed for her children's instruction (the conviction was reversed on appeal). Even more cases have revolved around the use of specific terminology, the inclusion of "dirty words." The interest is not in aesthetic taste but in morality; the apparent belief is that such language would actually make people less virtuous, that, if protective shields cannot be built against learning them, they should at least be defined as beyond the pale. Books as well as movies have been barred because they included one example of a forbidden term.

Of course, the censors have always had their vigorous opponents, also basing their case on prominently held values. Fundamental to them is the very idea of the First Amendment, the right of free expression. The curtailment of freedom in any printed matter is believed a potential for more general restrictions. Freedom, however, is more than a value in itself to them. Opposition to such censorship is motivated by the desire to defend and extend literary creativity. The censor is usually also the philistine, attempting to reduce literary expression to the level of the effete and the meaningless. The lists of books barred to the reading public in the United States, for a short time in one community or nationally for a long time, include a pantheon of literary masterpieces, symbolized by the two twentieth-century classics that provided significant test cases, Joyce's *Ulysses* and D. H. Lawrence's *Lady Chatterly's Lover*.

Many opponents of censorship are extremely hostile to "pornography," but they generally do not want anyone to have the right to determine someone else's reading options on the basis of subtle evanescent distinctions, especially law enforcement officials. In any case, proponents of censorship and legally empowered censoring officials have, typically, combined the most salacious trivia with recognized classics under the heading of "filthy" writing.[10]

Of course, the nature of the dispute has changed since Dreiser's *American Tragedy* was banned or Lillian Smith's *Strange Fruit* was under prosecution in Boston because of one example of an Anglo-Saxon four-letter word that is by now part of conventional usage. But it has remained a serious issue for the following reasons: contemporary literature, especially in England and the United States, has become franker in sexual reference; more people are reading now, especially in paperback form; courts have generally become more permissive in their rulings; and censorship groups, in reaction to all of this and in response to contemporary difficulties of all sorts, have vigorously sought the curtailment of "indecent" literature as a way of improving what they deem an immoral climate.

MODES OF CENSORSHIP

The process of decision-making, the multiplicity of legal and extra-legal ways by which printed works may be banned on the grounds of obscenity, is a unique feature of this phenomenon in the United States. For one thing, the roles of influencer and decision-maker may be combined in atypical fashion—a moralistic law enforcement official may take the initiative in "cleaning up" book stores, a private organization directly pressuring book dealers, and so on.[11] Police and prosecutors have had a vast array of laws available. Different court jurisdictions will convict or acquit for the same publication, at least until there is a Supreme Court ruling. To this day, the same works may be barred or permitted in different states or even in neighboring communities of the same state. To give one example, Henry Miller's *Tropic of Cancer* was "judged" in sixty different cases in different jurisdictions within one six-month period in the early 1960's with a variety of decisions resulting.[12] Such are the vagaries and complexities which have, for so long, prompted caution in both publishers and dealers. The federal government has been actively involved through its regulation of customs and the mail, with the appropriate administrative agency frequently acting as both prosecutor and judge. The post-master general has occasionally assumed the role of supercensor (this was altered in 1961 when enforcement of the relevant postal laws was turned over completely to the Department of Justice). Furthermore, new statutes defining obscenity as well as new legal mechanisms are constantly emerging, the latter sometimes in defiance of official doctrine and court decisions.[13]

Procensorship groups frequently consider action by public officials insufficient, especially in the light of particular Supreme Court rulings. Private, informal "censorship" is another much used tactic. By using lists, such as those of the "National Office for Decent Literature," local groups ask dealers to remove proscribed books and magazines. Refusal can mean publicly announced, abusive charges, accompanied by threatened boycotts. One device consists of the group's placing a "decent literature" sticker every month on the window of the store. If the sticker were absent any month, this would presumably imply that the establishment should not be patronized. Since most of the businesses sell printed material only as an auxiliary item—candy stores, supermarkets, and so on—this constitutes an extensive application of the idea of secondary boycott.

Frequently such lists do not mention the names of authors of books, merely the title and publisher. This symbolizes the nature of the selection process of forbidden works—omniscient judges labeling material about which those who act on their decisions know almost nothing. Under this aura of relative anonymity of that which is being judged, clear standards are necessarily absent and are largely irrelevant to most of those involved. The omnibus checklist becomes a pleasant substitute for the tortuous task of deciding what is proper or not, one of the most essential aspects of the entire issue.

COURT DECISIONS

Because of, among other things, the vagueness of legal standards and the multiplicity, and possible unconstitutionality, of procedures, the courts have assumed an atypically crucial role. In no other area under purview in this volume do their rulings have so much impact, direct and indirect. Some decisions have been concerned with methods of enforcement, and several acts of the police and prosecutors have been overturned on grounds of due process.[14] But the question of standards has been most important. The judges' value conflicts, their search for criteria, mirror the dilemma and contest of the rest of society. Whatever their inclinations, they have become the "supercensors."

The essence of their problem is to judge whether barring particular works, or penalizing those responsible for disseminating them, violates the First Amendment. In most such cases, the nature of specific statutes has rarely been the central issue. The legal dispute has revolved around the permissibility of application to specific writing. In fact, actual reference to the First Amendment probably did not appear in a Supreme Court decision until the historic Roth and Albertis decisions in 1957.[15] The apparent previous assumption was that such communication was, like "fighting words" and libel, "unprotected." Within all the complexities of these important rulings, they gave this belief a legal standing, clearly stating that obscenity was outside the domain of the First Amendment, as indicated by historical experience from the beginning of the Republic up to now, and by international agreements curtailing its transportation. The question became one of determining what was to be regarded as "obscene" and therefore punishable without violating the Bill of Rights. To some judges, there was no problem. To Justice Douglas, only such communication for which a "clear and present danger" of producing illegal acts could be demonstrated can be legally punished under the Constitution. Justice Black has been even more "absolutist," declaring, in a dissenting opinion, that the federal government has no constitutional power "to put any type of burden on speech and expression of ideas of any kind (as distinguished from conduct)." His, however, has been a minority opinion in the Court.

A brief history of the development of criteria for obscenity, as stipulated in a few major Court decisions, reveals much of a labyrinth of legal and value formulations through which it is necessary to journey to arrive at the desired "balance." [16] The ruling rationale, for some time, was the so-called Hickin decision in England in 1868, which defined as "obscene" anything with the "tendency to deprave and corrupt those whose minds are open to such immoral influences." In a special version of "common-law" practice, this became the norm in this country, although never included in that language in any American statute. Note the specific allegation of likely effects.

A series of judicial exceptions to the rule developed into the current formula of the Supreme Court. Recognized classics were excluded from the "obscene" category. "Vulgarity" was distinguished from "obscenity," earlier standards were not applicable to present-day works, a book must be judged as a whole, the likely effects on the "normal person" must supply the criterion, literary experts may testify on the artistic merits, and the impact on young people could not be used as a basis for restricting sales to the general reading public.

The decisions which codified most of the formulations occurred in the same year in the highly publicized cases of Roth and Albertis in 1957. Although they were generally hailed as something of a victory for libertarianism, it is interesting that the majority upheld the two convictions, for both defendants were judged to be writing or selling material beyond the protection assumed by the formula devised. (As already indicated, it was in connection with these two cases that Justice Brennan included the initial reference to the First Amendment.) To be judged obscene, and therefore "unprotected," a work must satisfy the conditions already indicated by previous decisions: the material, judged as a whole, must be appealing to the "prurient interests" of the average person based upon present-day standards of the community, and must be without any redeeming social importance. The terminology was extremely vague and potentially restrictive. Using the above conditions as a rationale, the court upheld the conviction of Ralph Ginzburg for distributing literature which, by a special combination of its actual content and the advertising blurb, was assumed to constitute an orientation to "prurient" interests. Yet, under their dicta, *Lady Chatterly's Lover* was finally cleared, and the sale of such works as *Tropic of Cancer, Candy,* and, at long last, *Fanny Hill* were legally permissible, at least in many areas. It is interesting that a few years after the Roth and Albertis decisions, the same formula was adopted in England, in line with their legal tradition, in the form of an act of Parliament.

What has emerged is the legal doctrine that anything but "hardcore pornography" cannot generally be censored under the First Amendment. This transforms the dilemma; it does not solve it. Judges must become literary experts, either evaluating a work personally or weighing the opinions of specialists. Drawing fine distinctions upon which legal sanctions will be based is a chore which few relish. Justices of the Supreme Court seem to perform this task with dutiful reluctance, apparently without the satisfaction of acting as enthusiastic sagacious defenders of civic virtues that marks their more typical stance.[17]

This torment does not seem a characteristic of the other major participants in the decision-making process, whether deciding themselves or influencing the decision.

THE CONTESTANTS: THEIR MOTIVATION AND BEHAVIOR

Judges are the crucial personnel in determining what happens in this type of civil liberties dispute, perhaps more decisive determinants in this area than in any of the others discussed. Besides the obvious fact that they make the ultimate, and more or less binding, decisions, frequently covering an entire category of material, they do attempt some precise clarification in a very ambiguous situation. Their rulings are legitimized opinions that set the tone of what can ensue, directly affecting the behavior of author, publisher, and dealer, as well as the various political disputants, even though the response may take the form of circumventing what they say, that is, by "private censorship" or writing different kinds of laws. But they do not take the initiative. The desire for judicial restraint seems to pervade most deliberations on this subject, whatever their general judicial orientations. Judges get test cases only because someone else has been concerned enough to make or enforce a law or to challenge its applicability to a particular work of literature.

If the judges appear typically obsessed by internal anguish over the complexities of the issue and wish they were not involved, the active proponents on either side are eager and certain. In fact, they cannot see the justice of the other viewpoint. The procensorship forces cannot perceive why their opponents are worried that suppression of "indecent literature" might affect important freedoms, and the opposition to censorship is amazed that the other side is so sure that any harm results from reading such literature. In essence, although the debate continues to be focused on contentions about possible "effects," this is not actually the latent substance of the dispute. It has been possible to marshall substantial expert testimony which asserts that there is no evidence for any harmful effects even from hard-core pornography, in fact, that there may be beneficial results—release of tensions, management of tensions, and so on.[18] Above all, the research findings tend to agree with the quip, attributed to both Governor Alfred E. Smith and Mayor Jimmy Walker, that no woman was "ever seduced by a book," that the most effective erotic stimulant is a member of the opposite sex.

All such rational, "fact" truths, however, carry little weight with those determined to eliminate what they deem "dangerous literature." They can hardly be moved by arguments about the lack of proven consequences, for they are motivated by self-evident "value" truths—such material is simply "filth," "an affront to common decency," and so on. That recognized classics are lumped alongside the most superficial girlie magazines is thus very appropriate. They are all simply "bad." Yet the idea of possible consequences remains, both implicitly and explicitly, as an important element of the motivation of those who work for censorship. Cleansing literature supplies a facile, quick, and ready method for combating various social evils—delinquency, immorality, and even Communism. In the language of Harry Golden, social and political programs require "planning, money, wisdom, and patience. How much easier it is to mount an anti-smut campaign." [19]

The procensorship cohort is generally very vocal and easily located. According to one estimate there are about two hundred such groups in the country, more or less formally organized.[20] They are now, as they were earlier, commonly associated with clergymen and religious organizations. Most recently, these groups are more likely to be Roman Catholic in this country, whereas they were formerly primarily associated with particular Protestant denominations. In neither case was there any inherent link with religious doctrine, and members of other faiths have usually joined forces with them. Furthermore, to keep the record straight, many religious officials and organizations have been vigorously opposed to these groups. Actually, the most publicized national organization is the "Citizens for Decent Literature," which has no official religious connections.

It should be apparent that pressure for censorship is associated with other relevant attitudes and values. The earlier relation with "uplift" reform ideologies is probably less important today than the identification with conformist, anti-deviance tendencies. This means a likely correlation with, in the contemporary conventional meaning of the term, political "conservatism" and even the "radical right." Campaigns against "indecent" literature can then carry political overtones and become associated with overt political struggles. Thus, one preliminary investigation in Iowa found that several respondents, if a minority, reported that a "decent literature" campaign began as a political partisan tactic and was emphasized by several candidates.[21] An organization in California, whose initials were spelled to read C.L.E.A.N., and whose membership, according to many observers, included many people usually associated with "radical right" causes, unsuccessfully attempted to pass a referendum so restrictive that it was opposed by public prosecutors. On the national scene, presidential candidate Richard Nixon included the drive against "indecent literature" in the goals enumerated in television spot commercials, and some opponents of the nomination of Justice Fortas as Chief Justice of the Supreme Court emphasized his vote in several "censorship" cases, in which his role was actually very secondary.[22]

The emotionally involved citizens as well as their pressure organizations do not constitute the only actors who can produce censorship, whether as influencers of public officials or as decision-makers in private censorship. Many public officials themselves, besides Supreme Court justices, make the relevant decisions —mayors, police, prosecutors, lower-court judges, legislators, or governors. What they do is a result of both their own values and their response to pressure. They may take an active role in censorship on the basis of their own beliefs, yield to the influences, or resist them in some way. Some officials are probably personally committed and actively participate in censorship efforts, either initiating them or avidly responding to pressure. For many, the oath of office appears to be a pledge to become protectors of public morality. Behavior toward distributors of "indecent literature" is a concomitant of reactions to demonstrators and bohemian deviants. The zeal sometimes devoted to enforcement of obscure ordinances, vigorous prosecution of offenders, or elaborate recoding of legislation, often with very little public prompting, suggests a profound personal sense of mission. The Comstockian belief system is still strong enough for some, despite the counter pressures and arguments.

The largest number of public officials, however, probably have no strong values in either direction and are thus subject to pressures. They yield to clamor for enforcing or writing laws against "indecency" because it seems so trivial that it is hardly worth the risk of being identified as a defender of "sin." State legislatures frequently pass new censorship bills unanimously without public hearings; in at least one case, several legislators admitted that they had not actually read the details.[23] Very few officials publicly resist pressures because of their own libertarian values, with the obvious exception of higher-court judges, who are required to decide cases on grounds of values. Some do make anti-censorship decisions—prosecutors who refuse to prosecute or governors who

veto legislation, usually on procedural grounds, such as the violation of due process in an arrest or in the administration of proposed
legislation. More generally, the entire issue has so little saliency for
them that they avoid any but the most casual public position and
readily yield to the most vigorous pressures.

It would seem that, in the absence of any significance of the
question for so many of the decision-makers, the procensorship
forces, with their clear commitments and vigorous activity, would
easily have their way. This does not happen because of the efforts
of their opponents, including potential victims, who can, among
other things, force legally binding higher-court decisions, and also
because of the relative unimportance of the issue to most of the
supporting public of the procensorship groups. Arrayed on the
other side are two groups that are sometimes combined, the conscious libertarians and those who have a professional and/or commercial interest in the question. All of them together hardly add
up to an obviously significant power base. Nevertheless, they do
win out because their values are so meaningful to them, because
of what they do, because they can appeal to widely held values
and legal norms, and because the structure of the Supreme Court
can be readily utilized. The libertarians are led by the ACLU
which, since it altered its original neutrality on the issue, has devoted itself as forcefully to this question as any other, particularly
in the area of its special competence, litigation. Civic groups, including those with religious affiliations, have frequently joined in
the campaigns. Ad hoc groups have sometimes been set up, such
as the "New Jersey Committee for the Right to Read." [24] The professional and business interests have been mobilized through organizations of writers and publishers, usually with the implicit
support of distributors and dealers. On the fringe are the almost
clandestine businessmen who print and sell the more clearly defined "pornographic" offerings; if nothing else they may become
the principal litigants in these cases. In defense of the indivisibility
of the freedom principle, those dedicated to humanistic values are
compelled to collaborate with the most crass and venal. In all of

these cases the response of the potential "victim" of suppression becomes crucial.

The courts are the major areas of contest and the brief the principal weapon, but some of the contestants are more involved in pressure activities surrounding legislation, administration, and private censorship. The most important tactic is sheer publicity. The public airing of disputes seems, by and of itself, a sufficient mechanism for thwarting censorship. The realization by the neutral, that is, the sympathetic and the frightened libertarian, that there are people against censorship who care a great deal creates the necessity for public debate, which can, among other things, engender caution among officials apathetic about rushing to conform to censorship pressures. That is why both procensorship groups and legislators strive to avoid public hearings on relevant bills. Publicity can then lead to an effective "tabling" of the legislation by appointing an "investigating committee." The victims are assured that there are those who will defend them. Procensorship groups, accordingly, tend to avoid any open confrontation with their opponents. In this area, as in so many others, the method of the suppressors tends to be secrecy whereas the libertarians tend toward arousing the public.[25]

Besides the other effects, publicity can dampen the ardor of those who support the procensorship groups. The saliency of the issue is usually too low for most of them to risk public encounter. The peripheral position of the question to most of them means that the procensorship groups can win support but cannot mobilize such support in any continuous effort.[26] Politicians who try to utilize the issue have too many other questions with potential impact to dwell on "indecent literature." Opinion polls, however, do show a sizable part of the population in favor of barring such material.[27] But few are bothered very much by its existence. This is probably why private censorship ultimately fails. One simply forgets to look for "decent literature" stickers. Many victims find it very easy to comply immediately and then usually go back to something resembling their old ways. In contrast, when subject to any kind of legal pressure, they may overconform, removing literature even after charges against its sale have been dropped.[28] But this too can easily change with the decline of procensorship pressures and the activities of censorship opponents.

What this adds up to is that the activism of the contending groups is generally decisive—zealous officials and procensorship citizen groups against their opponents. The zeal of the latter, however, tends to diminish the involvement of the former who are, at least in leadership, "respectable" people who want to avoid trouble. Much of the population is, even more than is typical in civil liberties questions, quite apathetic. The decisions of the higher courts, more or less legally binding and proclaiming legitimacy, thus become especially crucial.

MOVIES

External restraints on the content of American films, through some form of censorship or other devices, has been even more conspicuous than those on printed material. The audience for a single film is very vast, with a large proportion of young people. It is truly a mass medium, with each product known and available without much effort. (In contrast, books and magazines must be sought.) The pressures to control what appears on the screen would, understandably, be more extensive. The rationale behind censorship is thus similar to that for print, only more so. One obvious result is the application of more rigid standards.

But there are other differences. Movie censorship is more formally institutionalized, and, although many censoring decision-makers may take part, they can be readily located and their methods quite regularized. This is one of the reasons analysis of this subject is comparatively simple. Another reason is that the mechanism used is "prior restraint." Although supposedly in violation of the Anglo-Saxon tradition of common law, the practice has been upheld by the Supreme Court to this date, with the additional recent provision for proper procedural safeguards.[29] In addition, censorship was, for most of the history of American film making, merely an additional restraint to that exercised by the industry itself. The concentration of ownership (production, distribution, and exhibition) with its strong internal controls and its maximum market orientation, prevented free expression, a story told frequently enough. That is one of the reasons the "blacklist" had so little effect on what appeared in the pictures.

Three major decision-making bodies have participated in censoring films: state and local censoring agencies (which can also determine what foreign films can be shown), the industry's "self-censorship" organ, and the Catholic Legion of Decency. In addition, other government groups have attemped to influence content, with varying success. The armed services, particularly, have both the ability to decide what movies are shown on their bases and to deny permission to use their facilities for the film locales. Various citizen groups—religious, ethnic, and professional—have sought to remove "offensive" material before it appeared, as well as threatening and sometimes activating boycotts after such movies were released. Their impact has been, at most, peripheral and episodic.[30]

Only the three principal censoring groups have had a continuing effect. All, presumably, examine the content of every film somewhere in the process before release. Government censoring groups do not have to approve every film, but they do have the right to disapprove a particular film before it is shown in their localities. For a long time legal defense was very difficult because the Supreme Court ruled, in a 1915 decision, that movies were not "organs of public opinion," but "business pure and simple," and therefore not entitled to First Amendment protections.[31] The Court did not extend the "free speech" coverage to motion pictures until the early 1950's. The process has, since then, exhibited many similarities to what is typical for printed matter—a set of decisions case by case, a search for standards by the Supreme Court, and a wide variation in local practices (sometimes including circumvention of court rulings). The standards applied by the

Court have gradually approached those used for print—only the patently "obscene" is excludable, which means, among other things, that criteria like "immoral" or "indecent" are not applicable. All this came rather late in the game. Combined with the other forms of censoring controls and the internal mechanisms of each film company, the wide option of local censors in earlier times resulted in severe strictures on expression in movies.[32]

Formal censorship within the industry has been under the jurisdiction of its "code authority" since 1930, which examines all scenarios, suggests changes, and then gives its "seal" of approval. Because of the movie combine's tight control over all aspects of the industry, it was almost impossible to produce a financially successful film without a seal of approval. If not made by the major studios, a film without a seal could hardly be distributed and would find few theater outlets. The nature of the code is too devious to detail. It can be meaningfully summarized as an avoidance of the realistic and honest, with a dwelling on trivia and the presumed moralistic lesson. Included are such stipulations as: "Crime shall never be presented in such a way as to show sympathy with the crime," "lustful and open-mouth kissing . . . are not to be shown," and words such as "chippie," "goose," and "fairy" are barred.[33] Of course, neither the violent (with certain restrictions on some aspects) nor the suggestive were excluded.

The Catholic Legion of Decency has been far more institutionalized than any similar group attempting to censor printed material. It has been an integral part of the church organization rather than an unofficial adjunct, with support of religious leaders of other faiths. It makes judgments about almost every American film, with a classification systems that includes items such as "objectionable in part," "objectionable in its entirety," and so on. In addition, its officials may be called in by the studios for prior consultations to avoid later difficulties. The classification system might not be considered a form of censorship but merely a type of critical admonition to the potential audience, except for one additional feature—parishioners have been asked to take a pledge

not to see condemned movies and to proselytize others. Sometimes, the method of secondary boycott of theaters that show such
movies has been utilized. The standards used include such criteria as "salacious" and "indelicate." [34]

In these different ways, which required no pressuring by other
"influencers," free expression in American motion pictures has
been curtailed. The dread of government censorship, that is, of
becoming victims of more thorough suppression, has played some
part, especially because of the long existing fear of federal censorship and the lack of meaningful court protection until recently.
Even publicity about government action could be dangerous
whereas for books this may be the most effective form of publicity.
The industry has been very conscious of public relations. The reason is similar to the basis for its response to the Legion of
Decency—the need for a mass market, rather than a market that
is relatively specialized for each film. Too much is invested in each
movie to risk any possible loss of a significant audience, a reaction
which is roughly parallel to the near paranoia of the networks in
instituting the "blacklist." The code was the ultimate weapon of
the film industry to prevent this eventuality, buttressed by the
mechanisms within each studio.

In discussing books, one can refer to specific examples of books
that were unavailable as a result of censorship. This approach is
not applicable when discussing American film censorship because
Hollywood simply did not make movies that could be censored.
Of course, some films did not meet all the standards of the Catholic Legion of Decency or the extreme position of some local
censor, but there is both relevant information and impressionistic
support for some general conclusions. One can easily point to
"good" movies that were released, but every effort was made to
prevent the making of motion pictures that were genuinely profound and sincere. The principal fare was either banal or sensational or both, whatever the other redeeming artistic qualities that
might be found.[35] Obviously, institutionalized censorship was not
solely responsible for this state of affairs, but it intensified the

other inherent influences, especially since this type of restriction extended all the way to the exhibitors. Nothing like this was true of printed media.

It requires no extensive documentation to prove that all this has radically changed. American films are as "free" now as any media product in the world, though the "artistic" worth may not always be satisfying. The search for the sensational seems to have a wider option.[36] In any case, however, no one seems to be stopping anyone's efforts. The trend was gradual but complete, and the changed attitude of the courts had some effect. But one feature of most of the significant rulings reveals the more under-lying impetus for the shift; they generally covered foreign films. The increased audience for movies from abroad came at the same time as the beginning of serious television competition, with the resulting drastic reduction of movie audiences. Something different was needed to get some of the audience back. The "frank" movie, appealing either to sensibility or titillation, was an obvious device.

The economics of the industry was thus the major explanation for the alteration in filming, and this took many forms. Anti-trust prosecutions resulted in a divorce between theater and studio ownership, and distribution was also, to some extent, decentralized. "Art" theaters became an important source for patronage. Among other things, it was possible to release films without the seal of ap-proval, initially attemped by one Hollywood producer, Otto Prem-inger, in 1953, with distribution through United Artists, a type of cooperative of producers. When the film turned out to be finan-cially feasible and the exclusion of United Artists from the organ-ization of Hollywood producers had little effect, the code lost its sacred quality.[37]

Revised for the first time in 1956, to permit presentation of the subject of narcotics, the code no longer has any meaning. The Legion of Decency's attempt, in the early 1960's, to return to the "letter of the code," had no appreciable effect. The legion, it-self, although still very active, has actually altered its standards, with a greater concern for artistic values, and has apparently given up the sanction of a threatened boycott.[38] Perhaps the organization's spokesmen have changed their own evalutions, but it is also likely that they are less able to control the behavior of their followers.

The tenor of the times has also helped to eliminate so much of the earlier constraining censorship over American movies, as they have affected the easing of restrictions over printed matter. For movies, however, transformation was more the result of a complete alteration in the operations of the industry itself, especially the crucial decision-makers, who were prompted by the new internal organization. The influencers who stimulated the change were not so much the organized counterpressure groups as the unorganized audience itself. The movies represent one very singular example of our times where an unforeseen trend toward a classic market, consisting of many sellers and a variety of specialized buyers, fostered the extension of freedom of expression in an area where it had been severely restricted.[39]

LIBRARIES AND TEXTBOOKS

The two categories are logically combined for several reasons. Both include attempts at removal of "subversive" as well as "obscene" literature, which was not prominent in the other types of censorship discussed. Although both were particularly prominent during the McCarthy era, the interest was in content as well as the background of the author, an atypical manifestation of the times. Both involve some implicit concerns about "limited resources." Finally, since the question of school libraries has been a particularly significant issue, the pressures on libraries are similar to those directed at textbooks.

Disputes about textbooks were most evident in the 1950's. The demands on libraries remain, although they are not as common as throughout the 1950's. In these areas, the outside, potential "influencers," generally comprising a small group for whom the issues have had an acutely high salience, have been very important.

Among them, the "radical right" movements, even when these constituted a very deviant fringe in the 1950's, were especially crucial.[40]

The criticisms of textbooks, the demands that they either be appreciably altered or, in most cases, removed, clearly include the question of scarce resources. The student has no choice, the teacher is usually bound by school or community policy, and sometimes the state may make the decision. All citizens can be said to have a personal stake in what is selected. In many ways, it is thus not an obvious civil liberties issue. Limitations on textbook selection, however, can become an usurpation of the autonomy of professional educators and, therefore, of their freedom of expression. Those who attack particular texts are not arguing about pedagogical values but about presumed political slants instead. This, too, can be considered an appropriate basis for citizen intervention, that is, the citizens have a right to scrutinize the assigned reading material of elementary and secondary school students and to eliminate biases injurious to proper education. This would make the dispute one of educational *policy*. It becomes a problem relevant to civil liberties because of the precise nature of the criticisms. The anti-textbook forces do not typically seek the mere deletion of biases but rather the insertion of their own. Their most persistent tactic is to quote a few isolated remarks, which seem to suggest a particular political slant in what is otherwise a fairly "neutral" or "many-sided" discussion of controversial problems, particularly in social studies material.[41]

Because of the careful scrutiny of textbooks by the long chain of screening agencies and personnel, the possibility of anything resembling "subversion" creeping in is extremely remote. Similarly, publishers, because the market is so competitive and lucrative, are very cautious about creating any conceivable difficulties. Nevertheless, spokesmen for the radical right, who were sometimes joined by veterans' organizations, have prompted notorious cases about particular texts. One book, which was most subject to controversy, was Magruder's *American Government,* which had been very widely used for a long time. In fact, this book had been part of the education of some of the very people who started the campaigns against it.[42] State and city governing bodies, mostly in the South, ordered its removal from textbook lists.

Such pressures, however, have usually met with firm resistance, primarily because of the adamant stand of educators and educational administrators, sometimes backed by other state officials.[43] These pressures are simply regarded as invasions of the educators' domains, where they feel the record is so obviously "clean" (the texts contain very little that is "tainted") that only a few special zealots could possibly find anything suspect. As a result, the barring of particular textbooks, as a matter of policy, seems to have become less frequent.[44] But one subtle form of censorship does remain. The publishers may either revise books to conform to the wishes of the critics or look for substitutes because the market is too big to risk any antagonism. Unlike what is true in so many other areas of book publishing, a "select" market is not sufficient. As in the mass media, the maximum market is the objective.

Some suppression, therefore, has been and is still, to some extent, existent in the world of elementary and secondary textbooks, but it hardly poses one of the more dramatic issues for civil libertarians. After all, the differences between barred and approved books are probably very slight. Nevertheless, the subtle impact on writers and publishers cannot be ignored. To quote one of the most comprehensive accounts of the subject: "Publishers themselves acknowledge that they must walk a narrow path to avoid controversy. As a result, many books lack vitality and are too dull to interest the students. They treat controversial subjects superficially, or not at all." [45] The freedom of expression of textbook writers is curtailed on nonpedagogical grounds with the possible resultant vitiation of the educational process.

Attempts to remove books and periodicals from libraries have been more persistent and far-reaching, and can still be observed even now. School libraries are a particularly appropriate target. The pressuring influences may come from regular "radical right" organizations, ad hoc groups, veterans organizations and, sometimes, specific irate individuals. The objective is the elimination of both "subversive" and "obscene" material, the latter, as is typical, sometimes defined by the appearance of a few "dirty words." For presumed subversive works, the designation would, in the 1950's, be a matter of the record of the author as well as the actual content. In some situations, complaints would center on explicit "irreligious" content, but such charges were usually implicit in the other two types of allegation.

The campaigns sometimes engendered encompassing community conflicts. The record seems to indicate that the censorship efforts usually lose out ultimately, except when backed by very powerful "respectable" forces. A readily available interpretation would stress that librarians appear to exhibit more "tolerant" attitudes than other types of community leaders, as demonstrated in the national surveys of the mid-1950's, and that their professional organizations have been outspoken in affirming the autonomy of librarians—their obligation to choose books on the basis of merit and potential value without external restraints. Apparently, the values and role definitions of the actual decision-makers are the major obstacles to suppressive drives.

Several extensive studies, particularly Marjorie Fiske's account of interviews with librarians in California in the late 1950's, compel a revision of this analysis.[46] Many librarians do remove books on request and, more importantly, avoid purchasing "controversial" works. Furthermore, a large number do not expect sufficient support from professional associations if forced into a dispute. An additional finding is also significant, which is not evident from dramatized journalistic reports. Very few restrictions are a result of public disputes or strident demands, but, more typically, are responses to private requests or anticipatory caution. Individual complaints would not always produce a complete removal of the book; frequently, the librarian would use the device of compromise by placing it in a separate room, making it available only by a specific inquiry. Those who refused to buy particular books would not openly admit that they were reacting to potential pressures. Actually, the subtle pressures were more likely to come from within the system, that is, some element of the library administration itself, rather than from outside.

Many librarians thus seem to be cautious about getting and keeping material to which there was actual or potential objection, a reflection of their "straddling" the personal conflict between their professional ethics and values as opposed to the characteristic features of their roles. Librarians are primarily conscious of the fact that they are not the ultimate decision-makers; all selection policies can be subject to close scrutiny by the governing library boards, school administrations in school libraries, other government officials, and central library officials in large systems. They might be able to withstand the anxieties from such control except for the prevalence of an intense status ambiguity, accompanied by lack of faith in their professional bodies. It is significant that, in the California study, those with more job security, greater professional commitment, and more thorough professional training were more likely to resist informal pressures.[47] In addition, selection policy is very complex—what is removed or not purchased is only a small part of the total collection, and many other works are left out for a myriad of reasons. It is, therefore, unlikely that anyone but a deliberate investigator of the subject would learn what had happened.

This is not true when a public dispute emerges, however. The librarians, themselves, are less likely to yield, for this would be an admission that they are permitting those who are unqualified to enter their professional domain. More importantly, it prompts the marshalling of significant forces on the librarian's side: community leaders, higher decision-making bodies, other government officials, professional associations, and in one situation a large metropolitan newspaper. As is so frequently the case, the shift from secretive operations to open battle is valuable to the defense of freedom, even when its opponents start the struggle. The role of community "notables" is most important. The "respectable" citizens, in and out of government, hold the values of free expression important enough to defend them when confronted with a threat that is nearby, that is, the issues then become salient. They are also concerned about having "good libraries" and want "good" librarians, both of which are threatened by censorship campaigns. In some instances the publicity about the entire matter also compels their dedication; in essence, they do not want their communities to become "laughingstocks." This is particularly true if the community and the opposition to censorship are more "cosmopolitan." [48] The timorous librarians are then more secure in defending their selections.

In general, censorship efforts in libraries are more likely to be resisted when those who oppose them have power, clear and salient values, status security, and when the dispute is joined in frequent confrontation. The last point is quite essential. Few people care that much about what is included in library collections. Resource limitations are generic, and there is usually so little room that omission of a particular book has little effect on the totality of the collection. The larger libraries are part of cosmopolitan settings, for both librarians and readers, with an accompanying likelihood of resistance to any type of informal pressure. The inordinate caution of many librarians results in omission of specific items, a "nuisance" type of suppression rather than a pervasive threat. Censorship becomes a policy dispute only when some people care enough to make it one. When they do, the consequences are usually the affirmation of the librarians' freedom to select books, for the reasons given, except in small isolated communities or in the unusual situation where censorship efforts are backed by powerful and "established" community forces.[49]

14

Academic freedom

No symbol has been more sacred to libertarians than that of "academic freedom." At stake is one of the most precious values— the right of scholars to pursue and impart knowledge as they see fit. For them, the significance of such freedom is especially crucial because restricting scholars not only strikes at the personal representatives of "mind" itself, but also at those who are most likely to increase and disseminate knowledge. A society which limits the academics' area of inquiry and expression is hurting itself by reducing its potential for knowledge.

On the other hand, the academician, by his free-floating range of ideas, is, both by profession and personality, the most likely "subversive," encouraging skepticism of established orthodoxies and various "party lines." However pliable so many have been to become "idea men" for power-wielders and official doctrines, the possibility that they, or their institutions, will develop into querulous Socratic gadflies is endemic, no matter what the specific discipline. The academician is the most clearly definable intellectual with presumed "tender minds" as his captive audience. Certainly, the history of academic organizations lends credence to such concerns as well as the academicians' own fears, and, to carry out his professional role, he must be "free."

The focus of this discussion is on the faculties of institutions of higher education, leaving out problems of teachers in elementary and secondary schools and with only minor reference to the "rights" of students. Similarly, we do not, in line with our general emphasis, dwell at length on the possible effects of the "subtle" pressures on academic freedom, such as sponsored research.

HISTORICAL BACKGROUND

Historically, the concept of a free academic community had been associated with the idea of autonomy, that is, the university running its own affairs with minimal interferences from the outside. This notion is a continuation of the principle behind the chartered medieval university corporation, which was independent in its operation despite its church connection as long as it did not propagate heresy. For Americans, the model was the nineteenth-century German university, which, despite the fact that it was a governmental agency and expected political loyalty from the faculty, was considered an enclave that regulated itself as a collegium. The ideal form, at least, demanded that the outside world was not to interfere with its workings, but neither was the university to influence the outside world.[1]

Despite the libertarian tradition and the Bill of Rights, plus the general absence of suppression, colleges in early America were not too free. The famous American men of letters were rarely attached to colleges or universities; in contrast to today, more were full-time journalists. The institutions were largely religiously controlled and theologically oriented. Domination by administration and trustees tended to authoritarianism. Disputes were not more common largely because of the concordant views of the faculties and the governing bodies. Demands for faculty self-government, some of them achieved, were more an assertion of dignity and professional status than a struggle against orthodoxy.

The first widespread conflicts about the propagation of views pertained to scientists who exhibited any degree of sympathy with the ideas of Charles Darwin. Several were brought to trial before the school authorities, interrogated about their views in a fashion resembling heresy trials, and frequently dismissed. The pioneer American sociologist, William Graham Sumner, was pressured to remove Herbert Spencer's sociology text from his course at Yale because Spencer was a leading publicist of Darwin's evolutionary scheme.[2] In response, faculties consolidated in demanding some form of protection, including the doctrine of removal only for incompetence and the value of "scientific neutrality." It is important to note that the issue concerned the role of physical scientists, almost a direct continuation of the disputes in the Renaissance involving men like Galileo and Bruno. In effect, the autonomy of the physical scientists in their scholarship was soon almost completely assured. The arguments in their favor, similar to the ideological basis for the freedom of the German universities, were almost irresistible to an adherent of the American ethos. The practical results of their research would be limited if they were fettered in any way. Later difficulties in academia were rarely contests between physical science and religious fundamentalism or political orthodoxy. Generally, the subsequent heretics were more likely to be social scientists than any other group.

At the turn of the century, the issue of academic freedom was more sharply drawn on both sides. More faculties demanded, and sometimes received, some autonomy from the administration and also some voice in college government. The motivation for their behavior and their relative success was, in some measure, a result of the fact that they were now led by prominent intellectual spokesmen, particularly philosophers and social scientists. The administrators of the larger universities, at least, were in charge of prestigious institutions, and, whatever other attitudes prevailed, they wanted and needed distinguished scholars. Furthermore, the historical situation was very significant. This was the progressive era, during which academic intellectuals played an important political role. In line with the prevailing philosophy of the progressive movement, the faculties demanded more self-government.

This political posture, however, also involved intense criticism of the current political-economic reality and campaigns for change. Such a stance brought professors into an obvious collision with the powerful in government and business, with resultant demands for their silencing or removal. The classic pattern of entrenched interests attempting to stamp out dissenters in academia was more clearly realized in this period than at any other time in American history. To placate important financial contributors, notable scholars were removed from prestigious universities. On the other hand, many administrators, closely identified with professors and recognizing their importance to the institution, protected those under attack. In reviewing all the situations of those times, analysts insist that personalities of the participants and the power struggles were usually relevant above and beyond the public issue of academic freedom.[3]

Toward the latter part of the era, two events signified the further reaction of professors to the total situation. One was the publication, in 1918, of the first important critical analysis of American academia, Thorstein Veblen's "The Higher Learning in America," which was essentially an attack on both the bureaucratic and "promotional" modes of college administrators.[4] In 1914, almost nine hundred professors organized their inclusive professional society, the American Association of University Professors. Much of the history of the subject since then involves the role of the AAUP. It is of some importance that the organization, at the very beginning, was sponsored by many leading intellectuals and led by philosophers John Dewey and Arthur Lovejoy. In the original design, the defense of academic freedom was not the major purpose but, within a short time, it structured the attention of the organization. As Dewey put it: "the investigations of particular cases were literally thrust upon us"—a law professor who claimed he had been fired because of testimony before a government commission, a professor who believed he had been dismissed because of religious criticisms made to an off-campus group, and so on.[5] The AAUP founders were apparently previously unaware of the possible violations of academic freedom, however defined, or of the complexity of the problem. As a continuing attempt to solve both quandaries, Committee "A" on Academic Freedom and Tenure became, and has remained, the most important operating arm of the entire organization.

Shortly after the AAUP was started, the profession confronted a severe crisis—World War I.[6] The nature of the wartime atmosphere has already been described; academia was part of its orbit. Dismissals for public criticism of any aspects of the official war aims of the United States extended to the chairman of the Political Science Department of the University of Minnesota and the dean of the University of Virginia's School of Journalism. The most publicized incidents occurred at Columbia University under President Nicholas Murray Butler, who announced that "what had been tolerated before becomes intolerable now. What had been wrongheadedness was now sedition. What had been folly was now treason." [7] This attitude was apparently supported by the trustees, resulting in several dismissals and pressured resignations, highlighted by two of the most famous "cases" in the history of academic institutions, those of psychologist J. McKean Cattell and the famed historian, Charles Beard. In the face of its first and probably to this day most drastic test, the role of the AAUP was not very helpful. Many of its leaders were so heavily committed to the war effort that the organization officially sanctioned the removal of professors on grounds of various interferences with the war effort. The qualifying provisos—that penalties be modified in certain situations and that some form of due process be observed —were hardly sufficient to prevent the many abuses.

The AAUP was ultimately able to surmount its feeble wartime role, partly because the postwar return to academic tranquility and general academic freedom was fairly quick and smooth. Surprisingly, colleges were hardly affected by the postwar "Mitchell Palmer" atmosphere, with its extreme challenge to civil liberties. During the 1920's, "incidents" did occur, but professors generally continued to teach and do research unmolested, for there were few political clashes that could cause serious conflicts. Fundamentalist religious drives had little impact, at least in the larger and more prestigious institutions, and academic rebelliousness was usually confined, as was that of the general intellectual community, to attacks on the philistinism of the Babbitts.

In the 1930's, vigorous political dissent returned to academia, as elsewhere, with a few cases of firing of dissenters.[8] By then, however, the AAUP principles on "freedom" and "tenure" had been accepted by many administrations, at least informally. By 1940, the AAUP was able to work out a joint declaration of principles with the Association of American Colleges. Despite an occasional publicized case, the number of summary dismissals that could feasibly be interpreted as violations of academic freedom was comparatively small, and usually involved nontenured personnel. Unlike earlier periods, famous scholars were rarely touched. The era, however, concluded with one of the most notorious cases in the history of American academic life, involving one of the most famous intellectuals in the world, Bertrand Russell. In fact, the case stands out for its singularity. Russell has become an internationally controversial figure because of his recent political stands, but at that time he was attacked because of his alleged antagonism to "religion and morality." After a complex political and legal struggle, he was denied appointment at the College of the City of New York.[9] Note, the major ideas of one of the most prolific writers in human history were not the reason for his failure to be appointed; the refusal was based on a quite tangential issue, representing one of the last successful efforts of quasi-fundamentalist forces to pressure a major college. Despite the fears about the power of anti-intellectualism in America, nothing similar has since occurred.

In addition, the precursor of the pattern that was to become so conspicuous in the postwar period emerged in the early 1940's, also involving the New York City Colleges. A state legislative investigating committee disclosed that several persons on the faculty and administrative staffs were Communist party members, and these people were summarily dismissed.[10]

POST–WORLD WAR II AMERICA

To many observers, the two decades that supply the setting of most of our analyses was a time of serious threats to academic freedom. The keynote was the presumed "anti-intellectualism" of many strident political publics and their representatives in office, another manifestation of McCarthyism, supposedly continuing to this day. Anxious and authoritarian administrators readily submitted to the drives to stifle dissident voices, an especially grievous danger because of the tremendous growth of higher education. Furthermore, public opinion was more affirmative in its belief that dissident teachers be eliminated than was typical for most other "intolerant" attitudes.[11]

In a book published in 1955, the distinguished sociologist and political scientist, Robert MacIver, asserted that "it is hardly an exaggeration to say that the weight of authority in the United States is now adverse to the principle of intellectual freedom." [12] As he describes various "incidents" and lists the multiplicity of pressures against such freedoms—from governmental officials, governing boards, veterans' groups, self-styled patriotic organizations, and the apparent popularity of writers like William Buckley who demanded that alumni and trustees enforce religious and academic orthodoxies on campuses—he seems to substantiate the more casual impressions.

Other, more systematic investigations seem to corroborate his contentions. Lionel Lewis' study of all "cases" investigated by AAUP up to 1962 reveals a significant trend in the explanations for dismissals, as given by both the administration and the affected faculty member.[13] Whereas "problems of interpersonal relations" were the grounds in the majority of cases in the period from 1916 to 1932, the issue of "ideological position or compliance" was most prominent in the last period (1945–1962), affecting about half of the faculty members dismissed. The author thus insists that interference by the administration and trustees, which was probably spurred by specific outside pressures, had increased, and the view of the professor as a "hired hand" became more predominant.

Lazarsfeld's and Thielen's survey of almost twenty-five hundred teachers of social science in various colleges and universities seemed to offer further corroboration.[14] They reported almost one thousand separate "incidents." Almost 20 per cent explained that they had experienced some "caution" independently. The degree of "personal apprehension" varied with the specific question. Only 17 per cent thought the administration had a dossier on their political beliefs, and about 40 per cent worried about possible misrepresentation of political beliefs by students.

About a fifth of the "incidents" resulted in dismissals or forced resignations. Otherwise, the consequences, which were more difficult to substantiate, included such things as failure to be promoted or receive a merit salary increase or, very frequently, a simple admonishment from the president. In classifying what was at issue in these "incidents," almost three-fourths seemed to be "political" in nature. Twenty-nine per cent involved "Communist," "subversive," or "un-American" views; 44 per cent of the respondents reported "other" political issues, implying that attempted political censorship was much wider for college faculty than the rest of the population during the McCarthy era. Many teachers from southern schools reported difficulties in which race and segregation problems were clearly a part. A few cases were connected with the demands for religious orthodoxy at some denominational schools. In describing their own "cautions," many respondents admitted exercising restraint in publications and speeches and in assigning reading material. In expressing unpopular views, a common technique was to "hedge" any presentation with the disclaimer that these were simply views for discussion.

Does all of this, however, add up to an atmosphere of veritable academic terror in very recent times, possibly continuing to this day? Our answer is strongly negative. There were typical McCarthyite problems in academia but less extensive and influential than many have claimed, and they were special, nontraditional threats to academic freedom. Whatever the deficiencies of academic institutions and faculties, they were not primarily a result of external constraints on their autonomy. In fact, all discussions of "academic freedom" become very cloudy because of the usual failure to appreciate the complexities, including the murkiness of the concept itself.

MacIver's account is based upon several specific "incidents." Two of them, to which he devotes considerable attention, concern dismissal of presidents of two large state universities. Although these cases may be a significant part of a "sociology of academia" and although the attitudes of some participants revealed attitudes inimical to academic freedom, they were not academic freedom cases per se. The incumbency of an administrator should be viewed essentially as a substantive political issue, not as a civil liberties question. Several of the other troublesome situations were very concrete affairs, based upon the specific problems of a particular institution, which was usually rather small. The other cases Mac-Iver reports, and those which make up the bulk of "quality" colleges and universities censured by the AAUP, are reflections of McCarthyism on the campus.[15] In line with our persistent assertions about the nature of McCarthyism, the traditional elements of academic freedom, the teachers' unique rights of free expression, were rarely, as such, the major reasons for the dispute.

Most "cases" typically resulted from the following factors: present membership in the Communist party (which, in academia, did not seem to extend to any other "subversive" affiliation); behavior before legislative investigating committees, especially the refusal to answer questions; a raft of loyalty oaths; and invitations to "suspect" speakers to address campus groups (which were more likely to pertain to student organizations rather than faculty groups). Although the question of whether Communist party members should be on faculties was an issue that was hotly contested in academic circles, it was rarely necessary to take a definitive stand. Very few were ever "exposed," and their dismissals did not prompt any widespread academic protest. The major source of dispute was the removal of those accused of past membership, who generally took some version of the Fifth Amendment before inquiries.[16] In most cases, neither their present behavior nor their present beliefs were under attack.

The controversy about "loyalty oaths" evoked far more turmoil among faculties than among any other group, probably because of the academics' greater sensitivity to possible infringement of their unique civil liberties, their "academic freedom." The most publicized and researched as well as the most bizarre incident in the 1950's was the year-long battle over the oath at the University of California, which was, in essence, ultimately rescinded.[17] Nothing better revealed the trivia that tried so many souls during the McCarthy era, whose immediate impact was not a stifling of dissent but rather an unprecedented mobilization of faculty protest, and whose later result was the loss of several prominent or promising teachers. The university itself rapidly recovered from the turmoil and again became, at least until the student turmoil of the mid-1960's, an institution attractive to scholars.

Interviewed teachers in the Wagner-Thielens study reported other types of possibly suppressive administration behavior—cautioning faculty about research and extra-academic activities, bypassing them in promotions, screening applicants for faculty positions, and so on.[18] Such charges are probably, in many cases, quite valid, although it would be difficult to substantiate them with the best data available. In any case, these phenomena have been prevalent in American academia without the impact of "McCarthyite" pressures.

One other *pattern* of academic suppression, however, became prominent, the efforts directed at those who might, in whatever fashion, support the principle of integration in some southern institutions.[19] Several institutions did actually terminate the employment of prominent prointegration spokesmen and have been, or still are, "censured" by the AAUP for a considerable time. More frequent were the informal pressures against "external" activities. Attempts to hold a meeting to discuss civil rights were vetoed by presidents, in one case with a definite warning of possible legislative reprisals. Some were cautioned about the "wrong" type of research, publication, and choice of textbooks. The faculty was asked to list all outside organizational affiliations in one state university, until this was nullified by a Supreme Court decision. The pressures could become quite severe—abusive telephone calls at night, insults to their wives and children, and legal harassment. The pattern, of course, varied widely within the South, and has undoubtedly abated in the last few years.

Besides the special southern experiences, the publicized post-McCarthyite incidents do not imply any suppression of political or other significant intellectual dissidence. Perhaps the most dramatic recent example occurred at St. John's University in New York, where the governing Vincentian Order dismissed faculty members who were active in the campaign for more faculty government and, in most cases, in the organization of a chapter of the American Federation of Teachers.[20] Other cases also involve behavior of clearly authoritarian administrations. Otherwise, each case seems unique and generally includes many personal elements. One would expect that the current tensions—involving the war in Vietnam, student protests, demands of black students, and so on—would produce several "incidents" affecting the status of some dissident faculty members. What is most striking is the comparative lack of conspicuous pressures against dissidence on a national scale. The perplexing problems of American academia today can hardly be defined as "academic freedom" issues.

A closer look at the empirical studies reveals that the initial cursory assumption of widespread suppression in the earlier period does not hold up. The Lazarsfeld-Thielens study, after its accounts of "incidents," "cautions," "apprehensions," and so on, in the McCarthy era, offers this summary evaluation: "There is indeed widespread apprehension among these social science teachers, but in general it is hardly of a paralyzing nature; the heads of these men and women are 'bloody but unbowed.'"[21] Their data does lend some credence to this contention, and only a few examples are necessary. The "incidents" cover a widely varied and inclusive category, with a vast range of results. A fifth resulted in actual termination of employment. Both the nature and the consequences of the other situations could be very trivial, as well as probably interwoven with many other factors. Thus, "other" political incidents, besides those directly associated with "communism" or "subversion," seemed to affect a sizable number of teachers. Yet what was actually involved in many of the cases is revealed by a few concrete examples—bypassing a teacher for promotion because he was an avid New Deal exponent, administrators and trustees chastising fifty professors for signing a newspaper ad supporting Adlai Stevenson in 1952, and an administration criticizing the views of a "right of center" professor.

The observed, widespread apprehension did not always lead to *caution.* Only about 10 per cent of those interviewed, for instance, stated that their writings were affected. More importantly, apprehensive teachers were more likely to engage in "dangerous" activities. Why this seeming paradox? The apprehensive faculty members were more likely to be at bigger and/or "better" schools and were more cosmopolitan in their orientation. They also included more teachers who were confident in their administrations and had more status, that is, were secure in their professional identities and were more occupationally secure because of their reputations. Therefore, they had, as a group, fewer insecurities that might produce caution.

The authors suggest various reasons for their greater apprehension. As cosmopolites they were more sensitive to professional injury and would more likely be cognizant of all incidents. They worked in permissive and, frequently, heterogeneous institutions where more people are motivated to behave in a way which would create incidents. The "localities" and/or those in "poorer quality," more authoritarian institutions would be less likely to note, or to comment on, incidents that did occur, and fewer would be likely to occur because of the nature of the faculty and the constraining atmosphere. Nevertheless, a few incidents could make them very cautious. One more observation should be added. The reports of pressures were most prominent at tax-supported rather than private schools.

Lewis' study of AAUP investigations also requires more careful scrutiny. He noted an increase, over a period of time, in the number of situations in which the administration and trustees either removed or pressured the resignation of faculty members who were not "ideologically compliant." The findings may be only a result of a statistical artifact. The vast growth of higher education could simply have brought about more institutions in which problems of teacher opposition to administration is possible.

Perhaps, a significant part of the explanation is the greater self-assertion of many teachers as well as their increased numbers. Furthermore, the data does not include any breakdown of schools. This may be a significant variable. It is meaningful to hypothesize that a major proportion of those dismissed for their views, per se, were at the "inferior" and frequently more authoritarian schools. Offhand, it is difficult to think of many distinguished scholars removed from a prominent university in recent times because of ideas, a pattern for which there are many examples in the past. The few that might conceivably be so identified were affected by the unique operations of the McCarthy atmosphere.

The author's own cursory examination of administrations censured by the AAUP lends support to our contentions. Thirty-five were so designated in the ten-year period from 1958 to 1967. Only seven of these were, by a hasty inspection, large institutions with a likely "quality" evaluation. In the cases of all but one of these, the University of Illinois, AAUP action resulted from some manifestation of the McCarthyite style, particularly dismissals caused by behavior before a legislative committee. By 1961, only the University of Illinois remained on the censure list (censure followed the dismissal of a professor who advocated sexual "permissiveness" in a letter to the school paper). Nine of the remainder were obviously southern colleges. The others seemed to be generally small schools usually with, from the AAUP reports, authoritarian administrations (plus the special case of St. John's). The sixteen on the list in 1967 included no renowned educational institutions.[22]

One other source of evidence is significant. In their investigation of academia, published in 1958 as the *Academic Marketplace,* Caplow and McGill summarized interviews with two hundred faculty members in various schools, which included questions about situations of employment termination. They did not find a single instance where any apparent "academic freedom" issue was pertinent, even though some reported that *any* external political activity might affect opportunities for advancement.[23]

The general effect of recent trends has been to reinforce some of the styles of the inferior and authoritarian schools and to produce much concern and some carefulness among the more professionally secure in the "progressive" and quality schools. The incidents and the response both emphasize the specific features of the McCarthy era. In both the studies of social scientists and AAUP accounts, the type of behavior under attack, except in the South, rarely included beliefs and classroom activity and only occasionally research and published articles. It usually consisted of something "external," past and present political or other organizational affiliations, behavior before legislative bodies, and so on—the type of activity outside the scheme of the traditional values of the German university and something which AAUP was initially reluctant to make part of its credo.

McCarthyism did leave its mark on faculties of higher education, but not in the way usually emphasized. In general, freedom of inquiry and expression was not directly jeopardized by external threats. The tendency to avoid associations appeared less marked than among any other type of personnel subject to pressures. Unlike the formula that affected potential McCarthyite victims in other spheres, caution was not correlated with "success"; in fact, because of some special features of the academic career line, the reverse seemed to be true, that is, the "successful" were sufficiently secure in their academic positions or had very *"marketable" skills*.

What McCarthyism did to academia is an integral part of a major theme of our earlier discussions. Academic scholars not only yielded to the intensified political apathy and blandness but also many, particularly among social scientists, seemed to welcome it, that is, they misread the dangers as stemming from "too much politics." [24] This was the typical state of those who were genuinely politically concerned. For the others, for whom the saliency of political values was not too high, the adjustment was very easy, with subtle "cautions," which could not be detected easily by themselves or colleagues, an obvious result. Serious political dissent simply did not enter their intellectual perspectives because there were few impulses toward even considering such a perspective, especially since, again particularly among social scientists, their interests might well be structured by the nature of available research grants. If there were any bent toward dissident political activity, there was no viable mechanism for participation. With the possible "risks" attendant, it appeared to offer little but a quixotic adventure. The McCarthyite impact upon faculties was thus a latent consequence rather than a direct effect—the general national atmosphere tended to make them, too, relatively politically bland.

All this obviously changed in the 1960's. It is unnecessary to detail the role of professors of many types in the very recent variants of political protest, both as scholars and as citizens, becoming extreme barometric indicators of the change in national mood. And, as indicated, resulting reprisals have been very, very few. Nevertheless, "academic freedom" cases remain prominent. What is noteworthy is that they reveal no pattern except the continuation of authoritarian practices by many administrations. Otherwise, each case seems quite singular. All of them might be better understood from our attempted restatement of the entire problem, including both further examination of the bases for academic freedom or its absence, that is, the "independent variable" and a probe of the meaning of the "dependent variable," the concept of academic freedom itself.

GENERAL ANALYSIS

Although college faculties are, by disposition and training, dedicated to clarity and precision in the use of terminology, they have made academic freedom their own shibboleth, their professional value-laden slogan for mobilizing colleagues and appealing to other publics. This is quite understandable, for it represents an historic continuity with the age-old struggle for intellectual autonomy which is the groundwork for the life style of academics. Nevertheless, the sometimes facile application of the term conceals the many varying and complex types of problems masked by including all academic difficulties under the one heading. Many situations frequently identified as academic freedom cases are partially, or sometimes solely, a matter of judgments about competency, interpersonal relations, academic government, or a question of "job rights," which, for some other groups, might be readily defined as "collective bargaining issues." Naturally, in many cases these factors are closely enmeshed with academic freedom disputes but they must be analytically separated, and sometimes academic freedom is not genuinely at issue despite official and unofficial attempts to apply the label.

A summary report of the one hundred and twenty-four cases reported in the AAUP Bulletin up to 1953 is symbolic. Few apparently covered clear-cut violations of the rights of free expression. According to this analysis, "in almost two thirds, the issues were intramural and largely personal, hinging on the jealousy between a president and a professor, or the conflict between strong personalities, or the petty vindictiveness of someone in high office or—this was particularly true during the Depression—the decision to cut down on staff in an effort to economize." [25] Significantly, only a few "major" universities were involved.

Lionel Lewis' data would seem to imply that this pattern had later changed, and that "ideological compliance" had become a more prominent aspect of such cases. In the absence of precise indications of his coding techniques, it is impossible to contest his interpretation per se, except for the fact that the category included the McCarthyite phenomena, behavior before legislative bodies, which was the unique ingredient of the times. Another possible challenge, however, suggests itself. The ostensible issues may conceal some underlying features, which may or may not be revealed at all. The personality conflict, among faculty or with the administration, may have been the underlying reason for getting rid of a particular teacher, a process which occurs very frequently in other ways without becoming a case. Dissident views and actions will then be either an available excuse or will appear to be the major explanation to observers. To take a rather bizarre recent example, the removal of a professor of philosophy may have been partially prompted by his article on a trip to Mount Everest that antagonized professional mountain climbers, whose views were made known to the administration. One familiar type of situation rarely shows up in investigations, the intramural "power play," which the "losing" professor can turn into an academic freedom case.[26]

The question of "competence" is a thorny issue, which is very difficult to extricate in most cases and impossible to judge in others. It is frequently at least a relevant and sometimes a crucial feature, even if AAUP inquiries are basically only a result of possible infringement of academic freedom. The relation of academic freedom and an authoritarian administration is also complex. Sometimes it is obvious—a teacher is summarily fired because his unorthodox views displease those in power. More often, disputes cover the nature of college government, encompassing both faculty participation in decisions and protection from arbitrary treatment, or "freedom to" and "freedom from."

Despite tradition, official ideology, and some recent trends, a significant proportion of trustees, administrators, and faculty probably regard college teachers as professional employees rather than citizens of an academic commonwealth.[27] Recent developments have, however, probably produced more people who demand a greater voice in determination of policy as well as more institutions in which this is possible. The growth of the AAUP and the approval of much of its program by the Association of American Colleges have provided greater legitimation for those demands. In some institutions, this can result in a very dramatic clash, for it can be construed as an attack on the power of governing bodies, almost as a form of sedition. Defense of colleagues and students deemed subject to unfair treatment is still only "freedom from," which can be a sufficiently divisive issue. A campaign for more faculty participation in government is more challenging. Formerly, this was more likely to be the assertion of an entrenched academic activist, frequently in a large well-established and renowned institution. More recently, it has been more evident in authoritarian administrations, probably subject to many pressures, such as state and community colleges, schools of specific denominations, marginal private institutions, and some southern schools. The recent St. John's story is a conspicuous example.

In general, there is a close connection between the question of academic freedom and job rights. Even more than in any other problem area, civil liberties cannot be divorced from occupational security. A teacher cannot be free if his position on the job is threatened. That is why so much of the action of professional groups on academic freedom has, quite logically, been directed at job protection—symbolized and made concrete in the doctrine of "tenure." Essentially, this involves the stipulation that a teacher, whose competence has been legitimized over a specified time of full-time service at an institution, cannot be removed without formal hearings with due process. The prime purpose is to see that substantive rights of freedom of scholarship and teaching are protected by "procedural" rights. This has been extended, far beyond the original German model, to include the rights of free expression and association outside the university, the rights as "citizens." An important additional "right" is the freedom to comment and proselytize on internal academic organization.

Any attempt to "discipline" a teacher, which is typically a euphemism for firing, can thus have so many motivations. That is why due process, with all the usual legal protections, is defined as the quintessential condition for the maintenance of academic freedom, a subsection of the defense of job rights. If nothing else, a formalized judicial process compels some clarification of the issues, some stipulation, in quasi-legal terms, of what it is all about. All of this suggests a close similarity to collective bargaining methods.

Significant differences, however, readily suggest themselves. Procedural protections are usually available only to "tenured" faculty members, which, even by AAUP standards, is a standard taking much longer to achieve than the satisfactory "probation period" in most union-management contracts. In addition, procedural protections do not and probably cannot apply to promotions, let alone the murky area of "merit" pay increases. That is why possible reprisals by the method of denying promotion are very difficult to verify. To provide some safeguards, the AAUP has insisted on the doctrine of "proper notice"—that a faculty member be informed of nonappointment fairly early in the academic year

—and the possible participation of colleagues in making tenure and promotion decisions. In this instance, bureaucratization, which Veblen feared so much, is one of the professor's most important defensive mechanisms. Unlike what seems true in other areas, bureaucratic organization tends to implement the rights of freedom of expression and association. Without it, the faculty member is more likely subject to arbitrary treatment.

One other difference with the collective bargaining mode is consequential. The philosophy of the "better" faculty member, as exemplified in the AAUP orientation, includes a desire to participate in all academic decisions. perhaps even to be the principal governing voice. They want to be part of "management" and appropriately have some identification with that management, as long as nothing inimical to the faculty would be a result. Because of this and because of the traditional image of the scholarly "gentlemen," the AAUP has eschewed the militant combative stance. Instead, every effort is made to avoid an open confrontation. Investigations of "cases" are long, judicious, dignified, and careful. Attempts are made to get all interested parties to state their positions. Many people take part in the process, with an emphasis on including those who are not directly involved. For instance, many cases are under the jurisdiction of the national office rather than the local chapter concerned. Informal mediation is vigorously tried before a case is formally publicized and investigated. In one report written in 1934 it was estimated that, for every case written up in the AAUP Bulletin, there were three settled informally and quietly.[28] Most investigations include elements of "principle" as much as personal mistreatment. The ultimate weapon is "censure," a form of embarassment to administrators and an admonition to colleagues to avoid the institution. Censure is frequently removed when the "principles" are satisfied, even if the original "case" is left unsettled. This set of tactics may have had meaningful results, particularly in "quality" institutions, but may not be sufficient as teachers in more authoritarian institutions demand their rights. It is in such schools, particularly junior colleges, that the American Federation of College Teachers, with its more aggressive posture, appears to be assuming a significant role as defender of all aspects of academic freedom and other accompanying job rights.

GENERAL EVALUATION

Our summary assertion is that, with all the complexities involved, college faculties as a group have achieved greater job security and personal dignity, which encompasses academic freedom, over the past two decades. The impact of McCarthyite tendencies were special, limited, and episodic, and even the difficulties within some southern universities have become less pronounced. If academic freedom cases are still very prominent it is not because teachers are cowed but because more are asserting themselves in authoritarian institutions, as well as because of the obvious, inevitable conflicts within faculties and administration.

How, in the light of the attitudes of many teachers and administrators as well as the many external pressures, can this have happened? Even the "best" administrators and the most well-meaning trustees are not independent agents. The college and university survives and thrives only with outside support, particularly financial support. The administrator, even if not always the businessman-administrator type noted by Veblen, is, at best, a broker between the internal members—faculty and students—and the external influences—trustees and community power groups. Only the well-established private university, large public universities in some situations, and special types of small private colleges can be relatively immune. One of the more shocking observations about the South was that the institutions most constraining upon faculty and students active in desegregation movements were the small Negro colleges, both public and private, extremely vulnerable to the opinions of white donors and white legislators. Because of the nature of support from the outside and because of their own insecurity, many administrators became as readily frightened as a television executive in the blacklisting era. As described by one observer, "for some presidents, two phone calls and three letters constitute an avalanche of public opinion." [29]

The sources of external pressures have been diverse. At one time, business representatives, indirectly or directly through their positions on boards of trustees or in association with trustees, were prominent among those trying to curtail particular professors. This seems less evident recently. Religious groups, whether directly connected with a denominational school or not, were frequently active in attempting to silence a faculty member. Except for some fundamentalist groups, particularly in the South, this has also been less evident, probably because of the decreased importance of "heresy" as a present evil. The most publicized recent case involving a denominational school, that of St. John's in New York, was not based on doctrinal disagreement but on conflict with the power position of the governing religious order. In varying degrees at different times, the most conspicuous pressures, particularly since World War II, have openly come from political people, those in office and those in organized pressure groups, especially patriotic and veteran organizations in opposition to what they deem subversive tenets. In the South, this meant, above all, opposition to integration.

Why have the large private universities, with their typical concentration of business trustees, apparently been the most "free"? The possible answer to this question can furnish a clue to some of the reasons for the relative maintenance, in our assessment, of academic freedom. Perhaps the "sophisticated conservative" businessmen, on the one hand, have had few serious challenges to the legitimacy of their positions since World War II. On the other hand, they are becoming very appreciative of the importance of quality education and quality professors in furthering their major interest—the national destiny. Businessmen, including trustees, have, typically, not tried to intervene in faculty matters. Attempts to silence professors with "anti-business" views, once noticeable, has hardly been reported for some time.

If one also adds the fact that most state universities were relatively "free," except for an occasional abuse based upon the peculiar "McCarthyite" exigencies of the time, other features of the large institution may have enhanced the possibilities of internal freedom. Bureaucratization, with its attendant formal protections, is beneficial to internal freedoms in this situation. The educational administrator, carrying out the "promotion" role specified by Veblen, has generally felt the need to recruit and keep "quality" people in a very competitive market, which Veblen actually foresaw.[30] Because of these factors and because of the pressure of faculties and faculty organizations, it is likely that the degree of self-government has increased in the quality schools and many others. Symbolically, court decisions changed from an early view of all teachers as employees, to be hired and dismissed like all others, to their assigned role as "priests of our democracy," protected by the "preferred status" of the First Amendment.[31]

In general, the possible prevalence of anti-intellectualism is more than balanced by the need to have academic minds in the nation and in the burgeoning colleges. As fewer of the colleges remain small and "inferior," the possibilities of successful arbitrary administration tactics decrease. The faculties, on their part, have, through the "McCarthyite" annoyances, maintained their essential intellectual integrity and democratic values. In fact, as a group they were better able to withstand the suppressive pressures than most other sectors of society affected. This was partly a result of their accepted role definitions and the organizations dedicated to their fulfillment, partly a product of the situational needs of their institutions and partly a reflection of the job "dispensability" of academic notables. But it was also a matter of the structure of academia. The "bureaucratic" mechanism of tenure gave them a defensive device available to few others, except perhaps to some unionized industrial workers. The newer faculty members, the post-McCarthy generation, seems even more bent on self-assertion.

None of this is meant to imply a rosy-hued depiction of academic intellectuals. Many have, undoubtedly, failed to fulfill their possible functions as iconoclastic critics, pioneer scholars, devotees of the life of the mind, moral conscience of the community, and so on. The McCarthyite atmosphere did have some effect, not so much in frightening dissidents as to directing their vistas toward intellectual triviality. The large institution tends to protect teachers against abuses but it may also make them indifferent to larger, noncurricular concerns, such as the general direction of the university and the problems of the students.[32] Furthermore, many faculty members, particularly in the natural sciences and professional schools, are hardly avid proponents of academic freedom principles.[33] The problems of the "younger" and nontenured teachers and the danger of discrimination in promotion remain.

Pinpointing the "evils" of recent and contemporary faculties of higher education is not a difficult undertaking. Most of these, however, cannot be blamed, at least directly, on external restraints. They have come from ideological orientations and conscious decisions to get more rewards—climbing their promotional ladders, obtaining research grants, writing publishable scholarly works, and so on—as well as the always present personal rivalries.

POSTSCRIPT: STUDENTS AND THE CURRENT DISPUTES

The more dramatic disputes in colleges have increasingly centered around students rather than faculty. Dealing with the entire question of student "rights" would require a new chapter. Among the more pertinent issues relevant to freedom of expression and association that have prevailed from time to time are independence of the student press from administration or faculty control or censorship; freedom of student organizations to follow their own interests, particularly in terms of political interests; rights of student demonstration, a form of free assembly; and freedom of a student to express his views in class, on campus, and elsewhere, without retaliation. The first two types of problems—the rights of an autonomous press and extracurricular groups—were the bases for serious turmoil in many colleges for a long time but have ceased to be prominent recently. Whatever the reasons—student assertiveness itself, faculty support because of desire to have an intellectually alive student body, thus enhancing their own freedom, or the general "permissive" academic atmosphere—this type of First Amendment freedom seems to be a fairly well-established principle, at least for the time being. This requires a diminution of the formula of "loco parentis," the notion that students are juveniles under the charge of faculty and administration. The possibility of some sort of retaliation for expressed views, especially when it involves the withdrawal of academic reward—grades, honors, recommendations, and so on—is extremely difficult to detect. The question of punishment for demonstrations remains, of course, a crucial issue, probably more than ever before. In providing some viable formal stipulation for maintenance of both the last two rights, the only meaningful avenue seems to be an insistence on proper methods of due process.[34] For most institutions, this would require some changes, for many a substantial alteration of the on-going practices.

When these rights spill over into demands for "student power" and acts of confrontation, the entire question becomes much more complex. In both cases, the problem of "legitimacy" is posed to some extent. That is why this discussion of academic freedom does not include any consideration of student unrest, which was covered in the earlier account of the contemporary "legitimacy crisis." The most important "academic freedom" aspect has been the threat of scholarship and loan termination, which was already considered.

It may, however, emerge in a manner rarely considered seriously —that "student power" could become one obstacle to intellectual autonomy for the individual faculty, especially since the slogan for student power has sometimes included a demand for participation in hiring and firing. Conceivably, this could include the removal of tenure rights, judicial due process, and so on. The right of faculty to be "free" from student harassment has not been historically unknown, although naturally the reverse has been far more common. In fact, in post-Civil War America, sometimes students and trustees actually lined up together against the faculty.[35] This possibility seems farfetched today, but, whatever the movements toward student freedom and participation in academic decisions and whatever evaluation one has of these trends, this conceivable threat to faculty freedoms could become a future problem.

15

Some other issues: a miscellany

The recent civil liberties problems that have been analyzed have all been fairly pervasive—*many* people were in some way actually affected. Similarly, they usually represented some kind of disputes in which the participants, even if a minority of the populace, were sufficiently numerous. In most instances, the civil libertarian position was clearly on one side, whatever the other considerations that may have modified the views of particular individuals and groups.

A wide range of other issues, however, do not fit one or more of the above stipulations. Either the impact on a large number of people is not immediately apparent, fewer people are involved in the disputes than is even typical of most civil liberties questions, and/or the civil libertarian answer is complex. They can be grouped under three categories: freedom of expression versus other *social considerations*, freedom of expression versus other *individual* (and group) *rights*, and the question of *channels* of communication. Previous discussions have considered some of these features when obviously relevant but an extended examination is necessary to round out our account. Although some of these disputes are a major concern to particular commentators and provide serious problems for legal and libertarian organizations, the "threats" to freedom of expression and association they pose can generally be classified as "nuisances" rather than "pervasive" threats. For example, one is silenced at a particular time but the overall impact on the existence of such freedom is minimal. (Perhaps the major exception is the complex area of communication channels.)

FREEDOM OF EXPRESSION AND OTHER CONSIDERATIONS

Government Secrecy

Disputes about the respective merits of the public's "right to know" and the need for certain government operations to proceed without immediate and possibly harassing publicity have a long history. After all, the deliberations of the Constitutional Convention were held *in camera*. Restrictions on reports of legislative sessions were prominent in early America and in Britain. More recently, congressional committees have frequently gone into "executive session," with any official information about the details coming from "releases." The inner workings of executive offices are frequently unavailable to open scrutiny.[1]

Many of these restrictions are assertions of the "right of privacy," based on the fear of unnecessary embarrassment to individuals or premature and distorted disclosures of incipient proposals. Many victims of McCarthyism, in the most restricted sense, were sharply critical of the publicity given to information which, in terms of the need for proper policy formation, informal discussions, and the reputations of individuals, should best have been left secret. Those who disagreed emphasized the importance of an open record of events for a functioning democracy. The generic value question is whether any official actions of policy-making government officials is privileged. In actuality, the practice of "news leaks" has tended to make the issue somewhat academic—enough information does reach public attention. The commentary on this type of information, including possible distortion, becomes a form of free expression about these questions.

More serious are the issues revolving around the question of data which is defined as "classified" in military terms. What is covered by such a designation is itself subject to serious dispute. The principle is that dissemination of certain material, perhaps even knowledge of such data, would endanger the success of secret activities, might prove embarrassing to the nation, and so on. The secrecy of certain purely military facts is, of course, the most obvious and important type of restraint, and censorship, in its literal sense, is legally permissible without qualification. Similarly, organs of communication are expected to pursue and usually strive for a military "self-censorship."

Yet, even when the content is purely military, that is, there are no apparent political implications, the difference between what is permissible communication and what is not is hardly very sharp. In World War II, for instance, the *Chicago Tribune* was chastised for publishing the fact that American counterintelligence had broken the Japanese secret code, but apparently the paper's officials could not be prosecuted. When the line between policy and technical considerations becomes blurred or when the covert military operations become foreign-policy decisions, important issues are removed from public debate and a significant type of freedom of expression can thus be seriously curtailed. This has been a present danger since World War II and is a prominent source of apprehension for theorists of the "garrison society," amplified by reports of the clandestine activities of groups like the Central Intelligence Agency. The demands for secrecy, which people like Edwards Shils stipulated are required for the defense of freedom against the onslaught of the "Populist McCarthy" demands for disclosures, would thus turn out to provide a serious limitation on public liberties. What is surprising is that this has not been a very conspicuous *civil liberties* problem and has therefore not warranted too much attention in our discussion. In fact, it did not seem to become a public issue until the 1960's, possibly not until the U-2 incident of 1960.

Since then, there has been considerable discussion of the question of concealed information, "managed information," "credibility gap," and so forth. "Credibility gap," an example of "journalese" that obfuscates more than it clarifies, is a particularly confusing phenomenon. Applied principally to official reports and estimates of the war in Vietnam, it is presumed to imply that there is insufficient information or information that is too slanted for significant public discussion and public influence. On the other hand, this war is the most thoroughly reported and possibly the most thoroughly discussed war in history. If the allegation of inadequate and improper information is accurate, this would imply that whatever the efforts and facilities of all other bodies of the citizenry, only a few members of the executive branch of government and a few military officials are capable of supplying the kind of data that makes free expression and association around such vital issues possible. The actual course of events does not sustain this contention. Enough people, in various sections of American society, feel they have learned enough about the war to participate in the intense debate on the subject, influencing in some manner the course of a presidential election and perhaps the actual policy of the government. There has been sufficient opportunity for a variety of appraisals of what is happening in Southeast Asia to make the effect of any "managed news" very minimal. The danger to First Amendment freedoms from the war lies elsewhere, as otherwise discussed.

The threat to free expression posed by the dictates of "national security," in the literal and not in the typical euphemistic meaning of the term, is most pressing when the military-political decisions contain some element of "surprise." The most conspicuous examples were the Bay of Pigs invasion and the Cuban missile crisis in the Kennedy administration, and, to some extent, the intervention in the Dominican Republic under Johnson. In both the Cuban missile crisis and the Bay of Pigs invasion, important facts were withheld or distorted, and those who published prior information were officially chastised. In the Cuban missile situation, official pressure impelled newspapers to withhold material about to be published.[2]

The freedom of expression of the press was thus curtailed. The freedom of news consumers to discuss and organize was limited by the concealment of very relevant facts. What happened was a concomitant of several factors. It was not simply the garrison nature of society that was responsible for the demands for secrecy but rather the importance given to timing and concealment in such operations, so likely in the contemporary international setting. Other elements, however, were involved, particularly in the Bay of Pigs case. The role of the CIA meant that it would have to be clandestine, for the very essence of that organization means immunity from public debate, even when, as President Kennedy asserted, such debate might have prevented the debacle.[3] The structure of decision-making in such hands inherently limits the public's right to know, and therefore the free expression of those who could report on those decisions. Both the values of the people who operate the organization and the structure of the organization itself are inimical to some aspect of the exercise of this civil liberty.

All this could be a serious danger. Up to now, such manifestations of cold war barriers to free dissemination of important information have been singular events rather than pervasive phenomena. They may become more common, but the atmosphere of free discussion, structurally grounded in such features as some degree of congressional criticism and relatively free public media, provide something of a bulwark. For instance, some of the activities of the CIA have already been exposed. Even if the dangers from secretive decisions and withheld information are deeply rooted in our contemporary American society in its worldwide relations, they have not yet had the impact of the loyalty-security demands of the McCarthy era or the potential effect of the current legitimacy crisis, and thus do not warrant similar attention.

Secrecy of Private Groups

The operations of private groups are frequently of obvious public concern. Where and how to demarcate the distinction between what is genuinely private and what is in the public domain is extremely difficult. The clash between the demands for personal dignity and group autonomy versus the need for relevant facts on which to base free discussions is a perilous dilemma. To avoid getting into all the complex ramifications of the issue at this point, this brief discussion concentrates on one type of organization, the private business corporation. By the nature and scale of their operations, they are quasi-public bodies, whose influence on contemporary society is immeasurable. Nevertheless, by structure and operating ideology, they emphasize one canon of classic bureaucratic tenets, the hoarding of internal secrets. Free discourse about their internal life is very difficult. Even accounts in sophisticated business-oriented magazines, like *Fortune,* resemble the data from public relations handouts. What goes on inside the corporation is generally regarded as nobody else's business, including irate stockholders. What this means is that such significant data about one of the most crucial aspects of contemporary society is unavailable for public expression. This rarely becomes a genuine issue because of the almost universal and casual acceptance of this as a *given* condition, a fact of social life. The actions of corporate officials usually become matters of open public concern only when something nefarious is revealed, particularly if it may result in some harm to the consumers—in terms of prices, safety, and so on. The most common response of the corporate officials is to avoid disclosures, even to congressional committees if possible. Their adamancy rests on the ideological assumption that all information is privileged and that the corporate image must not deviate from the picture of a smoothly operating and nearly perfect monolithic facade. Those who attempt to expose and disclose may be subject to some variant of the carrot and the stick—the suggestion of a lucrative position or clandestine harassment.[4] The countervailing force is more of the same thing they are trying to suppress, exposés of tactics, undertaken by government officials or journalists, collaborating with or appealing to interested political publics. In any case, the secretiveness of those who manage such large repositories of accumulated wealth and power represents a continuing threat to freedom of expression, allayed primarily by some variant of what may be broadly defined as political action.

Advertising

Advertising presents an opposite alternative, a type of communication by businessmen whose "freedom" is threatened. Government regulatory agencies and prosecutor's offices may, under specific statutes, compel the cessation of any advertising or similar communication about consumer products, subject to appeals to the courts. Unquestionably, this constitutes legal suppression of free expression. In no other area of public discourse is there legal protection against exposure to falsehood or potential dangers, except for the complicated formula of a personal libel or slander suit. In this instance, libertarians are typically not opposed to such suppressions. In fact, many are likely to demand more restrictive actions. The demands for less restriction have usually come from business groups, ordinarily less oriented to First Amendment freedoms.[5]

The value disputes have been codified in legal form. Generally, advertising has not been considered "expression" under the First Amendment's protection. It can, therefore, be thoroughly controlled to protect "health and safety" without requiring anything like the "clear and present danger" stipulation. Similarly, commercial solicitations from house to house are not afforded the protection of religious and, presumably, political proselytizing.[6] The implication may come as a surprise. The efforts of some types of political publics as well as the acts of particular decision-makers have assigned communication of ideas a higher priority of legitimacy than commercial messages, an unexpected eventuality in our business-oriented society. Since the actual effect on the range of advertising messages has been minimal, the powerful business influencers have not attempted any extensive countercampaigns, with the exception of the present fight on cigarette advertising. Each specific dispute is simply met by the "victims" as each case arises. Even though interested publics may prod the responsible government officials, the decisions are typically *legal* rather than *political*. That is why the role of experts, ascertaining the validity of claims, is inordinately crucial.

In most of the publicized examples, the value conflicts are easily resolved. The desire to protect consumers from dangerous or fallacious assertions simply outweighs all other considerations. Sometimes, however, the facts are not clear-cut, particularly when the issue concerns advertised therapeutic techniques. Several questions are germane: Are the devices proposed helpful, are they actually harmful, or are the claims stated with appropriate caution? Two of the better known cases were those involving the presumed cancer-cure drug, Krebiozen, and Wilhelm Reich's "orgone" treatment.[7] If information about such conceivable "cures" is not widely disseminated, perhaps many people, including professionals, will be ignorant about something which may be very helpful. The decision is usually based on caution, in effect, of suppression of any definitive statements about therapeutic results not backed by substantial scientific evidence. To repeat, this is a unique phenomenon, in terms of both constitutional interpretations and the typical stand of libertarians.

PERSONAL RIGHTS

Media and "Fair Trial"

The conflict between the right to report on trials, or pretrial investigation versus the right to a fair trial—a conflict between the First Amendment, on the one hand, and the Fifth, Sixth, and Fourteenth Amendments, on the other hand—is an obvious dilemma in terms of both legal standards and crucial libertarian values. Any attempt to limit what communication media present constitutes a form of censorship, actually precensorship. Trials are supposed to be "public," with the historic justification that openness would protect the accused from Star Chamber tactics. The recent lesson of secretive administrative proceedings has made this all the more evident. Besides, the functioning of prosecution and judiciary are certainly within the domain of what the public has a right to know. The other side of the argument should be very obvious. "Trial by press" or radio or television has been a meaningful description of what occurred in many publicized cases.[8]

The Supreme Court has reversed several convictions on the grounds of possible prejudicial media publicity. One of the most relevant cases concerned the widely publicized conviction of Dr. Samuel Shephard for murdering his wife, set aside by the Court.[9] Among the reasons given for ordering a new trial were the press accounts of detailed comments by the police and prosecution about the defendant and about possible testimony. As a general admonition, the Court insisted that "legal trials are not like elections, to be won through the use of the meeting hall, the radio and the newspapers." This is the crux of the issue for the First Amendment freedoms. Trials are, in essence, "privileged" types of controversy for which some restriction on communication is in order. This is, in fact, one type of limitation that libertarians may be the first to demand, as shown by the role of the ACLU in the Shephard case.

A series of such incidents prompted proposals for severe legal restrictions on reports of trials, accordingly vigorously opposed by media officials as a dangerous and unwarranted form of censorship. In this instance, a satisfactory compromise has been obtained and the problem relatively "solved." An American Bar Association proposal, which would have placed the legal burden for restriction on law enforcement officials and defense counsels rather than the media, was apparently satisfactory to all concerned, a rare example of "consensus" in this type of sociopolitical problem.[10] In actuality, much of the difficulty has been obviated by the "self-censorship" of the media and, more importantly, by the policies adapted by police and prosecuting offices. Largely motivated by fears of unfavorable higher-court rulings, prosecuting offices both determine official performance and affect the general atmosphere, influencing the concept of what is proper behavior.

Yet potentially prejudicial comments are still communicated in the media, such as the background of an arrestee. In any case, even though the solution to this problem is, atypically, generally acceptable, many difficulties remain. The police attempts to keep radio and television reporters and, even more drastically, cameramen, from various spots at the convention or elsewhere in the city of Chicago during the 1968 Democratic National Convention can be justifiably considered an infringement of the public's right to know about a very pressing set of issues. Nevertheless, reporting and photographing are inevitably selective, and what is presented can be prejudicial to subsequent legal action against either involved citizens or the police.

Libel and Slander

The issues around the questions of libel and slander pose another value conflict for libertarians. The historical record reveals the potential danger to freedom of expression from suits and prosecutions under those headings. When public officials are involved, the history compels libertarians to be cautious about the entire process. Apprehension about possible litigation frequently forces publishers to seek legal advice before printing anything critical of anyone. On the other hand, "malicious" and false information can be injurious to a man's reputation and career, and thus becomes a weapon against his freedom to express himself and join with others. This was part of the intent as well as a frequent result of the "Communist" charges in the 1950's and 1960's. In several famous trials on those grounds, the plaintiff, by securing "compensatory" and punitive damages, was not only monetarily assuaged for personal injury but also, in effect, won the right to continue his previous writing, activity, and so on, without any repetition of the same treatment. The results could be a significant weapon for the victims of McCarthyism.[11]

The question of "group defamation" poses a more agonizing dilemma. Libertarians have been conspicuous in attempts to eliminate unfavorable allegations about any large sector of the population, particularly racial and religious groups. The obvious motivation is the desire to diminish derogatory stereotypes that furnish the justification for prejudice and discrimination.

The decision-makers are usually found somewhere in the judicial process, either judges or juries, although legislators have made some important statutory changes. Juries are, in fact, largely motivated by the instructions of the trial judges, who are, in turn, influenced primarily by the interpretations of appellate courts and the relevant laws. In other words, the legal framework generally determines the nature of the decision in this area, even though citizen jurors are very frequently the decision-makers.

Officially libelous statements are not, by Supreme Court rulings, constitutionally protected utterances.[12] The meaningful applicability of the concept is, however, severely limited. In civil suits the defense has many bulwarks. It can win its case, or at least be required to pay a very minimal sum, on the basis of such criteria as use of quotations, "truth" of statements, the right of "fair comment," or lack of "malicious intent." Finally, recent decisions have proclaimed that the "public life," not only of government officials and candidates for office but also of any person defined as a "public figure," can be fairly readily attacked without fear of a successful libel suit. Only when there is clear-cut evidence of a conscious and malicious use of false information can the plaintiff win his case, as occurred in the suit of Barry Goldwater against Ralph Ginzburg, the publisher of the magazine *In Fact*.[13] (Criminal libel convictions, with actual penalization by the state, are now rare.) According to some interpretations, libel protections are now less necessary because the original purpose, the provision of a legal alternative to private violent feuds, has no contemporary relevance. As a summary statement, the litigants and their attorneys are significant social actors in determining individual decisions, but the custodians of the law—legislators, judges, and possibly bar associations—have determined the general trend, with little intervention by citizen influencers. The direction taken has been "balanced" toward the side of "free expression," with attention to the need for protection against personal defamation limited to special obvious situations.

The question of "group libel" is more complex. The Supreme Court affirmed the right of the government to punish those who communicated certain types of defamatory material about groups on the grounds that these were "fighting words," capable of fomenting disorder, and thus not included within First Amendment strictures. In a ringing dissent in one of these cases, Justice Black warned that such judicial rulings would leave freedom of expression to the caprice of various government officials, a legal expression of the possible peril to civil liberties from suppression of militant opponents of civil rights.[14] Recent court decisions have not satisfied Black's "absolutist" position on this question, but they have restricted the possibility of convictions or civil judgments under group defamation statutes to the patently provocative and consciously malicious utterances, again indicating a judicial trend toward extolling the value of free expression over other considerations.[15]

Other types of noncriminal sanctions against alleged "prejudiced" communication, by nonjudicial governmental action or by private individuals or groups, remain available. This is particularly true of the airways. Among noticeable efforts are the attempts to prevent the specific type of communication (especially if it is a continuing program), either by actions of the station, the Federal Communications Commission, or the removal of a particular commentator from his job. An implicit and sometimes open corollary pressure is for the possible removal of the license from the station or channel. The most publicized recent incident concerned the reading of an alleged "anti-Semitic" poem of a student over the New York FM station, WBAI, accompanied by demands for the removal of the program of the man who read it.[16] The station's defense was that anyone had the right to conduct his own program and the station itself should have autonomy. In actuality, the entire issue was a concomitant of the far-reaching dispute between the New York teachers' union and a governing board of a school community in a black neighborhood. A complicated set of prob-

lems for both civil liberties and civil rights was thus closely enmeshed with a substantive political issue, as is so frequently the
case. For that reason, very little was done—any decision to alter
policy would imply some official stand on this issue.

This situation graphically illustrated the posing of the counter-
values of protection from defamation and the protection of First
Amendment freedoms, for the same station had been harassed, by
both governmental bodies and private individuals, for some of its
program content. The same phenomenon is characteristic of all
similar attempts at eliminating presumed prejudicial communication in all media, by formal and informal pressures. They all
present efforts at some form of censorship, which is generally
thwarted, frequently based upon very divisive clashes of strongly
held values and contending political forces. How serious these
clashes as well as the resulting censorship pressures become depends upon the solution of the substantive questions that under-
line them, especially the problems of black America.

Privacy

The right to privacy is not officially one of the First Amendment freedoms but, as stated by Justice Brandeis many years ago,
it is a basic "silent" freedom, whose violation can be a menace
to freedom of expression and association. Prying into the details
of one's life and person, present and past, obviously tends to
stifle expressions that may, at some time, be proscribed. Furthermore, it stimulates an atmosphere of generic fearfulness and the
emergence of appropriate personalities, as most evident in totalitarian societies. The "McCarthyite" threat to civil liberties was,
primarily, a utilization of this mode of operation, that is, compiling
a dossier on the person under attack. Our analysis of the phenomena further exemplifies the nature of the danger. The invasion
of *privacy* is not the same as the elimination of *secrecy*. In fact,
the most pervasive anti-libertarian results were a product of the
typical *secretive* quality of the processes, the Kafkaesque vista of
the entire situation. That is why the multiplicity of inquiries and
accompanying records by government and private groups is so

ominous. One has so little idea of who is gathering information, what is included, and how it may be used.

For the various reasons indicated earlier, the dossier has become a less prominent political weapon and therefore less of an apparent threat to civil liberties. At the same time, however, the amount of prying has actually magnified in scope and the methods of surveillance become more extensive.[17] Bureaucratization is the quintessential sociological explanation. Private and public bureaucracies demand copious personal data about their employees, "clients," and rivals to achieve the desired predictable, efficient, "smoothly functioning," and successful organization. At the moment, it is not the most conspicuous suppressive device against dissidents, but the potential needs no elaboration. The possible counterchecks include legal and judicial restrictions and pluralistic counterpressures against all aspects of accumulations of personal files. The actual impact on civil liberties depends upon the existing totality of political society, including the type of substantive problems with which it is confronted. Invasions of privacy will not, by themselves, cause any widespread suppression, but they do provide a means for making them more intensive and more pervasive.

This analysis, however, does not cover the only problems associated with the question of privacy. Others involve more definitive value conflicts, often expressed in legal forms. Is privacy of the home more important than the right to propagandize one's religious beliefs or to picket an opponent in a labor dispute? The courts have generally, but not universally, decided in favor of the "preferred position" of freedom of expression. Another complex conflict involves the right of reporters to conceal the sources of their information, in order to be able to tell their stories freely without danger to informants, and the "right to know" who was responsible for such information, especially if it might possibly include "defamatory" material. Apparently, the courts have demanded that such data must be revealed.[18] The "passive" right of privacy, such an important ingredient of freedom of expression and association, is posed against the fear of secrecy, which is also potentially inimical to such freedoms—a dilemma not easily resolved for society or for concerned individuals. The complexities of contemporary society prevent any ready solutions. By themselves, however, such problems present possible "nuisance" rather than "pervasive" threats to civil liberties, as long as the rest of the social-political system in the specific situational context is favorable to the maintenance of freedoms.

CHANNELS

Freedom of expression and association is viable only when some meaningful channel of communication is available. This aspect of current civil liberties problems has asserted itself at several points in this volume but has not been dealt with as such, largely because the emphasis has been on external negative sanctions and the divisive public issues with which they are associated, rather than structural limitations on communication. The latter subject is, nevertheless, pertinent to any attempt at a sociology of civil liberties. It is significant that an extensive account of impediments to the realization of First Amendment freedoms in this country, entitled *The First Freedom,* is mostly a discussion of organization of the mass media.[19]

In a discussion of the mass media, the channels of communication, of course, warrant special attention. In one way or another, they are *scarce* resources. Limitations on availability for certain expressions thus constitute a de facto type of "suppression." For the airways, this is obviously enmeshed with the question of external sanctions, that is, some form of censorship, for the extreme scarcity has meant that these channels are privileged public utilities under legal regulation. Some of this regulation is actually aimed at opening up the media for divergent viewpoints, as in the controversial "equal time" requirements and, to some extent, the vague admonition in federal statutes about "public service functions." But there are also efforts to avoid the "offensive," creating the possibilities of the kinds of disputes discussed in the chapter on censorship and under the heading of slander, which are potentially very restrictive because of the inclusive right of government intervention.

The most recent dispute, and perhaps the one which has prompted most concern among the officials of radio and television, is that over violence in the media, investigated both by a congressional committee and a specially appointed commission. The adamancy of network officials over this type of implied external pressures was quite different from their reactions to the blacklisting drives. Any attempt to intervene in their determination of content, either by the FCC or by congressional action, was striking at something very salient to their interests and values—their control over their programs. The possible value conflict for the interested public over violence in the media is probably more serious than the disputes over obscenity. More people, and more knowledgeable people, are concerned about the effect of the well-documented amount and type of violent action on television in particular. The debate over possible impact is more seriously joined so that sentiment for some type of restraint is more consequential. But any type of action by any branch of government, which, of course, legally "owns" the airways, seems unlikely. Probable hostility on libertarian grounds is only one potential motive for opposition. All the ideologies extolling the rights of "private enterprise" stand opposed.[20]

The more feasible pressure is for more "self-controls" within the industry as is, to some extent, true in a country like Great Britain, with its two publicly owned television channels. There is a "code" for broadcasters, as in the movies, but with little record of any meaningful attempts at enforcement and with essentially trivial admonitions. If seriously defined and administered, the code would then pose the problem of internal censorship, representing the most pressing issue of freedom of expression in the communication media—their internal organization controls. Those who decide what appears are exercising a possible de facto censorship, even though it does not involve any active external restraints. Except for the movies, it is very difficult to document the amount and type of such controls, especially since the question of judgment on matters of taste, significance, and popularity are present. More common is a kind of anticipatory socialization—the creators of communication will simply not present material to certain media officials which is not likely to be accepted. A few recent examples of direct controls are, however, available. The best known recent incident was the cancellation of the very popular Smothers Brothers' program by CBS because the performers had refused to submit tapes of future programs to the network. In one situation, a scheduled show was replaced by a "rerun" because of presumed objectionable material.[21] The entire question of control of "cultural" material thus becomes germane, including all aspects of "popular" and "mass culture," which would take us too far afield. What is relevant to civil libertarians, however, is the fact that, because of the scarcity of resources, certain types of expression can find no other significant outlet.

The range of issues was joined in the dispute over television coverage of the 1968 Democratic National Convention scene. If the networks did, as some have claimed, distort the depiction of events to present a picture unfavorable to Mayor Daley and, presumably, to Hubert Humphrey's candidacy, their combined monopoly of communication channels limited the actual free expression of other positions, at least at that time. If the networks were harassed for their reportorial expressions, the question of external censorship is present. Similarly, pressures against the noncommercial radio station WBAI in New York, already considered under the subject of slander, imply an attempt to thwart the freedom of the station management. But WBAI's choice of programs also involves some rejection of certain types of content, whatever the effort at "balancing," with or without FCC admonitions.

For the wireless media, the usual proposed solution is a variety of stations, the program for a genuinely free and open market of many "sellers" of ideas. This is possibly available in radio but hardly an option for network television, where government control of some sort is necessary. Nevertheless, the nature of such control is not obvious and poses the other dilemma for civil libertarians —government censorship. Rivalry through public and local television is another suggested answer but the question of control over content still remains. Even with more ultrahigh frequency channels, television space remains a scarce resource.

In actuality, divergent viewpoints have received more exposure in the wireless media in recent times than has been typical. The question of "choice," however, is still a problem, for the drive is still for market appeal and the emphasis is on the sensational and bizarre. The antidote is to be found not in particular media as such but in the total society. If pluralistic expression and association are somehow or somewhere available, divergent viewpoints will, in most cases, have some opportunity for wireless media expression. Their "newsworthiness" will compel some attention. (The result may, of course, be a distortion of dissident views or their relegation to the heretical, curious, or quaint. Assaying the resulting impact on popular opinions would require an analysis of the effects of the mass media, obviously beyond the scope of this volume.)

The other mass media in America present strangely divergent trends. As already described, freedom of expression has increased in American motion pictures, partly because of decentralization within the industry. On the other hand, the trend has been in the opposite direction among daily newspapers. The continuing concentration of ownership, the precipitous decline in the number of papers, has been conspicuous for a long time. In 1949, a national commission of scholarly notables issued a report on "A Free and Responsible Press." The findings highlighted the dangers from consolidation of ownership, without any effective controls, but declared that any government intervention would create at least equally dangerous perils for free expression. The best that could be offered was encouragement of rival and preferably nonprofit outlets for opinion and news, and a plea for "responsibility." Despite the comparative innocuousness of the proposals, newspaper editors and publishers vigorously attacked the report because of its findings.[22] If they were, perhaps, motivated by fears of pressures for government censorship, they were at least equally motivated by the challenge they saw to the public image of their businesses.

Nothing resulted from the report, and it has since almost been completely forgotten. It would have been quixotic to expect anything to happen. The structure of control and the economics of the industry, including, as in the wireless media, the possible influence of the advertisers, obviate any solutions. If one accepts the likelihood of bias and the lack of presentation of opposing vistas, particularly in purely "news" reports, the maintenance of freedom of meaningful expression is based on the other outlets in a relatively pluralistic society—other media (books and specialized journalism), personal and organizational communication, which also gets into the media, as well as communicating to people directly.[23] (Wireless media have also become something of an alternative to the press.) Actually, these have been surprisingly sufficient. For instance, "radicalisms" of various kinds were able to obtain a significant following, both in the 1930's and 1960's, without much presentation, at least initially, in the mass media or generally unfavorable attention. As long as there is some avenue of available open communication and as long as there is no external sanction, the dissident voice will be heard. If it has any appeal, it will have its supporters, with some sort of communication by the mass media themselves unless outright censorship is established, an unlikely eventuality in the immediate period in America. And since its audience is "interested," the saliency of the issues to them will, in many cases, act as a counterweight to the numerical preponderance of the casually involved mass audience.

16

Civil liberties in private organizations: the case of the labor unions

In contemporary American society, as in all complex societies, freedom of expression and association is predicated on the existence of a multiplicity of formal, relatively autonomous groups. They are the avenues of meaningful expression, the mechanisms by which liberties can be defended, the buffers between the citizen and the state, and the organized expressions of "pluralism." This motif has been dominant in all our discussions. Because of the proliferation of such formal associations and because of the impact of many of them on the lives of members and society at large, the problem of freedom *within* them has become a serious concern to civil libertarians. It is an area that warrants much more extensive investigation. For instance, the most powerful private group in the country, the private profit-making corporation, does not appear to be an appropriate setting for internal civil liberties, except when these freedoms are protected by some organization of employees.

Unfortunately, it is impossible to attempt any meaningful analysis of most private organizations because there is so little useful material. It is necessary to limit the discussion to one type of group —labor unions. The strong general interest in internal freedom in unions has provided a useful body of material for analysis. Unions, however, are also singled out for attention for other reasons. They constitute a significant type of private organization, probably involving more Americans directly than any other kind of organized group. But a specific examination of civil liberties problems in unions is not prompted merely by this fact or the availability of data, nor is it based upon any contention that abuses are more extensive. As emphasized in many discussions of "union democracy" in general, one expects more from organizations explicitly committed to democratic ideals, for which civil libertarians, both in and outside trade unions, have felt so much kinship. The American Civil Liberties Union, for instance, devoted a major part of its efforts over a long period to establishing the legitimacy of unions, that is, to affirm their civil liberties within the larger society. With conspicuous and dramatic exceptions, particularly in parts of the South, this effort has been achieved. It is, therefore, proper for those with libertarian values to turn at least some of their attention to discussing the question of freedom within unions, usually disassociating such concerns from the substantive issues of collective bargaining or union policy. Assessing a member in order to finance a campaign for a political position with which he disagrees is not a civil liberties question but penalizing him for publicly taking a stand against the union position is. Attention to the problem is further stimulated by the fact that unions are directly associated with jobs and, as we have emphasized at several points, threats of job losses or other work penalties have posed serious challenges to freedom of expression and association in recent times.

It is important to explain again that none of what follows implies that unions are any more suppressive of internal liberties than any similar organizations. But they are more important to their members than most organizations and are formally, and in their ideological pronouncements, "democratic organizations." For our purposes, they are also unique in other ways. The description of an ideal libertarian model for unions is quite complex. To what extent and in what way can members be permitted to organize factions within the union and what internal resources should be made available to them to present their views? The constitution of the International Brotherhood of Electrical Workers, hardly one of the "worst" examples in this respect, expressly forbids holding "outside meetings" in which union business is discussed and bars printed solicitations in the behalf of candidates in elections. The justification is the combat mobilization feature of unions, in essence, their resemblance to a permanent garrison society. The typical charge against those who violate such provisions is "dual unionism."

Meaningful freedom of expression implies access to communication with fellow citizens; freedom of association includes the right to organize at all times about any question, including opposition to incumbent leadership. The latter is, within a few legal strictures, assumed to be inviolate in civil society; the former may be limited by insufficient resources, which is, except for radio and television, typically outside the scope of formal legal provisions. But in the unions all formal communication and association are within the domain of their regulations. The ability to organize to elect candidates is by sanction of the union. Even when the right of speech at meetings is generally upheld, it may in fact be curtailed by such things as the formal agenda or by the inability of members to plan their comments in advance because of lack of prior information.

Do opposition members, furthermore, have the right to use the union press to express their positions or to use union mailing lists for mailing expressions of their opinion? Different unions have different regulations, but restriction is the more prevailing tendency and has been defined as a union option by court decision, as long as it is "reasonable" and "equally" applied to all.[1] In other words, an analysis of civil liberties within unions must extend beyond the search for restraints to an examination of the availability of mechanisms for free expression and association.

Such substantive rights are even more closely intertwined with procedural rights than in the general society. In fact, most publicized violations of "due process" within unions have been directed at dissenters, and the sanctions available to a union leadership are in some ways more inclusive. The union member, or group of members, is afforded some protection against restrictions and authoritarian abuse by the fact that union internal operations are, to some extent, regulated by the government. Such legislation as the Wagner National Labor Relations Act of 1935 and its subsequent amendments, the Landrum-Griffin Act of 1959, and various state laws contain provisions asserting the rights of members within their organizations. Under such legislation, administrative bodies like the United States Department of Labor, the National Labor Relations Board, and similar state bodies can and have occasionally intervened in defense of individual unionists and groups of unionists in opposition to the decisions of the organization and its leadership. Actually, the efforts of these government agencies has turned out to be minimal. In this area, only the courts have provided a significant check on some types of suppressive behavior.[2]

FEATURES WHICH LIMIT INTERNAL CIVIL LIBERTIES

The analysis which follows is predicated on an appreciation of the many endemic features that militate against civil liberties in these organizations, with their professed democratic values and the genuinely democratic orientation of much of the leadership and membership. The extreme anxiety of many paid officials about losing their jobs, which may extend to an almost paranoid fear of any opposition, has received sufficient attention.[3] If the leadership is "corrupt" in any definition of the term, suppression of disagreement will be much more vigorous. As potential or actual combat organizations, unions must discipline members. Thus, administrative agencies and the courts have affirmed their right to penalize members for crossing picket lines, for working under nonunion conditions, for making private agreements with employers, or even for refusing to pay assessments. In effect, these actions constitute illegal acts under union law. But can and should unions penalize members who openly attack the union or some union position, or, for that matter, the union leaders? In essence, can "unpatriotic utterances," often specified in such vague accusations as "causing dissension" and "creating disharmony," or "conduct unbecoming a union member," be punished? Court decisions have varied, but the general tendency is to permit penalties for specific anti-union acts in crucial situations, behavior which could be described as "treason," but not for "seditious libel," that is, "slandering" officials, and so forth. Nevertheless, members continue to be penalized under the latter charge, at least until there is a specific court ruling following an actual suit.[4]

On closer examination, an emphasis on the combative, quasi-garrison character of unions as the major explanation for internal suppression may be too facile. The manifest justifications of those who suppress may be too readily accepted as the actual latent cause. In fact, periods of external strain have often been the times of greatest internal freedom because of specific historical circumstances, the need to mobilize support, and/or the strength of opposition. External "peace" may, on the other hand, occasion extensive internal suppression. An entrenched leadership, administering a regularized and smoothly operating collective bargaining process, is fearful of dissent, especially if the arrangement with management includes any type of "corruption." In other words, the tendency toward close administrative harmony in union-management relations can be inimical to the liberties of union members. Management, adjusted to and preferring this type of relation, may not only approve internal suppression but may also actually collaborate unofficially by harassing dissidents on the job or by agreeing to collusive arrangements to discharge them.

In addition, unique features of American unions make the maintenance of civil liberties more difficult. The doctrine of exclusive bargaining, legitimized by the government in such laws as the Wagner Act and institutionalized among unions by "no raiding" agreements, means that a threatened or punished unionist has nowhere else to go in his trade. He cannot shop for another union. This has its ideological concomitant, which is also codified into union law. "Dual unionism" is considered one of the most serious personal accusations and grounds for formal discipline. By using a fairly strict interpretation, court decisions have accepted the charge as a valid reason for punishment but union officials have often successfully attempted to stretch the allegation to any effort at internal organization in opposition to the incumbent officials.[5]

The adjudication process and the sanctions available, the area of procedural rights, typically present further difficulties for the dissenter "brought up on charges" by the union leadership. It is common practice for the officials who made the charges to select the trial committee that judges the dissenters. Furthermore, decisions can be typically appealed only to the officials themselves, who thus, in several ways, are both prosecutors and judges. This obvious lack of any independent judiciary or jury is frequently accompanied by a lack of procedural safeguards, such as those listed in the Bill of Rights—precise charges, right to confront and cross-examine witnesses, obtain witnesses in one's own behalf, right of counsel, and so on. Rules of evidence are unclear and frequently unstated. Although none of this is applicable to all unions, at least it is a fairly widespread picture. Actual expulsion from the union is not too common. For one thing, the Taft-Hartley Law of 1947 stipulates that no union member can be expelled except for nonpayment of dues although some de facto removal from membership does occur under special circumstances, such as assignment to "second-class" membership status. But the range of available formal sanctions against dissidents is extensive. The dissenter may be removed from office (elected or appointed), denied certain membership rights for a specified period, be placed on probation, fined, and so on.

The informal sanctions available to incumbent officials can be more serious and more difficult to disclose and combat. The loss of jobs or blacklisting may be very subtle and without any definitive relationship to penalization for the opposition. The dissident may continue to get other jobs, which are, however, much inferior. He may be denied the use of grievance machinery. All these actions are officially barred by decisions of government agencies, but they are difficult to prove and require the sophisticated and expensive process of litigation. Finally, the use of illegal and extralegal actions, prompted and organized by the officials, even though less evident than in earlier periods and sometimes exaggerated by commentators, has been well documented—threats to self and family, physical assaults, or even actual murder, as in the story of two murdered officials of the painters' union on the West Coast a few years ago.[6]

What are the recourses for the punished dissident? A meaningful appeals system within his own union may not exist, and the possibility of appealing to the AFL-CIO itself is almost nonexistent, despite its official formulation of a code for ethical practices. He may mobilize the support of some of his colleagues, which can either help or hurt his cause in specific instances. Ultimately, however, he may be forced to go outside for help—to various government agencies, particularly the courts. But this requires initiative, effort, time, and expense, even if he is assisted by others. Initially, he is first required to go through all the complicated procedures of appeals within the union. Administrative agencies, like the Department of Labor and the National Labor Relations Board, rarely offer much help. As a result of a member's complaint about malpractices, the Department of Labor may set aside an internal union election and the National Labor Relations Board an election to certify the collective bargaining agent. But neither is likely to intervene to protect the member from individual penalties, even if the penalization is, by official allegation, a punishment for making the complaint to the government agency in the first place. The courts offer a better avenue for redress but this requires a formal suit, with all the obvious cost and delay that this entails. The courts may, in turn, send the entire case back to the union itself or to an administrative agency. Meanwhile, the aggrieved union member may be further harassed by official union action for going to the courts. In any case, unofficial sanctions are difficult to prove to the satisfaction of judicial criteria.

From all that has been said, it would seem that the possibilities for genuine internal civil liberties in unions is slight. It is easy to report enough recent cases of flagrant abuses to document this point. A few examples are illustrative.[7] Several occurred in the International Association of Machinists, whose president at that time was chairman of the AFL-CIO Ethical Practices Committee. Supporters of a dissident vice-president were fired from appointed union offices and charged with making "false and malicious statements" to the United States Department of Labor, the accused to be tried by a committee selected by the president of the union. In the same union, a member was expelled because his accusation that a district official was corrupt was judged a "slander." In the New York City painters' union, one local distributed handbills against the district president, attacking him for refusing to sanction a strike against wage cuts. As a result, several of the leaders of the local union were tried by a district committee; some were removed from office whereas others were barred from union activity.

Among the West Coast longshoremen (ILWU), a group of "B" men, a second-class citizenship status, protested the fact that they had not been promoted to "A" men. Many of the protesters were then fired with the active collaboration of management; there were no formal hearings, clear statement of charges, or any other procedures of due process. After an opposition candidate for secretary-treasurer of the National Maritime Union was physically beaten, he and a running mate were summarily "dropped" from the union rolls. (A few months earlier, the Department of Labor had decided to initiate action to void the election in which they were defeated.) One of the most dramatic cases was that of a member of a building service employees local in New York City, who opposed a dues increase back in 1949.

As a result, he lost his job, which also meant evacuation from his home where he had been a building superintendent. His persistent requests to government agencies resulted in several investigations. Officially, his charges of corruption against local officials have been sustained. But, meanwhile, he has frequently been threatened and actually assaulted physically, has not been able to get a job in the local, and has lost his pension rights.

These accounts are not offered as descriptions of prevailing patterns. They are presented as concrete illustrations of the previously listed types of factors that can limit civil liberties in unions—lack of procedural safeguards, union collaboration with management, opposition defined as sedition, penalties for appealing to government agencies, and the numerous official and unofficial sanctions available to the leadership. The denial of civil liberties to dissidents can then further reinforce the conditions that enhance suppression. The silencing of opponents removes the possibility of internal pluralistic checks on tendencies to stifle liberties.

To what extent is this portrayal of internal suppression a general statement about American unions? Is it true that unions are generally free and that these descriptions apply only to a minority, which is a significant number but still a deviant group? It would be extremely difficult to answer these questions with the best data conceivable. At present, it would be absolutely impossible and any attempt would be meaningless. There are too many varied unions—international, regional, and local.

In any case, such an assessment is not within the purpose of our discussion. Our objective has been to disclose the factors that tend to restrain or permit freedom of expression and association. Thus, it is only necessary at this point to indicate that relative freedom does exist in many unions. On the level of the international union, it is indicated by the recent incidence of contested elections for the major offices.[8] Some have been meaningful elections, with an actual turnover in office, whereas others have been merely "show" contests, with the incumbents able to use various mechanisms to secure their election. But this is beyond the scope of our analysis. Our interest is in "freedom from"—

the ability to communicate and organize dissent. Whether this will lead to the dissenters' ability to "win," that is, to gain office or establish policy, requires another type of analysis.

The situation in local unions is even more pertinent to this discussion, for it is here, close to the immediate job situation, that members are most likely to express disagreements. Whatever the level of "participation" and actual "membership control," studies of local unions do indicate frequent disputes and few penalties for the disputants.[9] One investigation of four large local unions in a major city, which was expressly oriented toward the question of "union democracy," was illustrative.[10] Few instances of contested elections were reported as well as few mechanisms for meaningful internal "pluralistic" groupings, but at the same time there was almost no evidence of any internal disciplining of dissidents. This is probably typical of many local unions. Because of the persistent fear of factionalism, internal official groupings were, with significant exception, not permitted or confined to election periods when they were usually informally organized. But this is of a different order than the forceful silencing of a critic or an opponent.

As a final support for the contention that the civil liberties situation in unions is not as bleak as implied earlier, it is interesting that, in all the cases of abuses described, the outcome was not the disappearance of dissent. Whatever the mechanisms used, opponents were capable to some degree of continuing their opposition. A review of the factors that can and do enhance the possibilities of internal civil liberties in unions becomes the next obvious section of this discussion.

FEATURES WHICH ENHANCE INTERNAL CIVIL LIBERTIES

The elements that can bolster civil liberties can be grouped into those features *internal* and *external* to the union itself. Under the first heading, the formal union structure and its stipulation in the constitution cannot be casually dismissed. Although many union constitutions are hardly acceptable to civil libertarians and also such formal provisions can obviously be circumvented, they do offer protection in many cases. They can and have helped assure free expression at meetings, some form of procedural safeguards, and have been utilized as a legal basis for court determination that a member's rights have been violated. In a few unions, the internal judicial system is quite extensive, with some form of due process and relatively independent judiciary, that is, trial by people other than union officers. The most developed example is that of the citizen's Public Review Board of the United Automobile Workers, whose decisions are binding on the union. Something similar has been adopted by several other unions.[11]

As already explained, internal opposition of some sort does exist in many unions at different levels, even though few approach the structural arrangement of the International Typographers Union, with its regularized two-party system.[12] Such dissent, of course, also requires appropriate values—of leaders, a significant number of members, or both. Again, the situation varies widely between and even within unions. Attitudes unfavorable to the maintenance of civil liberties are undoubtedly widespread. Yet many officials do want to be "democratic" in this sense, even if sometimes primarily for reasons of public relations, and, whatever the "apathy" so often noted, many unionists do desire and fight for internal freedoms. At one time, they were likely to incorporate such beliefs as part of a general political ideology. More recently, many unionists simply demand their rights as well as those of others because this is what they expect in and of unions, because they have been socialized to such values in a democratic society, and because assertion of dissident views is sometimes necessary in terms of their self-interests. Whatever the overall generalizations about union trends, noted by many observers, the number of rank-and-file individual members who vigorously struggle for civil liberties within their unions, often as a function of their demands for satisfaction of personal grievances, is a conspicuous phenomenon of recent times.[13] The earlier accounts of abuses are, on closer examination, a verification. There would have been no suppressions if there had been no dissidence, and the response of the affected "victims" was in most instances a continuation of their dissenting activity within and outside the union. (Again, the question of *motivation* to express oneself and associate actively with co-thinkers is shown to be a significant variable.)

In the story of the machinists' union, the staff personnel who were fired for their disagreements filed suit in court. The dissenting vice-president, whose opposition had started all the trouble, was subsequently elected secretary-treasurer of one of the regional organizations of the union. Those subject to discipline in the New York painters' union were generally successful in their appeals to the court, were able to get the reelection of the incumbent secretary-treasurer set aside, and ultimately to get their own man elected. The "B" men among the West Coast longshoremen have continued their campaign for reinstatement and equal status with extensive support from "A" members of their own local. What these examples illustrate is that the values of these victims of suppression prompt them to resist. With the help of those who are like-minded in some manner and the use of a variety of structural mechanisms available, they can become *influencers* who thwart oppressive acts or, if successful in maintaining or obtaining union office or establishing policy, the actual decision-makers. The result is, at least immediately, a more libertarian situation.

Of course, the attitudes and activities of interested members may not be enough, particularly because of the common strictures against regularized internal groupings. It has become increasingly necessary to look for *external* help in defense of internal liberties, either to decision-making government bodies or to interested citizens who can become influencers. As previously discussed, government administrative agencies have not been very helpful. Thus, the Landrum-Griffin Act of 1959, administered by the Department of Labor, has meant little to unions. Originally described as a "bill of rights" for union members, it has done little to protect them, just as it has hardly proven to be the "union-busting" legislation charged by opponents. Suppressions and arbitrary discipline have rarely been prevented or rescinded under its provisions.[14] Court decisions have, in this instance, provided the only significant government defense of individual liberties. Basing their opinions on a variety of statutes, judicial precedents, traditions of common law, and the union constitutions themselves, federal and state courts have frequently protected the rights of dissidents. Much of this has already been described but can be further amplified. "Slander" has been voided as a justification for punishment. Disagreement with officials has been defined as insufficient grounds for firing appointed staff personnel, and suspended members have been reinstated. Penalizations for appeals to government agencies have been set aside.

The "outside" individuals and groups, the influencers, who generally define themselves as "friends of labor," have been very helpful. By coming to the scene with "clean hands," they participate by publicizing abuses and demanding redress and, above all, by assisting in the complicated process of appeal to court suits, which, among other things, eases the aggrieved members' financial burdens. The list includes political figures (in and out of office), intellectuals, and journalists. One conspicuous instrument for uncovering violations of unionists' liberties and propagandizing for their elimination is the widely circulated newsletter, "Union Democracy in Action," from which much of our material is gathered. Since adjudication has become a principal method for redress and, as a corollary, for the prevention of future violations, those who aid in litigation have been very important—ad hoc "citizen" organizations, permanent bodies like the Workers Defense League, or individual lawyers who frequently volunteer their services without pay.[15] The affected "victims" and their collaborating work colleagues, however, are, probably more than in any of the other problem areas discussed, the singularly crucial social actors. Often without such external help, rank-and-file members, by their collective vigorous assertion of what they consider their rights (which may require a lengthy and costly legal process), have, in a significant number of situations, scotched attempts to stifle their freedom of expression and association.

In summary, despite the many conditions that militate against civil liberties within labor unions, they do exist and are likely to be maintained because of structural features within some unions, value commitments of some officials and members, and influence of government and private outsiders. Beliefs, laws, and structures for enforcing freedoms as well as pressures furnish the basic ingredients for civil liberties in unions, as in the larger society. Above all, the pluralistic counterstructures set up by dissident unionists, often very informally, provide the major bases for their defense of their civil liberties.

17

Some general propositions

The previous chapters analyzed recent and current American problems associated with freedom of expression and association, always attempting to use our analytical model as an orienting guide. Examining the specific areas under investigation was obviously not the only reason for this attempt. The object was to glean some general principles from this material and to test and further develop a few basic contentions.

The analysis of specific problem situations can now be more clearly viewed against a general historical backdrop, particularly in this country. Assuming a sufficient acceptance of libertarian values, however low in saliency and readily supplanted by other values, and a legal juridical system in some measure in accord with those values, the maintenance or thwarting of these civil libertics is seen as an outgrowth of specific *sets of decisions*. Such an approach offers a convenient analytical tool but a literal interpretation is replete with analytical dangers. To consider historical trends a mere cumulation of discrete events permits a casual slipping into a nominalist *reduction* fallacy. Social-political developments are global phenomena, the determinants of which are macroscopic factors rather than individual actions and concrete events.

Our hoped-for sociology of civil liberties, with its attention to dynamic processes in society, must then include a concern with modes of historical interpretation, particularly the contrast between the episodic details and the overall trends. At one extreme, one can adopt Tolstoy's vista and insist that history is nothing but the unfolding of a providential plan within which the situational details, however superficially consequential, are trival manifestations. On the other hand, one can accept the dictum of many historiographers that each historic happening, however significant, is something unique, resulting from so many converging factors, some of which are quite "accidental," that any generalizing formulas are meaningless. Both of these approaches define social science as all but impossible. A modification of each approach suggests our own interpretive scheme. There are master trends in societal development, even if many of them are limited to particular societies and historical epochs. In some types of inquiry, a concentration on these trends is sufficient for a cogent analysis. For the subject under discussion, it is hardly adequate. For instance, attempting to correlate the ebb and flow of civil liberties in American history with any other single historical trend would be a fruitless endeavor.

We must return to our analytical model, with its multivariate *field* approach. Each set of decisions relevant to civil liberties is a result of a confluence of many social factors that can be located, many of them representing major trends, namely, bureaucratization, or relatively continuing features of national life, such as the garrison society. The state of civil liberties does depend on a cumulation of these decisions but within the context of these social factors and their dynamic changes. In essence, we are asserting that man is neither a passive tool of social history nor a completely autonomous architect of his social development. To paraphrase an old philosophic dictum, men make their own history but only within the framework of social-historic constraints. Particularly in the areas and the times we are discussing, the option for consequential choice is always available, however structured by the social-political reality.

The McCarthyite suppressions were a reflection of a major trend, the garrison society, and a general historical situation, the cold war. But specific social actors, operating within and motivated by particular values, structures, and roles, were responsible for them. Similarly, other people, whose behavior can be similarly analyzed, collaborated with, accepted, or opposed them. Ultimately, some of them, working within a changed historic situation and both assisted by and encouraged by changes in some structures and values, terminated the McCarthyite phenomenon. Historical tendencies were conducive to all of these events but nothing was inevitable. In a more complex fashion, a similar analysis can be made of the still unsettled current "legitimacy crisis," and the discussions of other civil liberties problems are all based upon formulations that are somewhat akin. The distinction between "nuisance" and "pervasive" suppressions should now be clearer. The actions in "nuisance" situations, however affected by historical developments, are usually not in accord with any general historical trend and thus their overall impact is minimal. The "pervasive" suppressions, however, are implementations of historical trends, or rather of one of the several directions in which these trends can be steered.

All this suggests a further elaboration of the "indivisibility of freedom" principle. Evidence from the whole range of human history indicates that the assertion of the right of free expression and association tends to extend to all branches of society. This is not necessarily true when these rights are curtailed in some manner. "Nuisance" suppressions do not usually lead to widespread suppression. Even "pervasive" restraints, whatever their other effects, do not produce a thoroughly authoritarian society unless a relatively libertarian and democratic social-political-cultural system is completely altered.

Freedom of expression and association has been an intrinsic part of the American system, at least since the founding of the Republic, despite all the limitations, restrictions, obstacles, and problems. Some of the reasons for this have been explained. One can generally exercise one's freedom if one wants to, unless somebody stops him. The types of external restraints, the suppressions, vary with the situation, roles, values, and structures responsible as do the methods and structures for combating them. In summarizing recent American problems, a few general observations emerge.

1. The most serious threats to civil liberties have been those associated with the post-World War II garrison society. Suppression need not be an automatic concomitant of a nation mobilized for external conflict, as witness the case of the United States during World War II. A permanent orientation, however, represents a more severe danger to internal freedoms. The danger does not necessarily imply a completely authoritarian, let alone totalitarian, society, as some casual interpretations of the garrison concept suggest. Certainly, the United States has never, under any conditions, actually approached such a state.

2. The nature of the continuing conflict with the enemy, the cold war with the Communist world, has its unique qualities aside from its creation of the garrison society. Particularly when the struggle "hottens up," as during the wars in Korea and Vietnam, many perceive an ideological component and a foe or series of foes, presumed to be fanatical in the drive toward world conquest. But this was also true of World War II. To explain the McCarthyite strictures of the 1950's and the potential diminution of civil liberties from the current legitimacy crisis requires the addition of very specific situational elements—the appeal of the facile conspiracy explanation in the earlier period and the large-scale vigorous opposition to national policy today. Neither was present during the many "crises" of the early 1960's, which is one explanation for the absence of any pervasive threats to political freedoms at that time.

3. Determining and describing threats to civil liberties is not a simple task. The varied restraints, by government or private

groups, can be very complex and subtle and somewhat different for each problem area. The legal sanctions by the state, by imprisonment or a costly fine, have been a significant deprivation only for a few people affected by McCarthyism and for some victims of the present legitimacy crisis, although this can be the fate of many in the near future. In almost all the problem areas considered, the most common penalization or threatened penalization has been economic. Most prominent, of course, is the loss of a job and sometimes the resultant destruction of a career. In the present situation, this may take the form of loss of a college scholarship. Those businessmen who decide to suppress, particularly in the media, have been prompted by incoherent fears about loss of markets. The peril of job and career loss from dissident communication or association has been a significant deterrent to freedoms in this historical situation, one of both affluence and the emphasis on economic and job security. What one can lose looms very large. The right of free expression and association has therefore been so closely intertwined with job rights—in the loyalty-security programs, media blacklisting, academia, and internal union liberties—just to mention the most obvious examples.

4. Libertarian values, one of the most prevalent explanations for the relative presence or absence of civil liberties, are significant, although hardly singularly all important. Whatever the anti-libertarian attitudes revealed, the changes from time to time, and the low priority for much of the population, a sizable sector does possess some *general* adherence to the principle of free expression and association. Even the opinion surveys, which disclose so many anti-libertarian tendencies, show this to be in the case. This is particularly true of specific social actors who, by role prescription or other motivation, have been involved in disputes that relate to civil liberties problems in some way. Perhaps even more important is the maintenance of the desire for dissent, for which civil freedom is a necessary condition, throughout the McCarthyite period and much more evident since then. Suppression engenders quietude, which limits the motivation for dissidence and the avail-

ability of dissident ideas and colleagues, but never that thoroughly in recent America. In each of the problem areas considered, self-restraint has been a product of a particular type of external constraint. The McCarthyite suppressions were commonly accepted because of the absence of a politicalized atmosphere that would encourage meaningful opposition. Despite the prevalent political blandness, however, many a potential victim would still have been sufficiently motivated to talk and, more importantly, to participate and join, if not for the apprehension about possible suppression in the form of a threat to his job and career.

Of course, many did not yield—potential victims who maintained their values, actual victims who fought back, influencers who defended them and strove to change policy, and even some decision-makers who resisted the pressures for suppressive policies in some way. Since the McCarthyite controls were scarcely directed at ideas per se, very little effort at ideological affirmation was necessary for those who maintained any strong values. McCarthyism did have its lasting effects, to which we will return later. But the essential adherence to a democratic and more or less libertarian system of belief, with all the qualifications so often stipulated, remained. The value groundings for widespread public dissent in the later period were present and ready to emerge under the proper stimulus. Similarly, the analysis of other problem areas —censorship, academic freedom, and internal union fredom— indicated a sufficient adherence to First Amendment principles among many people, both as a general formula and as a justification of one's own rights, in some cases assuming a very high saliency for the social actors.

5. Civil liberties problems are closely enmeshed with substantive issues. The question of job rights is one obvious example. Academic freedom disputes are also closely tied in with such subjects as university government, interpersonal relations, and so on. The current crisis of legitimacy is directly related to attitudes and postures toward the war in Vietnam, the conditions of black America, the structure and policies of universities, and so

forth. The other problems lend themselves to similar analysis. Extricating the civil liberties aspects is a necessary analytical device, an abstract isolation of one dependent variable for better comprehension of the reality, but hardly an accurate description of the total reality. Too many discussions of civil liberties are not attentive to this complexity.

6. The legal-judicial features are significant but are not the all-important variables so commonly assumed, nor are their origins or impact subject to simple interpretations. They are one species of political decision and the bases for those decisions. Our own analyses buttress the long-range historical evidence that formalized and "just" structures and processes, resting on some form of due process, are essential for all civil liberties. But the statutes, administrative procedures, and judicial rulings under which they operate result from political processes—the perceptions and values of political role incumbents, the myriad types of pressures, the situational components, and so on. Those which are relevant to civil liberties are not a carbon-copy reflection of the libertarian or anti-libertarian attitudes of politicians or of any general public consensus. This is also true of court rulings, particularly of judicial review by appellate courts. Why judges rule as they do is one of the most difficult questions to answer and may be quite different for different areas under the civil liberties heading. In this instance, their legal philosophies in addition to their general value positions are probably very crucial, but political pressures and situational factors undoubtedly also play a part.

The impact of laws and administrative directives obviously depends on how they are executed, which is also determined by the types of factors listed above. The role of the courts, however, is a particularly important ingredient in this area. Appellate courts have rarely voided anti-libertarian laws and executive rules except those of a "nuisance" variety. But judges have sometimes effectively limited their meaning by procedural restrictions and interpretations about their applicability to specific situations, usually in terms of the Bill of Rights. For instance, court decisions have made most of the provisions of the McCarran Act of 1950 inoperative. On the other hand, some rulings have covered laws which had become largely irrelevant. In some situations, when the number of social actors meaningfully involved is unusually small and when the saliency for most publics is especially low, the courts have an inordinately crucial role, as in the area of "obscenity" censorship.

All legal stipulations, no matter by whom, also assume an aura of legitimacy, affecting not only all people who make legal decisions but also the opinions of the general public and the behavior of all others involved in the decision-making process. The Supreme Court thus becomes the "public educator" about what is permissible and what is outside the bounds of the values and formal restrictions of the Bill of Rights.

7. Decisions on civil liberties questions are political decisions, and the general fate of civil liberties is thus part of the political process. Their defense, therefore, requires more than the appropriate values of political decision-makers or the amorphous general public. Someone, for some reason, must want to maintain or extend these liberties and does something about it. Properly motivated and placed elites, however one interprets the term, do not seem to be the bulwarks that many commentators expect or hope for. An assessment of the controversy specified at the beginning of the volume is now in order. Civil liberties in contemporary American society, and in current complex societies generally, are not based upon the existence of the pluralism of self-contained elites but on political *conflict,* involving all those who are interested in whatever way and with whatever motivation. The maintenance of freedom requires people who are ready to do something to make it viable, and sufficient resources, accesses to decision-making processes, and the ability to appeal to the values and interests of wider publics to achieve their aims. The relative absence of any of these factors in their opponents, that is, those who favor some sort of oppression, can also determine the amount and type of freedom that exists. (Both sides, of course, have to

work within the situational context.) This is the common, quintessential finding of all the previous analyses.

8. The motivations on either side are, to a great extent, not directly related to pro- or anti-libertarian sentiments per se. The relevant social actors are frequently involved in order to defend or extend interests and values that are tangential to civil liberties questions. Culling the various analyses for available illustrations could produce a very extensive list of examples, and only a few need be mentioned. The various McCarthyites, whatever else impelled them, were bent on enhancing their political careers or at least making a full-time job of "anti-Communism." Administrators of the loyalty-security programs were, as much as anything else, responding to the bureaucratic pressures and restraints of their organizations. Union leaders defended the rights of "suspect" members because that is their essential function. (Note again the importance of job and career features.) Many trustees supported academic freedom for professors because it was necessary in order to retain and recruit quality personnel. The media executives yielded to blacklisting pressures because of anxieties about possible losses to their businesses. The movie officials accepted censorship for a long time for the same reason, and they effectively ended censorship in order to regain the audience lost to television and foreign films. The contestants in the current legitimacy crisis on either side assume their positions on the basis of a wide range of values that are crucial to them.

An analysis of civil liberties problems must also accent the latent consequences of whatever decisions are adopted. The cumulative effect on the general atmosphere is obviously important, as already elaborated at several points. Continuing suppressions produce other resultants. McCarthyite strictures helped reinforce the prevalent political blandness and were thus partly responsible for the "mindlessness" of the contemporary "new left," emerging on the political scene without a continuing heritage. Movie censorship vitiated movie content, and book censorship made literary classics unavailable to much of the reading public.

Denial of academic freedom deprived universities and their students of great scholars. The McCarthyite atmosphere encouraged the conservative bureaucrat rather than the autonomous official, particularly in the State Department. According to some commentators, the result was a scarcity of adequate information about many world problems. In other words, the importance of freedom as an *instrumental* value, its significance for the attainment of highly prized individual and collective ends, is borne out by the empirical evidence.

9. The rationally ordered *Weltanschauung,* most clearly symbolized by bureaucratic organization, is potentially both beneficial and very inimical to civil liberties. The attendant impersonality and formality can, as stated in John Roche's formulation, create a system of regularized justice.[1] In the problem areas under review, systems of job security such as those under union contracts and academic tenure regulations were fitting examples. Since suppressions were related to job pressures to such a large extent, any mechanism that ensures job status, that is, provides for removal only through formalized methods of due process, becomes an acutely important protective device against arbitrary harassment of the dissident or potentially dissident.

Several of the analyses also substantiate the many anti-libertarian tendencies typical of bureaucratic modes, especially those of the McCarthyite impact on civil liberties. They included inability of organizational personnel to question the objectives of the policies they administer; defensiveness about organizational decisions; secrecy of operations; rigid and fearfully conformist personnel; and the monolithic facade presented to all those affected by its operations. Widespread invasions of personal privacy become a frequently reported concomitant of the bureaucratic style. The most effective type of "antidote" to these features of bureaucracy is some form of pluralistic check, that is, some kind of internal or external countervailing force capable of resisting or even opposing the endemic "straight-line" hierarchal controls. For instance, the "evils" of the loyalty-security programs, the most blatant example of restrictions on freedoms by bureaucratic mechanisms, could be and were countered by some of the following: congressional committees (despite the fact that so many "liberal" analysts of the time cast Congress as the major villain); the courts; lawyers handling the cases of victims; journalists exposing glaring abuses; civil liberties organizations; the formal and informal associates of the "victims"; and the aroused political publics.

10. Clarity of values and perceptions makes a political issue, including one involving civil liberties, more salient. Those defending such liberties, either for themselves or others, will thus be motivated toward more vigorous actions. The psychological "field" of the particular situation, as well as the personal dispositions of the defenders, helps determine the degree of clarity or ambiguity. A regularized and predictable decision-making process, particularly one with juridical safeguards, is one of the elements that produces relative clarity. Diffuse anxieties from incomprehensible processes and sometimes people that cannot be located encourage submission to external restraints. "Big Brother" becomes more ominous when he is more anonymous. That is why civil libertarians are so conspicuously oriented toward orderly legal processes. This also explains why the model of bureaucratic organization found in administrative manuals can be beneficial to such freedoms and why existing operating bureaucracies, with their mysterious inner lives, are actually so inimical. In our analyses, McCarthyite suppressions were enhanced in large measure by the rampant vagueness of all that occurred to those personally involved as well as to the apprehensive publics. When the situation became more regularized and comprehensible, as in judicial and quasi-judicial settings, resistance to suppressions was more feasible.

11. Conflict is necessary to the maintenance of freedom of expression and association. Serious conflict, however, especially if it poses any questions of legitimacies and intense value conflict or the needs of a garrison society, may spur suppressions. No formula can go beyond this simple declaration and readily determine how much conflict is too much. It all depends on the "inter-

nal health" of society, a criterion very difficult to clarify and beyond the immediate possibility of this discussion. One must also reiterate an earlier proposition: that internal freedoms can be maintained in a "crisis" situation because, whatever the other motivations, suppressions will only exacerbate the crisis. Again, it becomes a matter of the decisiveness of the crisis in the eyes of relevant social actors and supporting publics. The comparative lack of external restraints in the current legitimacy crisis is, at least partially, a result of the desire to maintain civil peace. The demands for more restrictions are a product of the greater fears of some about the potential impact of that crisis.

12. A long-time popular ideological stance holds that freedoms are primarily threatened by "big government" that is far off and that control by small-scale local units is the major defense of liberties. Recently, both the "radical right" and the "new left" have popularized this new version of what can be appropriately labeled as neo-Populist, misplaced Jeffersonianism. As Jefferson's colleague, James Madison, pointed out so forcefully, the tyranny of a "small government" can be more complete than that of a larger body, for it may provide less of an option for either pluralistic insulation or pluralistic conflict.[2] American history offers many striking illustrations. Even if many have exaggerated the role of the Supreme Court as the bastion of civil liberties, this body of nine men, presumably far removed from "community control," has been instrumental in maintaining freedom of expression and association. Other highly organized national groups have also been important in protecting victims, such as trade unions. Civil liberties fundamentally rest on neither strategic elites nor "grass-roots" mandates but on some variant of competitive politics and the rules for their operation. Both are more likely to be of a type that would enhance freedoms in a *macroscopic* political system.

13. From what can be defined as the opposite vantage point, those who focus on some concept of the thesis of the "mass society" and the apparent accompanying tendency toward "con-

formity" present some cogent insights but do not offer a sufficient basis for a sociological analysis. A manipulated populace is less likely to want to express itself and organize with others and may not even possess the requisite knowledge and skills for meaningful communication of ideas. The "brainwashed" may be unable to offer any significant contribution, verbally or actively, to the solution of substantive problems. But what emerges from our analyses is supported by recent events in other parts of the world—enough people will try to exercise an equivalent of First Amendment freedoms *unless restrained by external sanctions.* The experiences of totalitarian countries are very pertinent. In opposition to the dire predictions of an automatically docile population, the easing of the threat of punishment is followed by widespread dissent, both personal and organized. A controlled society obviously limits and steers the content of that dissidence. But the most developed mechanisms of ideological mobilization have not, at least up to now, prevented the quest for divergent viewpoints in any complex society. In American society, as long as it remains relatively "open," whatever the impact of suppressions on national life and thought, a widespread impetus toward disagreements will always exist. One of the reasons is simply the functional necessity for some type of extensive knowledge, however the efforts to control it. An observable quest for independent ideas tends to follow. An early theme thus becomes very pertinent. The canons of scientific inquiry, even if poorly appreciated as such, create an inherent potential for demanding freedom of expression and association. Only some version of the "big stick" can, at least for a time, thwart this drive.

14. Similarly, relative unavailability of communication channels, particularly if based upon their structures and controls, obviously limits the dissemination of ideas and may even restrict the motivation for wanting to express them. But it does not stifle them. Divergent views can always find some mechanism of communication, for example, personal and small-scale media, which sometimes counter the impact of mass media thereby. Personal contact

and organizations are a meaningful counterforce to the influence of media, as frequently demonstrated. Dissidents will always find some significant communication device unless, to repeat our theme again, they are prevented from so doing by external sanctions. If their messages appeal to others, they will acquire a meaningful audience.

15. What seems to follow from the previous discussion is a rosy-hued, almost Pollyanna-like analysis of the typical and likely continuing state of freedom of expression and association. After all, these freedoms cannot be completely obliterated in contemporary complex society, and suppressions are likely to last for only a short time. In American society, only a drastic change would produce a completely nonlibertarian society. Such "all or none" presentations miss the essential point. The United States has developed and continues to maintain a relatively free political-social system on the basis of a particular combination of elements, which are both similar to and different from other "free societies." Suppressive actions, including those which are fairly pervasive, have not altered this basic feature.

The libertarian answer again involves a return to an early theme. Freedom and unfreedom are important values because of their consequences. Literary censorship can mean poorer literature or at least make better literature less available. Infringements of academic freedom mean an inferior university and less productive scholars. Limiting the freedom of dissidents reduces the opportunity for redressing personal and group grievances. Above all, suppression of freedom of expression and association reduces the opportunity for the kinds of contributions that can help solve substantive problems. Such freedoms do not, of course, guarantee solutions. Without them, however, the historical evidence clearly indicates that "mistakes" are less prone to challenge. The quaint and optimistic liberal contention that "truth" always wins out over "error" in open contest is quite naive. The chances of combating error, however, are magnified by the possibility of unfettered refutation. Furthermore, a free political atmosphere allows for that participation and communication by which existent evils are more readily combated, especially if "resources" are available for all contestants.

This is not meant as an "ideological" interpretation of history. Ideas are the expressions of forces and historical processes but they also have their reciprocal impact. Efforts to thwart their public formulation and the organized activity based upon them help make historical developments more injurious to human beings. Among other things, these efforts diminish the possibilities of creating or maintaining the type of society that permits and encourages freedoms themselves.

This rather simplistic exposition of what amounts to libertarian dogma can hardly be a comprehensive political manifesto. After all, we have emphasized that civil liberties problems are closely enmeshed with other considerations, frequently more salient to most people. Perhaps, under certain situations, some suppressions are "necessary." But societies, and particularly complex societies, suffer thereby. This volume is addressed to a probing of the social conditions that are related to freedom of expression and association, particularly as revealed by analysis of recent problem areas. Some of the programs, policies, perspectives, and so on, that can maintain or extend the favorable and limit the unfavorable features may be implicit. To state them in a more coherent and organized fashion would demand at least another book.

Notes

CHAPTER 1: AIMS AND IDEAS

1. Charles Lam Markmann, *The Noblest Cry: A History of the American Civil Liberties Union,* New York, 1965, p. 3.
2. The religious freedom aspect of the First Amendment is largely ignored, except when directly germane to the other freedoms, as was more typical in earlier times. Above all, the book contains no reference to the church-state issue, the type of First Amendment dispute that has probably meant as much to many people as those described.
3. The literature on this subject is much too vast for even a partial list. A fitting example of a cross-national comparison, which is limited because it contains little else except legal features, is Frede Castberg, *Freedom of Speech in the West,* Oslo, 1960.
4. Robin Williams, *American Society,* 2nd ed., New York, 1960, p. 256.
5. William Preston, Jr., "The Limits of Dissent: Contraction or Enlargement," paper delivered at meeting of American Historical Association, New York, December 1968.
6. There are too many prominent examples to list. Among the extreme presentations of this viewpoint are Everett Dean Martin, *Liberty,* New York, 1930; Ortega y Gasset, *The Revolt of the Masses,* New York, 1930; and Markmann, *The Noblest Cry.*
7. See particularly Edward Shils, *The Torment of Secrecy,* Glencoe. Ill., 1956, which is discussed at various times in this book. Also see several

of the contributors to Daniel Bell, ed., *The Radical Right,* Garden City, N.Y., 1964; David Truman, "The American System in Crisis," in Bernard E. Brown and John C. Wahlke, eds., *The American Political System,* Homewood, Ill., 1967, pp. 630–637.

8. For example, at least this is an implicit feature of *some* analyses of mass society, such as Ortega y Gasset, *Revolt of the Masses;* and William Kornhauser, *The Politics of Mass Society,* London, 1959.

9. Walter F. Berns, *Freedom, Virtue, and the First Amendment,* Chicago, 1955.

10. For instance, R. H. Tawney, *Equality,* New York, 1961.

11. Robin Williams, *American Society.*

12. Perhaps the most classic statement along these lines is that of John Stuart Mill, "On Liberty," *Essential Works of John Stuart Mill,* New York, 1965, pp. 249–360. Also see Henry Steele Commager, *Freedom, Loyalty, Dissent,* New York, 1954.

13. Examples of this type of analysis are too numerous to list. Several will be indicated in the historical discussions.

14. The term first came into use in the writings of Harold Lasswell. See Harold Lasswell, "The Garrison State and the Specialists in Violence," *American Journal of Sociology* (January 1941), reprinted in Arnold A. Rogow, ed., *Government and Politics,* New York, 1961, pp. 605–613. The use of the general concept had many earlier precedents, particularly Herbert Spencer, "Militant and Industrial Societies," in *The Principles of Sociology,* New York, 1896, vol. 2, part 5, 568–640. As used by both of these writers, it seemed to refer to a thoroughly mobilized and coordinated society, generally engaged in an actual war, resembling contemporary totalitarianism. This formulation referred to the ideal type, the end-product of a process which might never be reached. This is not the meaning usually implied, nor is this how it will be applied in this book. A garrisonized society threatens liberties but it does not necessarily eliminate them. Other features of the political-social system are also important, as are the specific situational factors, including the degree and type of "garrisonizing." Much of this discussion will be further developed at various points.

15. Seymour M. Lipset, *Political Man: The Social Basis of Politics,* Garden City, N.Y., 1965, Chapters 2 and 3.

16. Alexis de Tocqueville, *Democracy in America,* 2 vols., New York, 1956.

17. William Spinrad, "Power in Local Communities," *Social Problems,* XII (1965), 335–356.

CHAPTER 2: THE LESSONS OF WORLD HISTORY

1. For the Athenian experience, see Walter R. Agard, *What Democracy Meant to the Greeks,* Madison, Wisc., 1960, Chapter 5; Alfred Zimmern, *The Greek Commonwealth,* New York, 1961, Chapter 5. For Rome, see Michael Grant, *The World of Rome,* New York, 1960, Chapter 3. For medieval Europe, see Henri Pirenne, *Economic and Social History of Medieval Europe,* New York, 1937, Chapter 3.

2. Alan Harding, *A Social History of English Law,* Baltimore, 1966, Chapters 1 and 2.

3. Zechariah Chafee, Jr., *Free Speech in the United States,* Cambridge, Mass., 1954, pp. 498–499.

4. *Ibid.,* Chapter 13; also Irving Brant, *The Bill of Rights: Its Origin and Meaning,* Indianapolis, 1963, Chapters 7–10.

5. Francis Biddle, *The Fear of Freedom,* New York, 1951, pp. 45–53.

6. John Illo, "The Misreading of Milton," *Columbia University Forum,* VIII (1965), 38–42.

7. Agard, *What Democracy Meant to the Greeks,* Chapter 5; Zimmern, *The Greek Commonwealth,* Chapter 6.

8. Chafee, *Free Speech,* pp. 25–26; Brant, *The Bill of Rights,* pp. 81–86.

9. Freedom of religion did not extend to Catholics for some time, and formal restrictions against dissenters remained on the books. These were rarely enforced, however. See *ibid.,* Chapter 18.

10. Chafee, *Free Speech,* p. 499.

11. Wesley Camp, "The New Learning on the Left Bank," *Adelphi Quarterly,* Summer 1967, 11–19.

12. By using a variety of new and old legislation and precedents, as well as countless extralegal techniques, authorities engaged in a wide range of suppressive and oppressive acts. For instance, all political discussion was forbidden in Cambridge taverns. Licensing of printing presses was restored. Landlords were required to report the names of "republicans," and some people were even imprisoned for a remark said privately at dinner. See Biddle, *The Fear of Freedom.*

CHAPTER 3: CIVIL LIBERTIES IN AMERICAN HISTORY

1. The basic foundations in early America were those that de Tocqueville presented; see de Tocqueville, *Democracy in America.* The social factors favorable to freedom of expression and association at other points in American history are mentioned at various parts of this chapter and throughout the book.

2. Leonard Levy, *Legacy of Suppression: Freedom of Speech and Press in Early American History,* Cambridge, Mass., 1960.

3. *Ibid.,* p. 487.

4. *Ibid.,* p. 491.

5. Leonard Levy, *Jefferson and Civil Liberties: The Darker Side,* Cambridge, Mass., 1963.

6. For instance, Irving Brant, *The Bill of Rights.*

7. John P. Roche, *The Quest for the Dream,* New York, 1963; *Courts and Rights: The American Judiciary in Action,* 2nd ed., New York, 1966.

8. Preston, "The Limits of Dissent."

9. As a working definition, "pervasive" threats actually produce a significant depreciation of freedom of expression and/or association. External deprivations, or the likelihood of such deprivations, stifle the freedoms of many people, so much so that it becomes an evident part of the political-social atmosphere. "Nuisance" annoyances hurt particular people at particular times, but the general impact on society is, for whatever reasons, minimal. Obviously, the distinction is not clear-cut or the categorization precise. Nevertheless, it serves as a necessary device for extracting the total reality of civil liberties from the rhetorical reactions to specific incidents, however appropriate those reactions to the immediate purposes.

10. Chafee, *Free Speech.* Some interpretations do emphasize suppressive incidents and the intolerant atmosphere. See Leon Whipple, *The Story of Civil Liberty in the United States,* New York, 1927; Preston, "The Limits of Dissent"; Roche, *Quest for the Dream.* None of these books, however, actually reveals much actual *effective* pervasive suppression. To Roche, the explanation is the existence of pluralistic enclaves, i.e., the dissident would always find a haven among kindred spirits. This does not sufficiently account for the vast amount of open, free national political conflict. De Tocqueville's contemporary analysis, which considers all the pluralistic elements as well as laws, customs, and so on, is more insightful.

11. Perhaps even more dramatic was the fact that, despite the vast number who openly opposed the war in the North, none was apparently tried on any grounds in the postwar period.

12. The major exception was censorship of "obscene" literature, as later discussed.

13. It is interesting that the major political symbol of this atmosphere, President Warren G. Harding, pardoned most of those imprisoned under the restrictive policies of the administration of the "progressive" Woodrow Wilson.

14. For instance, Martin, *Liberty.*
15. Biddle, *The Fear of Freedom*, p. 38. For other discussions of the period, see Martin Spencer, "Democracy and the Rule of Law in America," unpublished Ph.D. dissertation, New School for Social Research, June 1969, Chapter 5; Chafee, *Free Speech*, pp. 23–28; Brant, *The Bill of Rights*, Chapter 23.
16. Among the many accounts of this subject, see Martin Spencer, "Democracy and the Rule of Law in America"; Thomas I. Emerson, David Haber, and Norman Dorsen, *Political and Civil Rights in the United States*, 3rd ed., Boston, 1967, I, 41–44.
17. See, for instance, Martin Spencer, "Democracy and the Rule of Law in America," for a crisp summary.
18. *Ibid.;* Chafee, *Free Speech*, pp. 228–231.
19. Spencer, "Democracy and the Rule of Law in America"; see also Chafee, *Free Speech*, pp. 224–231.
20. See Chapter 14, "Academic Freedom," *infra.*
21. For a somewhat contrary view, see Preston, "The Limits of Dissent." Preston's focus is on nuisance incidents, not on the pervasive atmosphere.
22. *Ibid.*
23. See Emerson, Haber, and Dorsen, *Political and Civil Rights*, pp. 45–48, for a brief summary.
24. See, particularly, Wood Gray, *The Hidden Civil War: The Story of the Copperheads*, New York, 1964.
25. *Ibid.*
26. Most of what follows comes from Chafee, *Free Speech, passim;* Donald Johnson, *The Challenge to American Freedoms: World War I and the Rise of the American Civil Liberties Union*, Lexington, Ky., 1963.
27. Chafee, *Free Speech*, p. 280.
28. Markmann, *The Noblest Cry;* Donald Johnson, *The Challenge to American Freedoms.*
29. In the case of the pro-Nazis, the judge died during the trial and the indictments were later dismissed.
30. The Socialist Workers party's most important area of influence was among the truck drivers in the Minneapolis area. President Dan Tobin of the Teamsters Union, who vigorously opposed this influence, was a close political associate of President Roosevelt. The defendants included not only much of the leadership of the SWP but also a large segment of their Minneapolis teamster contingent. The interpretation suggested was that the prosecution was primarily a political payoff of Roosevelt to Tobin. Supporting this interpretation is the fact that the

SWP was generally unharmed after the convictions. (See Preston, "The Limits of Dissent.") This threat to civil liberties was thus a response to quite tangential factors.

31. Many of the details will emerge in later discussions. Narrative accounts of the beginnings of what is described in the following paragraph are available in Biddle, *The Fear of Freedom;* Alan Barth, *The Loyalty of Free Men,* New York, 1951.

32. As explained at several points, a garrison society need not imply a completely controlled society. The concept means only that mobilization for actual or potential external conflict has a significant effect on all features of national life, particularly the political aspects.

33. The total, under any prosecution for "subversion," was about fifty by the mid-1960's. Several others were imprisoned for contempt before congressional committees, and so forth. In contrast, the estimate is that about three hundred went to prison in 1919 and 1920 alone. Milton R. Konvitz, *Expanding Liberties: Freedom's Gain in Post War America,* New York, 1966, pp. 157–158.

34. For instance, the Communist Control Act of 1954, which specifically declared that the Communist party, or any successor, is not entitled to any rights or privileges. See Chapter 4, "Courts and Civil Liberties," *infra,* for a description of what happened in attempts to administer the McCarran Act.

35. Roche does recognize this factor. For instance, he declares that "it has been the pressure of private demands for the expansion of freedom, the endless agitation of private organizations, which has paced the development of public policy" (Roche, *Quest for the Dream,* p. 267). But this is not the essential feature of his theoretical emphasis.

36. Biddle, *The Fear of Freedom,* p. 42.

CHAPTER 4: COURTS AND CIVIL LIBERTIES

1. See Chafee, *Free Speech,* Chapter 11.

2. Wallace Mendelson, "The First Amendment and the Judicial Process," in Martin M. Shapiro, ed., *The Supreme Court and Constitutional Rights,* Oakland, N.J., 1967, p. 37.

3. See Learned Hand, "The Bill of Rights," in Emerson, Haber, and Dorsen, *Political and Civil Rights,* pp. 21–24.

4. Wallace Mendelson, "On the Meaning of the First Amendment," in Shapiro, *The Supreme Court and Constitutional Rights,* p. 21.

5. The role of the Supreme Court became more significant in the 1930's when it decided that First Amendment restrictions were applicable to state governments. (Since then, it has also included many of the pro-

cedural rights of the United States Bill of Rights.) See particularly *Near vs. Minnesota*, 283 U.S. 697 (1931); *DeJong vs. Oregon*, 299 U.S. 353 (1937); *Palko vs. Connecticut*, 302 U.S. 319 (1937).

6. *Pennsylvania vs. Nelson*, 350 U.S. 497 (1956). Possible exceptions to this ruling are those in which state and local laws are more directly concerned with the question of public order.

7. *Schenck vs. United States*, 249 U.S. 47 (1919). The case concerned a man convicted under the 1917 Espionage Act.

8. See *Gitlow vs. New York*, 268 U.S. 652 (1925); *Whitney vs. California*, 274 U.S. 357 (1927).

9. *Dennis vs. United States*, 341 U.S. 494 (1951). Although two of the judges in the majority offered concurring opinions, the reasoning of the official position paraphrased a lower-court decision on the same case, written by Learned Hand, the well-known justice of the federal circuit court of appeals. He insisted that if there were a general "danger" it need not be "imminent" and that the "gravity of evil" could cancel out the improbability of achievement. Mere conspiracy to advocate violent overthrow of the government supplied sufficient grounds for government preventive action without violating the First Amendment. One need not prove the likelihood that such action would soon be attempted. Justices Hugo Black and William Douglas, using a more strict interpretation of the Holmes criteria, dissented.

10. See dissents in *Abrams vs. United States*, 250 U.S. 616 (1919); *Whitney vs. California*, 274 U.S. 357 (1927). See also the discussion in Samuel J. Konefsky, *The Legacy of Holmes and Brandeis: A Study in the Influence of Ideas*, New York, 1961, pp. 187–204.

11. *Yates vs. United States*, 354 U.S. 298 (1957).

12. *Scales vs. United States*, 367 U.S. 203 (1961); *Noto vs. United States*, 367 U.S. 290 (1961).

13. Particularly, *Herndon vs. Lowry*, 301 U.S. 242 (1937). While reversing the conviction of a Communist in the state of Georgia, the majority position, written by Justice Owen Roberts, further insisted that there must be an observable "apprehension of danger." The Herndon case was actually an exception, for it did involve a charge of possession of "Communist literature."

14. *Killbourne vs. Thompson*, 103 U.S. 168 (1881); *McGrain vs. Daugherty*, 273 U.S. 135 (1927).

15. Particularly *United States vs. Josephson*, 165 F2d 82 (1947).

16. *Berenblatt vs. United States*, 360 U.S. 109 (1959); *Wilkensen vs. United States*, 365 U.S. 399 (1961); *Braden vs. United States*, 365 U.S. 431 (1961).

17. *Watkins vs. United States*, 354 U.S. 178 (1957).

18. *Sweezy vs. New Hampshire*, 354 U.S. 234 (1957); *Gibson vs. Florida*

Legislative Investigation Committee, 372 U.S. 539 (1963); *Uphaus vs. Wyman,* 360 U.S. 72 (1959).

19. 127 F2d 847 (1954).
20. See *Quinn vs. United States,* 349 U.S. 155 (1955); *Bart vs. United States,* 349 U.S. 219 (1955); *Emspak vs. United States,* 349 U.S. 190 (1955). For later rulings, see *McPhaul vs. United States,* 364 U.S. 372 (1960).
21. Carl Beck, *Contempt of Congress: A Study of the Prosecutions Initiated by the Committee on Un-American Activities, 1945–1957,* New Orleans, 1959.
22. *Cole vs. Young,* 351 U.S. 536 (1956).
23. *Bailey vs. Richardson,* 182 F2d 46 (1950). The majority opinion claimed that, since dismissal from employment was not actually "punishment," due process was not essential. A dissenting judge disagreed. The Supreme Court upheld the lower-court decision without any written opinion: 341 U.S. 918 (1951). In one case, Justice Hugo Black declared that the Attorney General's list was a violation of the First Amendment: *Joint Anti-Fascist Refugee Committee vs. McGrath,* 341 U.S. 123 (1951). Justice William Douglas used his dissent in another case to declare that the program "condemns a man to a suspect class and outer darkness," and he attacked the role of the "faceless informer": *Peters vs. Hobby,* 349 U.S. 331 (1955).
24. See *Parker vs. Lester,* 227 F2d 708 (1955); *Greene vs. McElroy,* 360 U.S. 478 (1959); *Cafeteria and Restaurant Union vs. McElroy,* 367 U.S. 886 (1961).
25. *Joint Anti-Fascist Refugee Committee vs. McGrath.*
26. *Garner vs. Board of Public Works of Los Angeles,* 341 U.S. 716 (1951).
27. *Adler vs. Board of Education,* 342 U.S. 485 (1952). The law stipulated that members of organizations listed as subversive were ineligible for teaching positions in the public schools. In this instance, the list was to be compiled by the board of regents after appropriate hearings, including the right of appeal by such organizations.
28. *Weiman vs. Updegraff,* 344 U.S. 183 (1952).
29. *Shelton vs. Tucker,* 364 U.S. 479 (1960); *Cramp vs. Board of Public Instruction,* 368 U.S. 278 (1961); *Baggett vs. Bullitt,* 377 U.S. 360 (1964).
30. *Heckler vs. Shepard,* 234F Supp. 841 (1965).
31. *Elfenbrandt vs. Russell,* 384 U.S. 11 (1966); *Keyshian vs. Board of Regents,* 385 U.S. 589 (1967).
32. Subsequent efforts to reinstate loyalty programs, with or without the oath provisions, are too new for any court rulings, but it is likely that they will be similarly voided if passed. Positive oaths, those which

simply ask for some oath of allegiance, have been declared constitutionally permissible by the courts.

33. *Kent vs. Dulles,* 351 U.S. 116 (1958); *Aptheker vs. Secretary of State,* 378 U.S. 500 (1964); *Lamont vs. Postmaster General,* 381 U.S. 301 (1965).

34. *Albertson vs. Subversive Activities Control Board,* 382 U.S. 70 (1965). See the general discussion in Konvitz, *Expanding Liberties,* pp. 152–155. Perhaps the most potentially serious provision of the law, the possibility of detention camps in time of "emergency," has not yet been tested, although accounts of the existence of these camps have appeared.

35. The courts have yet to rule, at the time of this writing, on most of the legal issues related to the current legitimacy crisis.

36. This distinction is even more comprehensive than the previous concept of nuisance and pervasive threats. (See note 9, Chapter 3.) In the terminology used at this point, not only do the suppressions affect few people, but those directly involved are usually scarcely hurt, with lasting consequences very rare. Typically, at most they are annoyed. For instance, they may not make a speech at a particular time and place, but other times and places are readily available. Sometimes, the style of a speech may be forbidden, but the general content is permissible.

37. See George W. Spicer, *The Supreme Court and Fundamental Freedoms,* New York, 1959, pp. 34–41, for a description of several relevant rulings.

38. *Chaplinsky vs. New Hampshire,* 315 U.S. 568 (1942).

39. See Spicer, *The Supreme Court and Fundamental Freedoms,* pp. 43–45; *Kunz vs. New York,* 340 U.S. 290 (1951).

40. *Edwards vs. South Carolina,* 372 U.S. 290 (1961); *Brown vs. Louisiana,* 383 U.S. 131 (1966); also see Emerson, Haber, and Dorsen, *Political and Civil Rights,* pp. 480–481.

41. *Cox vs. Louisiana,* 379 U.S. 559 (1965); *Adderley vs. Florida,* 385 U.S. 39 (1966).

42. Justice Black, possibly the most libertarian Supreme Court justice in American history on free expression cases, has been adamant in insisting that such expressions need not be permissible in every place at every time.

43. For a systematic attempt at discerning the possible influence of Supreme Court justices on each other in civil liberties cases in one year, see S. Sidney Ulmer, "The Analysis of Behavior Patterns on the United States Supreme Court," in Rita James Simon, ed., *The Sociology of Law,* San Francisco, 1968, pp. 407–430. For a discussion of the impact of other relevant actors on Supreme Court decisions, see

Paul A. Freund, *The Supreme Court of the United States: Its Business, Purposes, Performances,* Cleveland, 1965, Chapter 6. The revived discipline of the sociology of law offers little help in understanding civil liberties decisions, at least up to now. The above reference is a rare exception. The subject of civil liberties is, in fact, hardly considered. See the other articles in Simon, *The Sociology of Law;* Edwin M. Schur, *Law and Society,* New York, 1968; William M. Evan, ed., *Law and Sociology,* New York, 1962.

44. Robert Dahl, "Decision-Making in a Democracy: The Supreme Court as Policy Maker," *Journal of Public Law,* VI (1957), 279–295.
45. For expositions of some of these ideas, see Alexander M. Bickel, *The Least Dangerous Branch: The Supreme Court at the Bar of Politics,* Indianapolis, 1962; Freund, *The Supreme Court of the United States.*
46. Bickel, *The Least Dangerous Branch,* p. 239.
47. Dahl, "Decision-Making in a Democracy."
48. See the accounts in Donald J. Kemper, *Decade of Fear: Senator Hennings and Civil Liberties,* Columbia, Mo., 1965. Although the focus is on the work of one particular senator, he had many allies in his efforts, among other things, to maintain the impact of these court rulings.
49. Mendelson, "The First Amendment."

CHAPTER 5: THE RELEVANCE OF PUBLIC OPINION

1. All of these figures are reported in Samuel A. Stouffer, *Communism, Conformity, and Civil Liberties,* New York, 1966, pp. 55–56.
2. *Ibid.,* p. 43.
3. *Ibid.,* p. 56.
4. Herbert Hyman, "England and America—Climates of Tolerance and Intolerance," in Daniel Bell, ed., *The Radical Right,* p. 286.
5. Stouffer, *Communism, Conformity, and Civil Liberties,* pp. 40–43. An even more interesting finding was indicated in August 1950 at the beginning of the Korean War. Almost 90 per cent of a national Gallup poll favored some forceable legal action against United States Communists if there were war with Russia: Athan Theoharis, "The Escalation of the Loyalty Program," in Barton J. Bernstein, ed., *Politics and Policies of the Truman Administration,* Chicago, 1970.
6. Stouffer, *Communism, Conformity, and Civil Liberties,* p. 56.
7. Hyman, "England and America."
8. Stouffer, *Communism, Conformity, and Civil Liberties.* p. 29.
9. *Ibid.,* p. 56.

10. "Minnesota Poll" Release, *Minneapolis Sunday Tribune,* December 13, 1953.
11. *Ibid.,* April 8, 1962.
12. Raymond W. Mack, "Do We Really Believe in the Bill of Rights?," *Social Problems,* III (1956), 264–269.
13. Stouffer, *Communism, Conformity, and Civil Liberties,* pp. 32–33.
14. Some libertarians may be even more apprehensive about public attitudes toward "censorship." A poll in Minnesota on November 11, 1956, revealed that over 70 per cent favored community permission before a movie could be shown. An inquiry made on December 20, 1966, found over half favoring licensing of bookstores to control sale of "obscene materials." Even among a generally libertarian college sample, almost half favored screening of "crime" comic books by a government agency before publication. Hanon C. Selvin and Warren O. Hagstrom, "Determinants of Support for Civil Liberties," in Seymour M. Lipset and Sheldon S. Wolin, eds., *The Berkeley Student Revolt,* Garden City, N.Y., 1965, p. 497.
15. For Northwestern material, see Mack, "Do We Really Believe in the Bill of Rights?" For Minnesota poll data, see citation in notes 10 and 11.
16. Stouffer, *Communism, Conformity, and Civil Liberties,* pp. 43–45.
17. *Ibid.,* pp. 31, 34, 42, 43.
18. *Ibid.,* pp. 30, 32, 43.
19. *Ibid.,* Chapters 4 and 5.
20. Mack, "Do We Really Believe in the Bill of Rights?"
21. Selvin and Hagstrom, "Determinants of Support for Civil Liberties."
22. Stouffer, *Communism, Conformity, and Civil Liberties,* Chapter 3.
23. Robert S. Lynd and Helen M. Lynd, *Middletown in Transition: A Study in Cultural Conflict,* New York, 1937, Chapter 12.
24. William Spinrad, "The Quest for an American Ethos," unpublished paper, Columbia University, Graduate Department of Anthropology, 1950.
25. Seymour M. Lipset, *The First New Nation,* New York, 1963. Although these citations refer to different periods of American history the general principle seems applicable at all times.
26. In analyzing the American historical experience, this is a principal theme of Martin Spencer, "Democracy and the Rule of Law in America," and is part of John Roche's analysis of recent America; see *Quest for the Dream.*
27. Among the relevant discussions on this general subject, see M. L. DeFleur and F. R. Westie, "Verbal Attitudes and Overt Acts," in Marie Jahoda and Neil Warren, eds., *Attitudes: Selected Readings,*

Baltimore, 1966, pp. 213–222; R. L. Gordon, "Attitude and Definition of the Situation," in *ibid.*, pp. 240–255; Stuart W. Cook and Claire Selltiz, "A Multiple Indicator Approach to Attitude Measurement," in *ibid.*, pp. 325–350.

28. Stouffer, *Communism, Conformity, and Civil Liberties*, Chapter 9.
29. Hyman, *England and America*, p. 288.
30. For purposes of this discussion, a full delineation of the possible meanings of "opinion," "attitudes," and "values," are avoided. Operationally, we define opinions and attitudes as identical concepts. Values are the substratum of generalized attitudes, of which specific opinions on a concrete issue are in some manner a meaningful representation. The one necessary proviso is that opinions may readily change with situations without any necessary alterations of basic values. Fundamental beliefs are not changed, but their application is different in the changed context.
31. Lipset, *Political Man*, Chapter 4.
32. Robert Merton, "Manifest and Latent Functions," *Social Theory and Social Structure*, Glencoe, Ill., 1949, pp. 21–81.
33. Stouffer, *Communism, Conformity, and Civil Liberties*, p. 166.
34. *Ibid.*, p. 158.
35. Little of the material in this chapter covers the more recent period, the 1960's. Because of the theme of this chapter, the difficult task of obtaining such data was not undertaken. Some information from public opinion surveys is, however, appended when specifically relevant.

CHAPTER 6: A WORKING ANALYTICAL MODEL

1. The terms "legitimate, "legitimacy," "legitimation," and so forth, have been and will continue to be used at so many points in our discussion that some attempt at clarification is in order. Historically, the concept has referred to the right of authority, a subject or subordinate's acceptance of orders from those who are assigned that role because of their formal position, regardless of whether one agrees with the substance of the order or not. Our elaboration of the concept covers all situations of accepted rights—to rule, to continue a social system, or to dissent. Legitimacy may further extend to, or be denied to, a document—a constitution—or a particular government decision, such as a statute. Denying legitimacy implies that one is placing any of these beyond the pale of acceptable behavior, with a belief that decisions are outside the approved rules or that the decision-maker is beyond the bounds of some *moral* considerations.

2. Decision-makers must have some power, i.e., resources to make their decisions meaningful. But they must also be properly motivated because of their role requirements, saliency of an issue, and so forth, as indicated throughout this volume.

3. The influencers may include a significant number of those directly affected, but many of them will, in most situations, be subject to indirect effects—those involving the general condition of civil liberties rather than the specific acts. In any case, these are distinctive analytical types, even if the same people may sometimes be included under more than one category.

4. See Chapter 13, "Censorship," *infra.*

5. Lipset, *Political Man,* Chapter 4.

6. Of course, this has been historically noted particularly in the postures of the powerful in response to the assertions of the downtrodden.

7. See Chapter 13, "Censorship," *infra.*

8. Muzafer Sherif and Carolyn W. Sherif, *Social Psychology,* New York, 1969, Chapters 10, 16, 17, *passim.*

9. De Tocqueville, *Democracy in America,* I, 282–290. Which lawyers are more likely to contribute their time to civil liberties questions would be an interesting subject for research. One possible variable is the amount of time available. Thus corporation lawyers may, somewhat surprisingly, include a conspicuous number of civil liberties lawyers, as symbolized by the long-term general counsel of the ACLU, Arthur Garfield Hays.

10. See Chapter 13, "Censorship," *infra.*

11. See Chapter 14, "Academic Freedom," *infra.* Perhaps this distinction is also applicable to lawyers. Civil liberties lawyers may be more cosmopolitan in outlook and in their reference groups.

12. See Chapter 13, "Censorship," *infra.*

13. Among the many analyses of this subject, see Robert Presthus, *The Organizational Society,* New York, 1962, Chapter 2; Robert Merton, "Bureaucratic Structure and Personality," in *Social Theory and Social Structure,* pp. 195–206.

14. See note 14, Chapter 1.

15. See Sherif and Sherif, *Social Psychology,* pp. 226–227, for a brief summary. The classic work is John Dollard, *Frustration and Aggression,* New Haven, 1939.

16. The number and types of actors vary, of course, with the type of dispute. It will generally be greater, on all sides, if the possible threat to freedom of expression and association is closer to the pervasive end of the pervasive-nuisance continuum because the relevant issues are salient to more people.

CHAPTER 7: WHAT WAS McCARTHYISM?

1. For an inclusive and critical summary of most of the relevant material, see Nelson W. Polsby, "Toward an Explanation of McCarthyism," in *Political Studies,* October 1960, reprinted in Nelson W. Polsby, Robert A. Dentler, and Paul A. Smith, eds., *Politics and Social Life: An Introduction to Political Behavior,* Boston, 1963, pp. 809–824; see also William Spinrad, review of Daniel Bell, ed., *The New American Right, Social Problems,* IV (1957), 339–343.

2. Polsby, "Toward an Explanation of McCarthyism."

3. Shils, *The Torment of Secrecy;* Bell, *The New American Right;* Truman, "The American System in Crisis."

4. Hook's position was that Communist party members are not simply people with dissident political views. They are *disciplined* participants in a cohesive organization demanding total allegiance, especially in the realm of ideas, directed—at least at that time—by a totalitarian state power. As such, they could not be permitted to occupy any position of trust, including teaching. Although the author has much sympathy with the motivation for this attitude, its implication, the doctrine of guilt by association, provided the ideological groundwork for McCarthyite strictures and the accompanying political blandness, the search for the hidden affiliations of countless individuals. See Sidney Hook, *Political Power and Personal Freedom,* New York, 1962, Chapters 20–22.

5. Alan Barth, *Government by Investigation,* New York, 1955, pp. 24–26, 53–57.

6. See Chapter 6, "The Relevance of Public Opinion," *supra.*

7. Political leaders who supported the McCarthyite tactics tended to be conservative Republicans. Empirical data indicates that this was true of their public supporters. See Polsby, "Toward an Explanation of McCarthyism." But policy orientations were not the rhetorical expressions by which the former sought support nor the reasons particular publics approved them.

8. For instance, the well-known columnist Westbrook Pegler complained that attendance was "melancholy and depressing" and called a Madison Square Garden rally a "turkey." None of this discussion implies that genuine radical right movements did not exist. But they were clearly fringe operations, with little relevance for most McCarthy supporters. None of the many studies of those who verbally supported Joseph McCarthy emphasizes personal involvement in such movements.

9. Social scientists, who, more than anyone else, should have been more

sensitive to the total reality, were very remiss. See a fuller discussion in Chapter 11, "The McCarthy Era: An Overview," *infra.*

10. See Chapter 3, "Historical Background in the United States," *supra.*

11. For instance, some authors in *The Radical Right* do not mention the Cold War at all; others refer to it only in passing. One analyst who does dwell sufficiently on the Cold War aspect is Samuel Lubell, *The Revolt of the Moderates,* New York, 1956.

12. Accounts of these historical developments are numerous. See, for instance, Biddle, *The Fear of Freedom.* One recent account particularly emphasizes the active role of the Truman administration in fostering such policies (Theoharis, "Escalation of the Loyalty Program"). Although his documentation provides very valuable material, he tends to offer his own conspiracy theory, i.e., the Democratic administration's political direction was primarily responsible for the suppressions, while tending to play down the situationally provided impulsions. Such an interpretation is as limited as that of most analyses of McCarthyism, which dwell primarily on the active role of a few congressmen and other political malcontents.

13. That Joseph McCarthy's personal intervention in campaigns often elected the candidate he supported was a commonly accepted truism. This contention has been substantially refuted. (See Polsby, "Toward an Explanation of McCarthyism.") Republican victories in the mid-1950's were undoubtedly helped by the frustrations over the Cold War, in which the charge of communism in government might have been a constituent element. (See Lubell, *The Revolt of the Moderates.*) But the impact of this attitude would probably have been almost as evident without the Joe McCarthy-type charges.

14. Obviously, this is not a description of all or even most liberals, a very inclusive categorization in any case. A symbolic representation of this tendency was that of the intellectuals associated with the Congress for Cultural Freedom. See, for instance, Hook, *Political Power and Personal Freedom.*

15. One of the most graphic illustrations of this blandness was the 1956 presidential election campaign, when supporters of both President Eisenhower and Adlai Stevenson could find no dramatic issues; many of the usually sophisticated were forced to emphasize Eisenhower's health and Stevenson's divorce.

16. The elimination of Communist party influence in a few unions, as much a result of internal pressures as external McCarthyite pressures, had a minuscule effect on the total labor movement. The impact on the internal organization of unions was also not too significant. Too many other factors were involved. (See Chapter 16, "Civil Liberties in

Private Organizations: The Case of the Labor Unions," *infra.* Similarly, congressional investigations and loyalty-security programs produced little change in unions, partly because, as later indicated, they were in many ways resented. Attempts by legislative investigations to find subversives in pacifist and civil rights movements were nuisances and had no appreciable consequences, i.e., both grew in numbers, with sufficient widespread, popular, and even respectable support.

CHAPTER 8: LEGISLATIVE COMMITTEE INVESTIGATIONS

1. Interestingly, the state investigations sometimes covered a wider scope than those of congressional groups. The Broyles Committee in Illinois, for instance, spent a great deal of time probing into textbooks. Among the more publicized similar groups were the Teney Committee in California and the Ober Committee in Maryland. See Biddle, *The Fear of Freedom.*
2. Rather than list the voluminous literature at this point, specific reference to published material is left for those points in the text where it is immediately relevant. The behavior of each of the committees was not identical, but the prevailing patterns were very similar.
3. See *ibid.,* pp. 110–123. Many discussions of all these investigating committees stress the intent of many investigations to malign "New Dealers," "Fair Dealers," and so forth, as somehow tainted with subversion. But the inquiries after World War II rarely dealt with stands on domestic political issues, as will be seen. The major drive has been to expose personal backgrounds and personal associations. The ostensible purpose has thus not been to attack opponents for political disagreement but for some participation, witting or innocent, in an anti-American conspiracy.
4. James Burnham, "The Investigating Power of Congress," in William F. Buckley and the editors of *National Review,* eds., *The Committee and Its Critics: A Calm Review of the House Committee on Un-American Activities,* New York, 1962, p. 37.
5. Alan Barth, *Government by Investigation,* p. 23; Telford Taylor, *Grand Inquest: The Story of Congressional Investigation,* New York, 1955, pp. 143–147.
6. Buckley, *The Committee and Its Critics.*
7. Barth, *Government by Investigation,* pp. 46–57, 95–111.
8. One of the most famous incidents was that of 110 California public schoolteachers subpoenaed by HUAC in 1959, whose names appeared in the press. Most were not given an opportunity to reply and their files were turned over to county school officials. Two years later,

more than a third were not teaching in California. See Walter Goodman, *The Committee: The Extraordinary Career of the House Committee on Un-American Activities*, New York, 1968, pp.
425–427; "The
Case Against the House Un-American Activities Committee," published
by the American Civil Liberties Union, pp. 12–13; on other incidents,
see *ibid.*, pp. 14–17.

9. *Ibid.*, p. 18. See discussion, pp. 17–36.
10. See, for instance, "Security and Constitutional Rights," *Hearings of the
Subcommittee on Constitutional Rights of the U.S. Senate Committee
on the Judiciary*, 86th Cong., July 2, 1959, an account of the hearings
of a subcommittee on the subject under the chairmanship of Senator
Thomas Hennings of Missouri. Similar hearings by subcommittees
under the chairmanships of Senators Hubert Humphrey and Olin
Johnston exhibited the same type of atmosphere. See also accounts in
Kemper, *Decade of Fear*.
11. Taylor, *Grand Inquest*, p. 120.
12. *Ibid.*, pp. 80–82; Barth, *Government by Investigation*, pp. 187–190;
James Wechsler, *Age of Suspicion*, New York, 1953.
13. See Chapter 5, "The Relevance of Public Opinion," *supra*.
14. See Chapter 4, "Courts and Civil Liberties," *supra*.
15. The relevant case was *Slochower vs. Board of Education*, 350 U.S. 551
(1956). For a discussion of the implication of taking the "Fifth," see
Taylor, *Grand Inquest*, p. 210. For varying views on the subject, see
Goodman, *The Committee*, pp. 351–356. As will be later discussed, the
dismissal of teachers who invoked the privilege was probably the
major McCarthyite impact on American colleges. See Chapter 14,
"Academic Freedom," *infra*.
16. Carl Beck, *Contempt of Congress*, pp. 217–240. Beck considers citations by all the congressional anti-subversive committees through 1958.
One famous example was that of playwright Arthur Miller, who refused to disclose the names of those who might have been associated
with "Communist activities" many years earlier. Miller was convicted
of contempt, but the case was thrown out on appeal on technical
grounds. Whatever difficulties he may subsequently have faced, Miller
seemed to fare better than those who "took the Fifth." One discussion
of the activities of HUAC specifically estimated that, of 130 people
prosecuted for contempt because of their behavior before the committee over a seventeen-year period, "fewer than a dozen have finally
been convicted" (Vern Countryman, review of Walter Goodman, *The
Committee, New York Review of Books*, December 5, 1968, p. 20).
After the *Berenblatt* Supreme Court decision in 1959, which accepted
the propriety of congressional questions about "Communist affiliations," and several similar subsequent rulings, the pertinency claim

became less useful. By then, however, the nature of the inquiries and the response had changed, as later described, and many contempt convictions were set aside on procedural grounds (Goodman, *The Committee*, pp. 421–422).

17. In the interrogation of John Cogley for writing his report on entertainment blacklisting, the questioners emphasized that his assistant had been Michael Harrington, later to become famous as the author of *The Other America*. The HUAC hearing implied that the report was probably tainted because of Harrington's "socialist" ideas, *ibid.*, p. 383.

18. Senator Robert Taft, titular leader of the Senate Republicans, who was never personally involved in these investigations, once instructed his political colleagues, "If one case doesn't work, then bring up another" (Polsby, "Toward an Explaantion of McCarthyism," p. 817).

19. Richard Rovere, *Senator Joe McCarthy*, New York, 1959.

20. One "friendly witness" was actually offered a contract as a consultant with HUAC before he had testified. See Richard Eder, "Job Offer Linked to House Hearing," *New York Times*, October 29, 1967.

21. Harvey Matusow, *False Witness*, New York, 1955.

22. See Buckley, *The Committee and Its Critics*.

23. See Goodman, *The Committee*, pp. 435–481.

24. In the 1967 congressional session, ninety-two representatives voted for a motion which would have compelled HUAC to justify its appropriations at an open hearing; forty-three voted against the appropriation itself, *ibid.*, p. 489.

25. "New Dimensions—New Challenges," *46th Annual Report* (July 1, 1965–January 1, 1967), American Civil Liberties Union, pp. 29–30.

26. Goodman, *The Committee*, Chapters 15–17.

27. On the Stamler case, see *ibid.*, pp. 457–464.

CHAPTER 9: THE LOYALTY-SECURITY PROGRAMS

1. Harold N. Hyman, *To Try Men's Souls: Loyalty Tests in American History*, Berkeley, 1959.

2. Congress, as part of the Hatch Act of 1939, which lists several items limiting the political activity of federal civil service employees, added the proviso denying employment to a member of any organization "which advocates overthrow of our Constitutional form of government in the United States." The same proviso was appended to most appropriation bills passed thereafter and was codified into a general law in 1955. (Some agencies insisted on a sworn affidavit to that

effect with obvious criminal penalties for those who perjured themselves. Since 1949, this has been a regular practice in most agencies. This makes the decision a matter for judicial action. Possibly because of the difficulties inherent, prosecution under these acts has apparently been rare.) In 1940 and 1941, Congress instructed the Secretaries of War, Navy, and State to dismiss all those considered security risks. An investigation by the Attorney General in 1942 resulted in the dismissal of thirty-six federal employees. (See John H. Schaar, *Loyalty in America*, Berkeley, 1957, pp. 132–137.) Between 1940 and 1944, almost 275,000 cases were investigated, and 1,180, or about .0157 per cent of all federal employees, were discharged because of presumed disloyalty. In other words, the loyalty-security programs in the federal government meant little until the executive branch acted on its own, whatever the pressures elsewhere.

The first significant step was President Truman's Executive Order of March 1947, establishing a comprehensive federal loyalty program for civil service employees. The purpose was to refuse or terminate employment if "on all the evidence, reasonable grounds exist for belief that the person involved is disloyal to the Government of the United States" (Ralph S. Brown, Jr., *Loyalty and Security: Employment Tests in the United States*, New Haven, 1958, p. 385). The list of subversive organizations followed. Each employee or potential employee was to be investigated; the actual decision on his case was up to the head of the particular agency, although special staff personnel usually did most of the relevant work and generally made the appropriate decisions. Appeal was possible, through the agency itself, then to a general loyalty review board, and possibly to the courts. See *ibid.*, Chapters 1 and 2, *passim.*

The security criterion was originally an extension of a 1950 act of Congress, reasserting a wartime provision which gave particular department heads the right to dismiss any employee in the interests of national security. More than half of all federal employees were covered by this statute, which did provide for formalized procedures, including a hearing, for tenured civil service personnel. The standards for these sensitive agencies were based on the simple criterion of what is "necessary or advisable in the interest of the national security of the United States" (*ibid.*, p. 31).

President Eisenhower's 1953 Executive Order extended the program to all employees of the federal executive branch, with the language that employment should be "clearly consistent with the interests of national security" (*ibid.*). Note that there were no formalized procedures stipulated for prospective employees. (The loyalty review board was abolished.) After the Supreme Court's 1956 decision in *Cole vs.*

Young, the security formula was applicable only to sensitive agencies, but that meant that a major part of all federal employees were still included.

3. *Ibid.,* Chapters 3 and 4. American employees of international agencies, like the United Nations, were also subject to the same type of scrutiny.

4. *Ibid.,* p. 181.

5. See *ibid.,* Chapter 2, for a description of the typical procedures and some concrete illustrations; also David Fellman, "The Loyalty Defendants," *Wisconsin Law Review,* IV (1957), 4–39; Eleanor Bontecou, *The Federal Loyalty-Security Program,* Ithaca, N.Y., 1953; Charlotte A. Kaufman and Herbert Kaufman, "Some Problems of Treatment Arising from the Federal Loyalty and Security Programs," *American Journal of Orthopsychiatry,* XXV (1955), 813–824; Schaar, *Loyalty in America,* pp. 130–174; Testimony of Ralph S. Brown, Jr., *Hearings Before the Subcommittee on Security and Constitutional Rights,* pp. 947–961; Testimony of Joseph L. Rauh, Jr., *Security and Constitutional Rights,* pp. 962–977.

6. The most publicized cases of this sort were those of several prominent State Department employees—John Stewart Service, John Paton Davies, and John Carter Vincent. Among the many accounts, see Brown, *Loyalty and Security,* pp. 367–369. The famous story of atomic scientist J. Robert Oppenheimer is even better known; see *ibid.,* pp. 279–282; Joseph Boskin and Fred Krinsky, *The Oppenheimer Affair,* Beverly Hills, Calif., 1968; Joseph and Stewart Alsop, "The Case of Robert Oppenheimer," *Harper's,* October 1954, pp. 25–45.

7. See the citations in note 8 for a discussion of cases which indicate such examples. Also Maurice Goldbloom, "A Case Study in Due Process," *Commentary,* March 1956, pp. 250–256.

8. *Case Studies in Personal Security,* collected under the direction of Adam Yarmolinsky, Washington, D.C., Bureau of National Affairs, Inc., August 1955; Jack G. Day, "Problems of Trial Practice in Loyalty and Security Cases," *Ohio State Law Journal,* CLXXXI (1957), 359–382; Michael C. Slotnick, "The Anathema of the Security Risk," *University of Miami Law Review,* XVII (1962–63), 10–50; Bruno Stein, "Loyalty and Security Cases in Arbitration," *Industrial and Labor Relations Review,* XVII (1963), 96–113; Lloyd K. Garrison, "Some Observations on the Loyalty-Security Hearings," *University of Chicago Law Review,* XXIII (1955), 126–153; Bontecou, *The Federal Loyalty-Security Program;* Brown, *Loyalty and Security,* pp. 41–45, 365–370, Appendix B by Ralph S. Brown and Robert Bower, "Tabulation of Data from Case Studies Collected by the Fund for the Republic"; Schaar, *Loyalty in America;* Harry Fleischman, "Labor and Civil Liberties," *AFL-CIO American Federationist,* March 1963.

9. Brown and Bower, "Tabulation of Data Collected by Fund for the Republic," in Brown, *Loyalty and Security,* pp. 269, 277.
10. Rauh, testimony, in *Security and Constitutional Rights.*
11. See *Security and Constitutional Rights,* pp. 978–979; Schaar, *Loyalty in America,* pp. 151–156.
12. Goldbloom, "A Case Study in Due Process."
13. See the detailed account in Olive H. Golden, "Administration of the Attorney-General's List of Subversive Organizations: The Case of the Workers Party–Independent Socialist League," unpublished M.A. thesis, University of Chicago, 1962.
14. Brown, *Loyalty and Security,* pp. 49–50.
15. Brown and Bower, "Tabulation of Data Collected by Fund for the Republic."
16. Fleischman, "Labor and Civil Liberties"; Harry Fleischman, Joyce Lewis Kornbluth, and Benjamin D. Segal, "Security, Civil Liberties, and Unions," Publication 31, American Federation of Labor and Congress of Industrial Organizations, September 1957; Rauh, testimony, in *Security and Constitutional Rights.* Brown, *Loyalty and Security,* pp. 138–141. For the role of the union in the case of an Air Force reservist "security risk," see "The Exception or the Rule," *UAW Ammunition,* November 1953, pp. 11–13.
17. Joseph P. Blank, "Security Risk," *Look,* May 17, 1955; Fred W. Friendly, *Due to Circumstances Beyond Our Control,* New York, 1967, pp. 3–22.
18. Brown, *Loyalty and Security,* pp. 24, 182; Brown and Bower, "Tabulation of Data Collected by Fund for the Republic"; Garrison, "Some Observations on the Loyalty-Security Hearings."
19. Brown, *Loyalty and Security,* pp. 185–189, 26; Kaufman and Kaufman, "Problems of Treatment from the Loyalty and Security Programs."
20. Brown, *Loyalty and Security,* pp. 81–91.
21. Yarmolinsky, *Case Studies in Personal Security.*
22. Marie Jahoda and Stuart W. Cook, "Security Measures and Freedom of Thought: An Exploratory Study of the Impact of Loyalty and Security Programs," *Yale Law Journal,* LXI (1952), 295–330.
23. *Ibid.,* p. 307.
24. *Ibid.,* p. 314.
25. *Ibid.,* p. 317.
26. Albert Einstein's supposed advice to young men not to seek a career in science because of security regulations did, conceivably, change the professional aspirations of some people. But the supply of creative scientific personnel, even those accepting positions utilizing classified material, seems to have been ample.

27. Note some of the variations presented in Brown, *Loyalty and Security, passim.*
28. Some of those subject to "security hearings" before senatorial confirmation committees included Director of Bureau of Standards Robert Conden, Ambassador to Russia Charles Bohlen, and Assistant Secretary of Defense Anna Rosenberg.
29. Schaar, *Loyalty in America.*
30. See Garrison, "Some Observations on the Loyalty-Security Hearings," p. 137, on the "new profession of security officers with vested interests in perpetuating the existing regime."
31. Fleischman, "Labor and Civil Liberties."
32. *Ibid.,* Rauh, *op. cit.,* pp. 962–997; Fleischman, Kornblut, and Segal, "Security, Civil Liberties, and Unions."
33. William F. Tompkins, "Substantive Recommendations of the Reports, an Internal View," *Ohio State Law Journal,* XVIII (1957), 317–330; Robert N. Shamansky, "Freedom and the Report of the Commission on Government Security," *ibid.,* pp. 331–358. The Bar Association recommendations were published in 1956. The report of the government commission, selected by the President, President of the Senate, and Speaker of the House, appeared in 1957.
34. Schaar, *Loyalty in America,* p. 179.
35. Alan F. Westin, "Reviewing the Loyalty Controversy," *Commentary,* December 1959, p. 528.
36. For story of "disclaimer" affidavit, see "The Disclaimer Affidavit, A Validation," *AAUP Bulletin,* XLVIII (1962), 324–329. On Medicare oath, see "Civil Liberties," CCXLII (December 1966). To indicate the change in attitudes of political leaders, the Senate passed a bill in 1967, introduced by Senator Sam Ervin of North Carolina, which would prevent all government agencies, except the FBI and CIA, from investigating the private lives of their employees ("Senators Ban Probes of Most U.S. Employees," *Newsday,* September 14, 1967). The loyalty-security efforts, however, continue to show up in strange places. Recently, published reports have revealed that the Department of Health, Education and Welfare has kept its own blacklist of those barred on such grounds from serving as advisers ("Scientists Decry HEW Blacklisting," *New York Times,* October 13, 1969). Interviews with several of those scientists disclosed that they had never made an application for such positions, so the effect has probably been minimal. The Department has responded by declaring it will examine its procedures.
37. Personal letter to author, quoted with permission of Alan Westin.
38. *United States vs. Rodell* (1967). See account in *Harvard Law Review,* LXXXI (1968), 43.

39. Tompkins, "Substantive Recommendations of the Reports, p. 323.
40. Slotnick, "The Anathema of the Security Risk."
41. A recent attempt by the ACLU to learn about the current loyalty-security situation from federal officials was able to locate little substantive information, almost implying that it was hardly relevant at this time. See Linda L. Watkins, "Survey of the Loyalty-Security Programs and Suitability Programs of the Federal Government," Communication to Free Speech Committee of the American Civil Liberties Union, January 13, 1969. The larger memberships of government employees' unions may be another reason for the decline in enforcing loyalty-security programs.

CHAPTER 10: BLACKLISTING

1. The major sources of information are the studies of blacklisting sponsored by the Fund for the Republic: John Cogley, *Report on Blacklisting, Vol. I—Movies, Vol. II—Radio-Television,* Fund for the Republic, 1956. Additional material for the earliest period of blacklisting comes from Merle Miller, *The Judges and the Judged,* Garden City, N.Y., 1952. A leading source for data about the period after the Cogley volumes are the two descriptions of the successful libel suit of one of the prominent blacklisted personnel, John Henry Faulk. One is the account by his famous lawyer, Louis Nizer, *The Jury Returns,* Garden City, N.Y., 1966, Chapter 4. The other is by Faulk himself, *Fear on Trial,* New York, 1964.
2. Perhaps the published reports, which were so critical of the process, may have avoided the more patently obvious cases of subversive records. Yet Cogley's account of movie blacklisting does point out that most of those affected in this medium were not "innocents."
3. Nizer, *The Jury Returns,* pp. 326–331.
4. Cogley, *Radio-Television,* p. 31. In January 1966, almost a decade and a half after her case, Miss Muir actually discussed it on a television talk show called "Girl Talk." The network on which it appeared, however, insisted on censoring out ("bleeping") any reference to the names of individuals and groups directly involved, presumably for fear of libel suits. Many commentators were too upset at the deletions to note the significance of the event. Obviously, for such a discussion to appear at all, the blacklisting phenomenon, as a regularized process, had to be long since gone. No effort was made to suppress the history, partly because such an attempt would create even more of a furor but also because the networks themselves had been relatively unaffected by the entire process. But what most everyone failed to emphasize

was that Miss Muir had never been rehired, for this would have been a tacit, official admission that the networks had actually barred her. The network executives would not prevent anyone else from making accusations, but they would, as a matter of policy, like to forget the whole thing.

5. Cogley, *Radio-Television,* p. 166.
6. *Ibid.,* p. 162.
7. The most publicized example was that of Philip Loeb of the television serial, "The Goldbergs." The accounts of ruined careers of performers, some of them explicitly named and others referred to anonymously, appear throughout the Cogley volume. See also Merle Miller, *The Judges and the Judged.*
8. Marie Jahoda, "Anti-Communism and Employment Policies," in Cogley, *Radio-Television,* pp. 248–250.
9. Nizer, *The Jury Returns,* pp. 225–238.
10. For instance, Robert Kintner, president of the American Broadcasting Company, refused to respond to pressures to bar, of all people, famed "stripper" Gypsy Rose Lee. He not only held his job but also subsequently became president of NBC. Prominent newscasters, like Edward R. Murrow and Howard K. Smith, were under constant attack from blacklisters; their careers were not affected. See Cogley, *Radio-Television,* pp. 24, 80–88; see also Jahoda, "Anti-Communism and Employment Policies," p. 256; Friendly, *Due to Circumstances Beyond Our Control,* Chapter 2.
11. Jahoda, "Anti-Communism and Employment Policies," p. 226.
12. Cogley, *Radio-Television,* p. 31. In addition, letters sent to General Foods were overwhelmingly against Miss Muir's dismissal. See Miller, *The Judges and the Judged,* pp. 40–41.
13. Cogley, *Radio-Television,* p. 108.
14. *Ibid.*
15. Perhaps some newscasters' careers were hurt by the attacks of the blacklisters, but the evidence is not striking, i.e., too many other factors may have been involved. See Cogley, *Radio-Television,* pp. 71–88; Friendly, *Due to Circumstances Beyond Our Control,* Chapter 2, *passim.* Both, however, indicate many examples to the contrary— commentators retained despite the many pressures. Similarly, controversial news programs were not barred by the networks despite even more vigorous pressures. See *ibid.*
16. Jahoda, "Anti-Communism and Employment Policies," p. 236.
17. Cogley, *Radio-Television,* p. 125. Her explanation that she had been influenced by her grandfather seemed to end the matter, a solution quite out of line with the typical tortuous experiences of most suspect personnel.

18. Cogley, *Radio-Television,* p. 162; "AFTRA Asks Blacklist Ban in Contracts," *New York Post,* September 28, 1956; Nizer, *The Jury Returns,* pp. 225–236; Faulk, *Fear on Trial,* Chapters 2 and 3.

19. Folk singer Pete Seeger did not appear on a network program for seventeen years. Dancer Paul Draper and harmonica player Larry Adler have, to the knowledge of the author, never appeared since their cases became *causes célèbres* early in the 1950's. Jean Muir has appeared only on special discussion programs. There may be others. But these are previously blacklisted people, not newly barred personnel. Examples of unofficial pressures may still be found, but there is no evidence of any definite policy, including clearance procedures, and so forth, since at least the early 1960's.

20. Nizer, *The Jury Returns,* Chapter 4; Faulk, *Fear on Trial.* The defense chose two varying lines of argument—there was no blacklist and the elimination of subversives was necessary. Such apparently contradictory positions were typical of those who defended the process. Faulk's case was bolstered by the prominent entertainment people who testified in his behalf, such as David Susskind, Garry Moore, and Tony Randall. The size of the judgment was considerably reduced on appeal to a higher court, but the plaintiff and his counsels still considered the result a substantial victory. Network officials on the stand merely insisted that Faulk did not appear because of declining audience appeal, an argument which, in the eyes of the jury, his counsels seemed to refute. For the officials to take any other position would have been to admit that they were blacklisting. As will be seen, movie executives were typically very open in their affirmations that they were denying employment to subversives.

21. See Cogley, *Movies,* for most of the details. A significant proportion of the blacklisted personnel was publicly identified, especially since so many appeared before or were named in congressional investigations. See some of the accounts in Walter Goodman's history of HUAC: Goodman, *The Committee,* especially, pp. 207–225, 297–309.

22. Pictures starring Judy Holliday were picketed by members of the Catholic War Veterans because she had been listed in *Red Channels.* Her studio officials questioned her, were convinced of her loyalty, and started a public relations campaign to redeem her. She finally appeared before the Senate's Internal Security Subcommittee, testified that she had always been an anti-Communist but had been duped into supporting Communist-front organizations, and promised to be careful in the future. That was all. A small group called the "Wage Earners Committee" attempted to exert pressure against top Hollywood officials, like producer Stanley Kramer and MGM head Doré Schary, by picketing their movies. Both filed suit on grounds of libel; a court

order stopped the picketing. Cogley, *Movies,* pp. 113–116. See also the cases of writer Abe Burrows, pp. 168–169, director John Huston and actor José Ferrer, pp. 157–158, and actor-dancer Gene Kelly, p. 159.

23. Emanating from a meeting at New York's Waldorf Astoria Hotel, it is commonly identified as the "Waldorf Statement." See *ibid.,* pp. 21–23.

24. Quote from Millard Lampell, "I Think I Ought to Mention I Was Blacklisted," *New York Times,* August 21, 1966, Section D.

25. The opposite, an intense hostility against those who informed, was, as would be expected, probably more typical. See Goodman, *The Committee,* pp. 297–309, 392. A conspicuous example was the break in the personal and artistic associations of playwright Arthur Miller and director Elia Kazan, who did name names. Yet their story also revealed how such breaches could be healed. Within a few years, Miller was writing plays for the Lincoln Center Repertory Theatre, directed by Kazan.

26. Dorothy B. Jones, "Communism and the Movies: A Study of Film Content," in Cogley, *Movies,* pp. 196–278.

27. Omnibus charges of connections with organizations and individuals vaguely defined as subversive appear to have been less common in Hollywood (*ibid., passim*). Similarly, the likely avoidance of such associations was not a prominently reported phenomenon.

28. Some of those who defended the blacklisting procedures in all media, as well as those who merely criticized the Cogley volumes, pointed to the fact that "Communists" exercised their own kind of blacklist against some of their opponents. Cogley accepts this as probable, but explains that such procedures were occasional, informal acts rather than regularized practices.

CHAPTER 11: THE McCARTHY ERA: AN OVERVIEW

1. For instance, Bell, *The Radical Right;* Shils, *The Torment of Secrecy,* Truman, "The American System in Crisis."

2. Michael Paul Rogin, *The Intellectuals and McCarthy: The Radical Specter,* Cambridge, Mass., 1967.

3. Shils, *The Torment of Secrecy;* Bell, *The Radical Right.*

4. C. Wright Mills, *The Power Elite,* New York, 1959; *White Collar,* New York, 1951; David Riesman, wtih Reuel Denney and Nathan Glazer, *The Lonely Crowd,* New Haven, 1950. For Riesman's analysis of McCarthyism, see his collaborative article with Nathan Glazer, "The Intellectuals and the Discontented Classes," in Bell, *The Radical*

Right, pp. 105–135. Mills's casual discussion of McCarthyism, almost in passing, in *The Power Elite,* pp. 232–233, supports the status anxiety interpretation.

5. Marie Jahoda, "Psychological Issues in Civil Liberties," *American Psychologist,* V (1956), 234–240.

6. William Whyte, *The Organization Man,* Garden City, N.Y., 1957.

7. The formal, impersonal, and legalistic protections that bureaucratic structures are presumed to emphasize offered some barriers to suppression in academic circles, particularly the existence of tenure systems. See Chapter 14, "Academic Freedom," *infra.* In the case of the loyalty-security programs, they were generally absent, except that formal stipulations offered a device for those appealing decisions made against them and provided a basis for court decisions which checked some of the abuses.

8. With all the changes that have occurred and the apparent emergence of new styles of politics, the social basis of vote choice in the 1968 election was very close to what was typical of the 1930's, to the astonishment of many commentators. See Samuel Lubell, "The Voters Speak," release of United Features Syndicate, October 30, 1968.

9. Arthur Koestler, *Darkness at Noon,* New York, 1941.

CHAPTER 12: THE PROBLEMS OF THE MID-1960's: THE CRISIS OF LEGITIMACY

1. See Chapter 4, "Courts and Civil Liberties," *supra.*

2. "Civil Liberties Reporter," New Jersey Civil Liberties Union, May 1968. For an account of the vigilante group involved, see Paul Goldberger, "Tony Imperiale Stands Vigilant for Law and Order," *New York Times Magazine,* September 29, 1968.

3. The national population cross-section was even hostile to the earlier, more acceptable forms of militant demonstrations. Two-thirds were against freedom riders in 1961 and 1963, and almost the same proportion opposed school boycotts in 1965. Two-thirds were, in general, against all civil rights and student demonstrations in 1965. After several waves of ghetto outbursts had become a common national experience, 81 per cent believed, in August 1967, that no police brutality had been evident. See Hazel Erskine, "The Polls—Demonstrations and Race Riots," *Public Opinion Quarterly,* XXXI (1967–68), 655–677.

4. Edward A. Suchman, Robin M. Williams, Jr., and Rose A. Goldsen, "Student Reaction to Impending Military Service," *American Sociological Review,* XVIII (1953), 293–304.

5. A periodical newsletter called *Resist,* which contains the added caption: "A Call to Resist Illegitimate Authority," presents the following argument in support of a group that had burned draft card files: "Some property, like some laws and some actions of our government, is illegitimate, and people of conscience have a right and a responsibility to take action against it." *Resist,* Cambridge, Mass., Newsletter, October 1968, p. 5.

6. The complex issues have been further exacerbated by such unique manifestations among servicemen as the formation of a labor union for military personnel, the publication of underground newspapers, and organized demonstrations. One example of the latter, a sit-down strike of twenty-seven soldiers in a stockade, resulted in an average sentence for the three on trial of fifteen years. (See Paul Feldman, "Injustice at Presidio," *New America,* March 20, 1969.) This seems to reflect a typical reaction of military commanders in such situations, as described by one observer, "by following the routine it knows so well —overkill." (Robert Sherill, "Must the Citizen Give Up His Civil Liberties When He Joins the Army?," *New York Times Magazine,* May 18, 1969, p. 21.) Any meeting or extensive discussion of the public issue that is so pressingly relevant to them, the war itself, is officially stifled. As explained by one officer: "I think we all recognize that it is an unpopular war. . . . And the more of this sort of thing that goes on, the harder it is for us to maintain authority both here, in training our men, and also in the battlefield. . . . So at a certain point we have to say: 'these activities are all right but beyond that you cannot go,' because otherwise we will have an undisciplined rabble" (*ibid.,* p. 26). Propaganda for peace is defined as one of the practices beyond the permissible. The dispute is thus another, special form of the legitimacy crisis, the legally protected option for expression versus the right of the military to develop the most effective fighting force, a dilemma always present in a democracy at arms but brought to what seems an ultimate in value and personal choice in this situation.

7. This was the publicized case of Captain Howard Levy, a medical officer convicted of disobeying a lawful order to provide special training for Green Beret soldiers going to Vietnam. Actually, evidence at his trial revealed that this charge developed after action against him had already started, and the contemplated accusation because of his action was originally only dereliction of duty, which would have resulted in a reprimand. But the other indictments, of which he was also convicted, were apparently the major elements of his case, and probably prompted the original action. "Civil Liberties," July 1967.

8. The Supreme Court denied this allegation by upholding the law. See *United States vs. O'Brian,* 88 Supreme Court, 16:73 (1968).
9. "Spock Guilty, Plans Appeal," *Bergen Record,* June 15, 1968. The convictions were overturned by a federal court of appeals on what amounted to the prosecutor's failure to prove genuine active involvement in organized appeals to avoid the draft. The basic constitutional issues are thus unresolved. ("U.S. Court Upsets Spock Conviction," *New York Times,* July 12, 1969.) For a general analysis of the case, see Fred Graham, "The Case Against Spock, et al." *New York Times,* January 16, 1968, Section E.
10. Because the directives were not legally binding, a federal district court declared it could not overturn them. See "Draft Rule Suit Lost by Students," *New York Times,* March 8, 1968.
11. Whatever the provocations, the capriciousness of the violence against particular demonstrators is one of the most frightening eventualities. A shocking illustration was the beating of women participating in the Pentagon confrontation of the fall of 1967, at a time and place where the militancy of the demonstrators appeared to be at low ebb. See Norman Mailer, *The Armies of the Night,* New York, 1968, pp. 298–316.
12. "Dove Curbs Are Sought by Reagan," *Bergen Record,* October 26, 1967, p. 5.
13. Donald Sullivan, "Rutgers Dispute Looms as Central Issue in New Jersey," *New York Times,* October 17, 1965. Attempts of various groups, led by the local American Legion post, to pressure the University of California at San Diego to remove Herbert Marcuse, defined as a "guru of the New Left," from his faculty position at the university have failed ("Legion Asks Marcuse Probe," *Bergen Record,* August 16, 1968). Other cases of nontenured faculty members, or those denied promotion, have been reported. Without attempting any evaluation of what seem to be complex situations, what is noteworthy is that there have been so few of them.
14. Seymour M. Lipset and Paul Seabury, "The Lessons of Berkeley," in Lipset and Wolin, *The Berkeley Student Revolt,* p. 349.
15. Sheldon S. Wolin and John H. Schaar, "The Abuses of the Multiversity," *ibid.,* p. 363.
16. See *Crisis at Columbia: Report of the Fact Finding Commission on Columbia Disturbances,* New York, 1968.
17. For an account of the student New Left on campuses which crisply summarizes much of the existing commentary on the subject, see Kenneth Keniston, "You Have to Grow Up in Scarsdale to Know How Bad Things Really Are," *New York Times Magazine,* April 27, 1969.

Keniston particularly emphasizes their virtues, both personally and in their aims. Even though each situation has been quite different, including the amount and type of disruption that ensued and the administration reaction to it, a very common popular attitude was recently succinctly summarized by Governor Thomas McCall of Oregon: "Americans are fed up to their eardrums and eyeballs" ("Campus Disorders Bring Demands for States to Act," *New York Times,* May 4, 1969, p. 1). Such sentiments are probably particularly prevalent among those with no direct contact with academic institutions.

18. Such statutes have not been enforced by college administrators, probably for some combination of technical, strategic, and moral reasons. As a reaction, legislators have sought to bring pressure on school administrators by demanding that they submit regulations on this matter to the United States commissioner of education.

19. Quoted in Grayson Kirk, "A Message to Alumni, Parents, and Other Friends at Columbia," June 1, 1968, p. 5.

20. Jerry Rubin, "American Mythology," *Delphian* (student publication), Adelphi University, February 28, 1969, p. 11.

21. Arnold Forster and Benjamin R. Epstein, *Danger on the Right,* New York, 1964; selections written about the situation, as of 1962, in Bell, *The Radical Right;* Harold M. Proshansky and Richard I. Evans, eds., "American Political Extremism in the 1960's," *Journal of Social Issues,* XIX (1963).

22. Daniel Walker, *Rights in Conflict,* New York, 1968; Norman Mailer, *Miami and the Siege of Chicago,* New York, 1968.

23. *Report of the National Advisory Commission on Civil Disorders,* New York, 1968.

24. Keniston, "You Have to Grow Up in Scarsdale."

25. Several studies, for instance, indicated a significant sentiment for George Wallace in 1968 among traditionally Democratic industrial trade unionists. Many of these ultimately voted for Humphrey, but their earlier sentiments were very indicative. See Samuel Lubell, "The Voters Speak," release of United Features Syndicate, November 12, 1968.

26. Gordon K. Haskell, "Problems in the ACLU," *Dissent,* XV (1968), pp. 229–232; "Civil Liberties," July 1968, pp. 1, 3.

27. To give one example, the number of members increased from 90,000 to 110,000 in the one year, 1967 ("Civil Liberties," July 1968, p. 6). Since the organization has recently taken stands on what can be defined as substantive rather than civil-libertarian questions, other motives for joining may be involved. Others have probably left the organization for the same reason. The general adherence to the de-

fense of civil liberties by so many committed Americans remains, nevertheless, an obvious interpretation of this statistic.

28. For faculty attitudes toward students, see *Crisis at Columbia;* Allen H. Barton, "The Columbia Crisis: Campus, Vietnam, and the Ghetto," Columbia University Bureau of Applied Social Research, July 1, 1968. For a sympathetic attitude toward ghetto rioters by an official government source, see *Report of the National Advisory Commission on Civil Disorders.* One recent development, to which we have been able to devote little attention, is the growing popularity of "guerrilla warfare" tactics among some protesters—bombings and so forth. Obviously, this can widen the demand for suppression of protest groups.

CHAPTER 13: CENSORSHIP

1. David H. Bayley, *Public Liberties in the New States,* Chicago, 1964. For the recent French experience, see Herbert R. Lottman, "Letter from Paris," *New York Times Book Review,* September 1, 1969.

2. For instance, there is little evidence that anyone condemned Chaucer's *Canterbury Tales* for his inclusion of the "Miller's Tale" and the "Reeve's Tale," whose bawdiness and vulgar language are more shocking than most things condemned by decent literature groups today. The question of controls over violence in all media is excluded in this discussion because of many special complexities. Some attention is given to the question in relation to television content in Chapter 15, "Some Other Issues," *infra.*

3. Morris L. Ernst and Alan U. Schwartz, *Censorship: The Search for the Obscene,* New York, 1964, Chapters 1–3.

4. H. Frank Way, Jr., *Liberty in the Balance: Current Issues in Civil Liberties,* New York, 1964, pp. 31–32.

5. Konvitz, *Expanding Liberties,* p. 199.

6. Way, *Liberty in the Balance,* p. 36.

7. *Ibid.,* pp. 34–35.

8. Ernst and Schwartz, *Censorship,* p. 68.

9. Markmann, *The Noblest Cry,* pp. 298–302.

10. A casual examination of one list of objectionable works, that in the "National Office for Decent Literature" newsletter of the fall of 1964, reveals such conglomerate listings as Robert Lindner's breezy account of his experiences as a psychotherapist, *The Fifty-Minute Hour,* interspersed between items entitled *$50 a Night* and *Flesh.*

11. At one time in American history, the roles of decision-maker and influencer were actually legally combined, significantly, in the person

of Anthony Comstock and his organization. Under a federal law passed in 1873, Comstock was appointed a special agent of the Post Office with police powers. His "Society for the Suppression of Vice" received part of the fines collected from convicted violators of the law. Private censorship was thus legally enforced (Ernst and Schwartz, *Censorship*, p. 33).

12. See Konvitz, *Expanding Liberties*, pp. 214–216. As an extreme example, a Los Angeles trial produced a conviction, while one hundred miles to the south, in San Diego, a similar trial led to an acquittal. A 1964 Supreme Court decision terminated this confusion.

13. The New York State Legislature passed a bill, vetoed by the governor, which would punish any storekeeper for allowing a minor, unaccompanied by an adult, to come into his premises if he sold objectionable literature. In New Jersey, a bill which would have made the presentation of any specified parts of the human body illegal was passed unanimously by both houses of the legislature. (Reporters quipped that the graphic descriptions in the legislation, freely available, would drive pornography for sale off the market.) The bill was finally vetoed by the governor on constitutional grounds. The legislature of the same state adopted a law making it criminal to "exploit lust for commercial gain." Despite previous court rulings, a bookstore clerk was arrested in St. Louis for selling *Candy*. The metropolitan Airports Commission in Minneapolis barred Henry Miller's works from airport newsstands, basing the decision simply on their own opinion that they were objectionable. (See Civil Liberties," October 1966, pp. 3–4.)

14. A complex setup was that devised in Rhode Island in 1956. A five-man commission to "encourage morality in youth" was assigned the task of "educating" the public about obscene material and recommending prosecution for violation of state obscenity laws. In practice, notices from the commission to booksellers were usually followed by a visit from a policeman, who sought to learn why proscribed books were not removed. The dealer usually complied. Bantam Books appealed all the way to the Supreme Court, where a majority declared that such informal sanctions were in violation of due process (Ernst and Schwartz, *Censorship*, pp. 237–240).

15. *Roth vs. United States* and *Albertis vs. United Statees* 354 U.S. 476 (1957).

16. See accounts in Ernst and Schwartz, *Censorship;* Konvitz, *Expanding Liberties*, pp. 168–242.

17. See discussion in *ibid.*, pp. 229–242.

18. The Institute for Sex Research, popularly identified with its founder, Dr. Alfred Kinsey, studied 2,721 men, 1,356 of them serving prison

terms for sex crimes. The conclusions were, in the words of Dr. Paul Gebhard, one of the collaborators: "Few are in any way inspired by pornography . . . their disinterested and indeed scornful attitude toward pornography was perhaps best summed up by a fairly typical prisoner who told me 'you can't do nuttin with a pitcher.' . . . Not one of the men interviewed seemed to have gone to prison as a result of exposure to pornography, either immediately before his crime or even at some distant time in his adolescence" (Paul Gebhard, "The 1965 Kinsey Report: Our Dangerous Sex Laws," *Ladies' Home Journal,* May 1965, p. 64).

To discern the opinions of those who should have the most direct knowledge, the "New Jersey Committee for the Right to Read" mailed questionnaires to all listed psychiatrists and to a large proportion of psychologists in the state; the overwhelming majority of both responded. The research was prompted by particular pending legislation. Some questions referred to the legislation, but all were directed at probing more general attitudes. Only a few of these professional practitioners remembered a single case of a patient who was "provoked into anti-social behavior as a result of sexually oriented literature." The overwhelming majority thought that the type of "sexually-oriented literature" to be barred in the proposed bill "might have a value for some individuals, and might in these cases serve to minimize anti-social behavior by providing a vicarious outlet." A large majority thought that the exclusion of such material from libraries and stores would not encourage a "healthy and accurate view of sex by the young person." Few thought that the passage of proposed legislation would contribute to the improvement of juvenile mental health. A decisive majority felt that "concealment of sexual and anatomical information might tend to promote a pathological degree of curiosity." Most declared that there should be no limitation of reading matter for juveniles or that such limitation should come only from the parents. (See "A Survey of New Jersey Psychiatrists and Psychologists Pertaining to the Proscription by Legislation of Sexually Oriented Publications for Persons Under 18 Years," Final Report, January 1967, New Jersey Committee for the Right to Read.)

19. Harry Golden, "Charlotte's Anti-Smut Unit," *Paterson (N.J.) News,* February 15, 1965, p. 35.
20. Laura Clarke, "A History of the New Jersey Committee for the Right to Read," unpublished M.A. thesis, Montclair State College, 1966.
21. "The Censorship of Periodicals and Books and Its Relationship to the Community Legal Process," a research proposal submitted by Joseph Tanenhaus, George Robert Boynton, and Douglas Edmonds, Political Science Department, University of Iowa, September 26, 1966, p. 10.

Although the author has not yet seen any of the completed results of this study, it seems to promise an unusually productive research undertaking in the entire area of the sociology of civil liberties.

22. The proposed legislation declared that district and city attorneys *must* prosecute whenever any citizen charges a work with obscenity, or face removal from office. This extensive proposal, revealing the intense passion on the subject of at least a few people, was probably unconstitutional. As such, it was opposed by several prosecutors of large cities and was defeated at the polls. See "Civil Liberties"; Walter Winfield, "Politics of Smut," *Nation,* April 18, 1966, pp. 456–459. On Fortas, see Saul Freedman, "New Fortas Hearings Spotlight Those Films," *New York Post,* September 13, 1968.

23. For an example in New Jersey, see "Civil Liberties," October 1966.

24. See Laura Clarke, "A History of the New Jersey Committee for the Right to Read," for a description of the history and activity of the organization.

25. For examples of all the above, see *ibid.,* Chapter 3.

26. A fitting example was provided by a much-reported campaign in the Yorkville section of New York City. Organized by local clergymen, with widespread local citizen participation and approval of government officials, the immediate results were well-attended meetings as well as planned and executed legal and informal actions against neighborhood dealers selling proscribed material. But, despite the initial fanfare, fewer and fewer people came to the meetings and less and less was done. The entire operation soon dissipated, even though the campaign officially continued. See Murray Kempton, "Impurities in Yorkville," *New Republic,* March 16, 1963, pp. 10–17.

27. See Chapter 5, "The Relevance of Public Opinion," *supra.*

28. Research proposal, "The Censorship of Periodicals and Books," p. 8.

29. The most significant recent case was *Times Film Corp. vs. Chicago* 365 U.S. 43 (1961). The court, however, subsequently ruled that the burden of proof was on the censoring agency and that a court order was necessary to prevent the showing of a film that was barred (*Freedman vs. Maryland,* No. 690 October Term, 1964).

30. Murray Schumach, *The Face on the Cutting Room Floor,* New York, 1964, pp. 83–116. Some government agencies, like the United States Information Agency and the Defense Department, have attempted to alter the content of specific films, at most producing minor variations.

31. *Mutual Film Corporation vs. Industrial Commission of Ohio,* 239 U.S. 230 (1915).

32. A comprehensive detailed summary is Ira H. Carmen's, *Movies, Censorship and the Law,* Ann Arbor, 1966.

33. "The Motion Picture Production Code," Motion Picture Association

of America, Inc., December 1956, pp. 2, 4; for a discussion of the code, see Schumach, *The Face on the Cutting Room Floor*, pp. 33–48.

34. Harold Gardner, *Catholic Viewpoint on Censorship*, Garden City, N.Y., 1958, p. 84. For other discussion of the Legion of Decency, see Schumach, *The Face on the Cutting Room Floor*, pp. 84–93.

35. See the discussion in Schumach, *The Face on the Cutting Room Floor*, pp. 44ff.

36. The line between artistic integrity and pandering to crude tastes is difficult to determine. The author does, however, agree with many critics that a significant number of American and foreign films seem to be directed at titillation and morbidity rather than authentic expression. A conspicuously blatant example which we have personally seen was *The Detective*, starring Frank Sinatra.

37. The picture, an adaptation of the play, "The Moon Is Blue," was actually without a seal for the now unbelievable reason that it included the word "virgin."

38. Schumach, *The Face on the Cutting Room Floor*, 90–93.

39. The production code, as modified in 1966, is only the continuation of a ritualistic formality, including such admonitions as "restraint and care shall be exercised." The new system of classification, by which the industry officially designates films according to their suitability for younger audiences, is a method that has long been prevalent in many countries. Whatever one's personal opinion of the process, it is not, in reality, a significant form of censorship, i.e., it has hardly curtailed the production or exhibitions of any projected movies. See Robert Windeler, "Hollywood Is Preparing a Broad Film Classification System," *New York Times*, September 21, 1968.

40. See Edward N. Saveth, "What to Do About Dangerous Textbooks," *Commentary*, February 1952, pp. 99–106.

41. *Ibid.;* Benjamin Fine, "The Truth About Schoolbook Censorship," *Parents Magazine*, December 1952, reprinted in Robert B. Downs, ed., *The First Freedom*, Chicago, 1960, pp. 349–353.

42. *Ibid.;* Saveth, "What to Do About Dangerous Textbooks."

43. Fine, "The Truth About Schoolbook Censorship"; Zena Horn, "The Teacher and the Threat of Book Censorship," *Teaching About the Bill of Rights*, Proceedings of the 6th Annual Institute for Social Studies Teachers, Paterson (N.J.) State College, 1964, pp. 17–22.

44. This interpretation is based mostly on negative evidence—the apparent absence of the publicized controversies of the past.

45. Jack Nelson and Gene Robers, Jr., *The Censors and the Schools*, Boston, 1963, cited by Horn, "The Teacher and the Threat of Book Censorship," p. 20.

46. Marjorie Fiske, *Book Selection and Censorship;* Robert Shaplen, "Scars-

dale's Battle of the Books," *Commentary,* December 1950, pp. 530–540, reprinted in *The First Freedom,* pp. 359–370; James Rorty, "The Librarians Take a Stand," *Commentary,* June 1955, pp. 541–549, reprinted in *ibid.,* pp. 303–310; E. W. Temblen, "They Play It Safe: North Carolina Librarian Report of Survey," *Library Journal,* XC (1965), 2495–2498; F. Castagna, "Climate of Intellectual Freedom: Why Is It Always So Bad in California?," *American Library Association Bulletin,* LIX (1965), 27–33; Henry Madden, "On the Firing Line in a Bad Climate," *American Library Association Bulletin,* LV (1961), 33–34; B. Collins, "Ordeal at Long Beach," *Library Journal,* XC (1965), 2486–2490. Some of these are accounts of publicized disputes in which some of the general community was involved. Others are reports of the librarians themselves. The more dramatic conflicts are a minor element in the vistas of the librarians studied, as later indicated.

47. Fiske, *Book Selection and Censorship.*
48. See accounts in Shaplen, "Scarsdale's Battle of the Books"; Rorty, "The Librarians Take a Stand"; analysis in Fiske, *Book Selection and Censorship.*
49. See examples of the latter in *ibid.*

CHAPTER 14: ACADEMIC FREEDOM

1. The basis for most of the historical material through World War I is Richard Hofstadter and Walter P. Metzger, *The Development of Academic Freedom in the United States,* New York, 1955.
2. *Ibid.,* pp. 335–338.
3. Economist Henry C. Adams was dismissed from Cornell for delivering a pro-labor speech; the famous labor economist John R. Commons lost his job at Indiana University; Edward A. Ross, one of the distinguished American pioneer sociologists, was forced to resign at Stanford University because of pressure from Mrs. Stanford, wife of the railroad magnate who founded the university. On the other hand, both Commons and Ross had long and distinguished careers at the University of Wisconsin (*ibid.,* Chapter 9).
4. Thorstein Veblen, *The Higher Learning in America,* New York, 1957.
5. Quoted in Hofstadter and Metzger, *The Development of Academic Freedom,* p. 479.
6. *Ibid.,* Chapter 10.
7. *Ibid.,* p. 499.
8. James Wechsler, *Revolt on the Campus,* New York, 1935.

9. See account in Robert M. MacIver, *Academic Freedom in Our Time,* New York, 1955, pp. 154–156.

10. *Ibid.,* pp. 144–146. World War II produced few threats to academic freedom, a counterpart of the absence of infringements of freedom of expression generally, and, for the same reason, the lack of opposition to the war. About the only significant case was that of Professor George Hartmann of Teachers College, Columbia University, who, as a socialist-pacifist, opposed the United States' entry into the war beforehand and then became associated with a "Peace Now" campaign. With all the procedural complexities typical of such situations, including disputes about contract provisions and tenure rights, the administration's attempt to ease him out was revoked by the courts. When Hartmann obtained another teaching position, the legal conflict was resolved by an out-of-court settlement (*ibid.,* pp. 144–146).

11. See Chapter 5, "The Relevance of Public Opinion," *supra.*

12. MacIver, *Academic Freedom in Our Time,* p. 127.

13. Lionel Lewis, "The Academic Axe," *Social Problems,* XII (1964) 151–158.

14. Paul F. Lazarsfeld and Wagner Thielens, Jr., *The Academic Mind,* Glencoe, Ill., 1958. Most of the material that immediately follows is from Chapters 2–4.

15. The two presidents were Rainey of the University of Texas and Stoddard of the University of Illinois. Rainey was removed by the governing board after a long series of wrangles over the board's interference in internal affairs—selection of administrators, textbook choice, and research projects. Amidst the usual charges of possible subversion, the existence of a power struggle was very apparent. The board simply wanted to run the university, without interference from either administrators or faculty. It is interesting that several board members criticized the idea of tenure and referred to the AAUP as the "professors' CIO union" (MacIver, *Academic Freedom in Our Time,* pp. 74–75, 90–95).

Stoddard was pressured into resigning after the university had been publicly accused of being a haven for "reds, pinks, and communists" by a member of the state legislature, and Stoddard had been publicly criticized by the governing board for his role in the development of UNESCO. But intramural disputes exacerbated the situation—an open conflict among the faculty at the School of Commerce in which Stoddard was identified with the "winning" side, and his unwillingness to permit the utilization of the university facilities for research on the controversial drug, Krebiozen, by Dr. Ivy, the head of the Medical School. (It is conceivable that a claim could be made that Stoddard infringed on Dr. Ivy's "academic freedom.")

One of the most prominent *causes célèbres* occurred at Olivet College in Michigan, a progressive liberal arts college in what could readily be described as a very conservative community. The governing board, officially associated with the Congregational Church, included people who were upset by the political views of some faculty members, including the Socialist party candidate for Vice-President of the United States in 1948. In addition, the financial strain became serious. A corporation lawyer was appointed president to straighten everything out. His method was to ignore faculty autonomy and to fire particular professors, starting with one accused of being a socialist but, more importantly, chastised for wearing a beret in town. This obvious move in the direction of every type of conformism wrecked the academic standing of a promising college. It was not, however, a typical McCarthyite phenomenon. *Ibid.*, pp. 147–149.

16. AAUP censure of large universities in this period was usually based on such grounds. That dismissals of current Communist party members produced little faculty resentment is illustrated by events at the University of Washington in the late 1940's, when a state legislative committee named ten faculty members as present or former members of the Communist party. In this case, due process was observed. A faculty committee determined that only two were still currently members. The president then recommended their dismissal, plus that of one of the others for different reasons. Only the latter move resulted in faculty protest. *Ibid.*, pp. 179–182.

17. See George R. Stewart, *The Year of the Oath*, Garden City, N.Y., 1950.

18. Lazarsfeld and Thielens, *The Academic Mind*, Chapter 10.

19. William P. Fidler, "Academic Freedom in the South Today," *AAUP Bulletin*, LI (1965), 413–421; Lazarsfeld and Thielens, *The Academic Mind, passim*, especially pp. 331–335; "Academic Freedom in Mississippi: A Report of a Special Committee," *AAUP Bulletin*, LI (1965), 341–356.

20. "Students and Teachers Picket St. John's," *New York Times*, December 19, 1965; "Academic Freedom and Tenure: St. John's University, New York," *AAUP Bulletin*, LII (1966), 12–19.

21. Lazarsfeld and Thielens, *The Academic Mind*, p. 195. For the material that follows, see *ibid., passim*.

22. The material was gathered from the issues of the *AAUP Bulletin*, March 1958 to June 1967. Among the larger "quality" institutions earlier censured were the University of California, Rutgers University, Ohio State University, and New York University. Those on the list in 1967 represent the more common type of school included, represented by such examples as Benedict College, Alcorn Mechanical and

Engineering College, University of South Florida, and Sam Houston State College. The quality designation, used by Lazarsfeld and Thielens, is based upon criteria such as volumes in library, proportion of Ph.D.'s on the faculty, and ratio of annual budget to number of students. That the type of university we have so described would be relatively high on these criteria is simply assumed from the obvious nature of such institutions, a sufficient indicator for our immediate purposes.

23. Theodore Caplow and Reece J. McGee, *The Academic Marketplace,* Garden City, N.Y., 1958, pp. 40, 195.

24. See Chapter 11, "The McCarthy Era: An Overview," *supra.*

25. Hofstadter and Metzger, *The Development of Academic Freedom,* p. 492.

26. To take a well-known historical example of dissidence as an excuse, Cattell's removal from Columbia during World War I was officially a result of his anti-war actions, but it is reasonable to believe that authorities were out to "get him" for his generally "brash, tactless, and offensive" behavior (Hofstadter and Metzger, *The Development of Academic Freedom,* p. 499). For the Mount Everest story, see "Academic Freedom and Tenure; Tufts University," *AAUP Bulletin,* LII (1966), 24–31. That personality conflicts and power plays are transformed into academic freedom cases is difficult to validate by typical reports, even official AAUP inquiries. Perhaps the best suggestive material comes from novelists. See particularly, Mary McCarthy, *The Groves of Academe,* New York, 1951.

27. For faculty attitudes, see Lionel Lewis, "Faculty Support of Academic Freedom and Self-Government," *Social Problems,* XV (1956), 450–461. The findings are too detailed and varied to report, but they are of such a nature as to produce apprehension among those favoring the two types of freedoms. For instance, of five hundred polled faculty at a large state university, only slightly fewer than half believed a university should defend teachers expressing various "controversial views." Only a fifth believed that faculties should participate in selection and appointment of other faculty members. Attitudes were correlated with the particular disciplines taught—social science and humanities teachers were much more for faculty rights than physical science teachers and those in professional schools, for instance. Such survey data, while valuable, ignore the saliency dimension, a typical defect of such studies. What one would do if there were an actual issue is thus not apparent.

For attitudes of trustees, see Rodney T. Hartnett, "College and University Trustees: Their Backgrounds, Roles, and Educational Attitudes," Princeton New Jersey, Educational Testing Service, 1965. Of more than five hundred trustees queried, 64 per cent believed administrators and/or trustees should have sole responsibility in determining tenure, but a decisive majority would give faculty authority over curricular matters. Other findings are generally similar. Of additional interest is the fact that the public junior college trustees were least likely to grant faculty authority, whereas the selective (quality) private university trustees were most likely to grant such authority.

28. Hofstadter and Metzger, *The Development of Academic Freedom*, p. 491.
29. David Fellman, "The Association's Agenda," *AAUP Bulletin*, LII (1966), 108.
30. Veblen, *Higher Learning*, pp. 128–130.
31. See discussion in Konvitz, *Expanding Liberties*, Chapter 3.
32. See criticism of Columbia faculty on this score in *Crisis at Columbia*.
33. See Lewis, "Faculty Support of Academic Freedom and Self Government."
34. For a comprehensive discussion of the subject, see Sol Jacobson, "Student and Due Process: A Study in Contrasts at the City University of New York," *AAUP Bulletin*, LII (1966), 196–204.
35. Hofstadter and Metzger, *The Development of Academic Freedom*, pp. 306–311; for a general historical description of faculty "subordination" to students, see Walter Laqueur, "Reflections on Youth Movements," *Commentary*, June 1969, pp. 33–41.

CHAPTER 15: SOME OTHER ISSUES: A MISCELLANY

1. For a comprehensive historical account, see James R. Wiggins, *Freedom or Secrecy*, rev. ed., New York, 1964.
2. Arnold Beichman, "The Unmanageable Issue Behind 'Managed News,'" *Columbia University Forum*, VI (1963), 4–10; Victor Bernstein and Jesse Gordon, "The Press and the Bay of Pigs," *Columbia University Forum*, X (1967), 4–13.
3. *Ibid.*, p. 10.
4. Even those who attempt to disclose information about an aspect of the company's operation that is of special relevance to the consuming public, the actual products, may be subject to harassment. Witness the private investigations of crusader Ralph Nader (*New York Times,* April 20, 1969).
5. Witness, for instance, the disputes about cigarette advertising (*Wall Street Journal*, April 23, 1969).
6. "Freedom of Expression in a Commercial Context," *Harvard Law Review*, LXXVIII (1965), 1191–1211.

7. For the Reich story, see *New York Times,* September 11, 1960. For the Krebiozen story, see *ibid.,* January 13, 15, 1960.

8. See Anthony Lewis, "The Case of 'Trial by Press'," *New York Times Magazine,* October 18, 1964,

9. See "Free Press v. Fair Trial," "Civil Liberties," November 1966.

10. *Ibid.*

11. Besides the suit of John Henry Faulk, discussed in Chapter 10, "Blacklisting" (*supra*), some of the more famous suits were those involving prominent journalists on both sides—James Wechsler against Walter Winchell and Quentin Reynolds against Westbrook Pegler. The latter case, which provided the plot for the Broadway play *A Case of Libel,* is described by Reynolds' lawyer, Louis Nizer, in his series of reminiscences, *My Life in Court,* New York, 1963, Chapter 1.

12. For a detailed description of the history of legal decisions on libel, see Robert H. Phelps and E. Douglas Hamilton, *Libel: Risks and Responsibilities,* New York, 1966. For an interesting recent case, a suit of a sociologist against "right-wing" critics, see Arnold Rose, *Libel and Academic Freedom,* Minneapolis, 1968.

13. For the legal background of the case, see "For Goldwater, the Problem Is to Prove Malice," *New York Times,* May 12, 1968. Goldwater won a $75,000 judgment at the trial.

14. His dissent occurred in response to one of the most significant rulings on this question, *Beauharnais vs. Illinois,* 343 U.S. 250 (1952).

15. See discussions in Emerson, Haber, and Dorsen, *Political and Civil Rights,* pp. 568–615.

16. *New York Times,* January 23, 1969.

17. For a thorough description and analysis, see Alan F. Westin, *Privacy and Freedom,* New York, 1967; "Hearings of Subcommittee on Administrative Practice and Procedure," U.S. Senate Judiciary Committee, 89th Cong.

18. The case involved reporter Marie Torre, given a jail sentence for refusing to disclose the network official who made a comment about Judy Garland. See *New York Times,* June 21, 1959.

19. Morris Ernst, *The First Freedom,* New York, 1946.

20. See *New York Times,* March 13, 1967, for attitudes of network officials.

21. The apparent objectionable material was folk singer Joan Baez's reference to her husband, about to begin a prison sentence as a draft violator. For a discussion of the entire question of internal network censorship, see Nicholas Johnson, "The Silent Screen," *TV Guide,* July 5, 1969, pp. 6–13. Among the types of controls he lists is the avoidance of references to anything that might be inimical to sponsors. Significantly, news and discussion programs have been much less

affected than those defined as entertainment, except for their possible elimination because of low audience ratings, an issue very closely enmeshed with the subject of mass culture. Also see Friendly, *Due to Circumstances Beyond Our Control.*

22. Edward Engberg, "A Free and Responsible Press: Where Are They Now?," *The Center Magazine,* I (1967), 22–27, 98–102.

23. Interestingly, the number of magazines in the United States is increasing, despite the folding of several well-known publications. See Philip H. Dougherty, "What Future for Magazines," *New York Times,* April 27, 1969, Section 3.

CHAPTER 16: CIVIL LIBERTIES IN PRIVATE ORGANIZATIONS: THE CASE OF THE LABOR UNIONS

1. J. B. Atelson, "Union Members' Rights of Free Speech and Assembly," *Minnesota Law Review,* LI (1967), 403–490.

2. In actuality, the administrative agencies have turned out to be bodies through which protesting unionists must go before making their court appeals. Many illustrations appear in the issues of *Union Democracy in Action,* Nos. 7–35. The issues of this newsletter, edited by Herman W. Benson, have been an extremely valuable source for all aspects of this chapter. See also Paul E. Sultan, *The Disenchanted Unionist,* New York, 1962.

3. See, for instance, Seymour M. Lipset, "The Political Process in Trade Unions: A Theoretical Statement," in Morroe Berger, *et al.,* eds., *Freedom and Control in Modern Society,* New York, pp. 82–124.

4. For material on government rulings, see Sultan, *The Disenchanted Unionist,* Chapters 9 and 10; *Union Democracy in Action.* For an account of a union trial of a dissident member on what amounted to a charge of "seditious libel" against union officials, see *Union Democracy in Action,* Nos. 12, 21, 30.

5. Sultan, *The Disenchanted Unionist.*

6. See accounts in Sultan, *The Disenchanted Unionist, passim;* for the San Francisco story, see *Union Democracy in Action,* No. 20, and the series of articles by Frederick C. Porter, *Washington Post,* April 24–27, 1966.

7. The data for the accounts that follow are primarily from the issues of *Union Democracy in Action.*

8. Among the unions in which incumbent international presidents were defeated were the International Union of Electric Workers, United Steel Workers, and the American Federation of State, County and Municipal Workers. In other unions, incumbent presidents either re-

tired or withdrew fom a contest in the face of significant opposition, for instance in the oil workers' union and rubber workers' union.

9. The authors of works based upon the studies are typically very upset at many features observed in local unions, particularly those which imply some diminution of democratic principles. Yet actual external restraints against dissidence are hardly ever reported. Apparently, the type of incidents we have earlier described, particularly those coming from the issues of *Union Democracy in Action,* may not be that general but are prevalent enough to be germane to our analysis. For studies of local unions, see, among others, Leonard Sayles and George Strauss, *The Local Union,* New York, 1953.

10. Alice H. Cook, *Union Democracy: Practice and Ideal,* Ithaca, N.Y., 1963.

11. For an analysis of the work of the UAW Public Review Board in its first three years of operation, see Jack Stieber, Walter E. Oberer, and Michael Harrington, "Democracy and Public Review: An Analysis of the UAW Public Review Board," a report to the Center for the Study of Democratic Institutions. Other unions that have created something similar are the American Federation of Teachers and the Association of Western Pulp and Paper Workers.

12. Seymour M. Lipset, Martin A. Trow, and James S. Coleman, *Union Democracy,* New York, 1956.

13. See issues of *Union Democracy in Action;* Stanley Weir, "U.S.A., The Labor Revolt," *International Socialist Journal,* IV (1967), 279–296, 456–473.

14. Sultan, *The Disenchanted Unionist; Union Democracy in Action.*

15. Internal union operations constitute one area of civil liberties problems in which the American Civil Liberties Union has not, at least up to this writing, been very active. It has made several policy statements and has sometimes submitted "friend of the court" briefs, but has rarely, if ever, provided counsel for aggrieved union members.

CHAPTER 17: SOME GENERAL PROPOSITIONS

1. See Chapter 3, "Historical Background in the United States," *supra.*

2. James Madison, "The Union as a Safeguard Against Domestic Factions," from *The Federalist,* No. 10, reprinted in Hillman Bishop and Samuel Hendel, eds., *Basic Issues of American Democracy,* New York, 1956, pp. 47–53. One of the basic themes in Madison's classic document is the danger of factionalism, somewhat opposed to our emphasis on the necessity of conflict for civil liberties. His insistence, however, on the tendency to squelch opposition in small democracies is very apropos.

Index

354   *INDEX*

A Note on the Author

William Spinrad was born in New York City and studied at the City College of New York and at Columbia University. His writings have appeared in the *American Sociological Review, Social Problems, Dissent, Public Opinion Quarterly,* and the *British Journal of Sociology.* He is now Professor of Sociology at Adelphi University.